Dickens's plots have often been dismissed as conventional or cheaply sensational; Anny Sadrin argues that they should rather be seen as the significant embodiment of one of Dickens's central preoccupations: the dramatized rituals of succession. Through sustained readings of individual texts Professor Sadrin shows how the simple pattern of quest for father which characterizes *Oliver Twist* develops in Dickens's later novels into an extended exploration of the triple inheritance of looks, name and property. Increasing intricacies of plot represent growing tension between conflicting forces in the parent–child relationship: the wish to belong and the wish to break free, the desperate quest for identity and the fear of shameful identification, the filial piety of Telemachus and the parricidal yearnings of Oedipus. Throughout, Dickens is using plot to account for the complex process of reinstatement and revaluation which enables rightful heirs to take their rightful place in the family and society.

European Studies in English Literature

Parentage and inheritance in the novels of Charles Dickens

European Studies in English Literature

SERIES EDITORS
Ulrich Broich, Professor of English, University of Munich
Herbert Grabes, Professor of English, University of Giessen
Dieter Mehl, Professor of English, University of Bonn

Roger Asselineau, Professor Emeritus of American Literature, University of Paris-Sorbonne
Paul-Gabriel Boucé, Professor of English, University of Sorbonne-Nouvelle
Robert Ellrodt, Professor of English, University of Sorbonne-Nouvelle
Sylvère Monod, Professor Emeritus of English, University of Sorbonne-Nouvelle

This series is devoted to publishing translations in English of the best works written in European languages on English literature. These may be first-rate books recently published in their original versions, or they may be classic studies which have influenced the course of scholarship in their world while never having been available in English before.

TRANSLATIONS PUBLISHED
Walter Pater: The Aesthetic Moment by Wolfgang Iser
The Symbolist Tradition in English Literature: A Study of Pre-Raphaelitism and 'Fin de Siècle' by Lothar Hönnighausen
The Theory and Analysis of Drama by Manfred Pfister
Oscar Wilde: The Works of a Conformist Rebel by Norbert Kohl
The Fall of Women in Early English Narrative Verse by Götz Schmitz
The Rise of the English Street Ballad 1550–1650 by Natascha Würzbach
Romantic Verse Narrative: The History of a Genre by Hermann Fischer
Shakespeare's Festive World by François Laroque
The Eighteenth-Century Mock Heroic Poem by Ulrich Broich
The Middle English Mystery Play: A Study in Dramatic Speech and Form by Hans-Jürgen Diller
Parentage and Inheritance in the Novels of Charles Dickens by Anny Sadrin

Parentage and inheritance
in the novels of Charles Dickens

Anny Sadrin

University of Burgundy, Dijon

CAMBRIDGE
UNIVERSITY PRESS

CAMBRIDGE UNIVERSITY PRESS
Cambridge, New York, Melbourne, Madrid, Cape Town, Singapore,
São Paulo, Delhi, Dubai, Tokyo, Mexico City

Cambridge University Press
The Edinburgh Building, Cambridge CB2 8RU, UK

Published in the United States of America by Cambridge University Press, New York

www.cambridge.org
Information on this title: www.cambridge.org/9780521172325

First published 1994
First paperback edition 2010

A catalogue record for this publication is available from the British Library

Library of Congress Cataloguing in Publication Data

Sadrin, Anny, 1935-
    Parentage and inheritance in the novels of Charles Dickens / Anny
Sadrin.
        p.   cm. - (European studies in English literature)
    Includes bibliographical references and index.
    ISBN 0 521 39086 9 (hardback)
    1. Dickens, Charles, 1812-1870 - Criticism and interpretation.
2. Parent and child in literature. 3. Domestic fiction, English -
History and criticism. 4. Inheritance and succession in literature.
5. Children in literature. 6. Parents in literature.
7. Family in literature. I. Title. II. Series.
PR4592.P34S23 1994
823'.8 - dc20 93-30387 CIP

ISBN 978-0-521-39086-6 Hardback
ISBN 978-0-521-17232-5 Paperback

For Sylvère Monod

Contents

Preface and acknowledgements

This might begin like a Dickens novel: 'Thirteen years ago, Marseilles lay burning in the sun, one day', when I returned from a Corsican holiday on my way to Paris for my viva. The 'Thèse de Doctorat d'Etat', *L'Etre et l'avoir dans les romans de Charles Dickens*, had been directed by Sylvère Monod and was successfully defended at the Sorbonne Nouvelle in September 1980. An unrevised version was published five years later by Didier Erudition (Paris, 1985), a loose baggy monster, much longer than this book which is a translation of the first of its three parts, 'Patronyme, patrimoine'. On being invited to provide a slimmer volume in English, I decided that, rather than shorten the whole thing, I would do the translation of a complete section, and this one seemed to me the most obvious choice as its subject lies at the very centre of Dickens's preoccupations. Inheriting the father's name and the father's property is crucial in determining the ontological status of all his heroes, a necessary step for them towards self-knowledge, self-definition and self-acceptance.

At the time when I first started my research, the Dickens plot was almost unanimously – and to my mind, undeservedly – dismissed as conventional or cheaply sensational. In my own reading of those inheritance stories, the intricacies of plot seemed on the contrary to be fully justified, the result of complex and contradictory forces at work which I set out to analyse: the wish to belong and the wish to break free, the quest for identity and the fear of disgraceful identification, the innate filial piety of Telemachus and the parricidal yearnings of Oedipus. With the upsurge of new critical theory, fresh readings of Dickens have been made since then, some of which occasionally overlap with mine, but none, to my knowledge, centres like this book on the rituals of succession. Convergences therefore, rather than putting me off, have been an incentive for me to go on with this new project.

My translation is not literal. Translating oneself is a most difficult and depressing task and, to avoid schizophrenia, I often chose to keep the spirit rather than the letter of the French version. Some alterations were inevitable anyway since the introductory chapters had to be reoriented. Odd pieces of the two parts left out have, in any case, found their way into this new book: my analysis of the inheritance of looks in *Bleak House* is adapted from two chapters of the middle section, 'Miroirs diaboliques', 'Portraits symboliques'; the passages on hermetics in my study of *Our Mutual Friend* were lifted bodily from a chapter of part three on metaphors and metamorphosis entitled 'Le Mythe de Midas'. The chapter devoted to *Great Expectations* has a story of its own. Some of it appeared in my monograph on this novel for the Unwin Critical Library (1988) and went through some rewriting and updating at the time. For all the other chapters I chose to stick to the original version, updating it only in occasional footnotes and in my references to those novels of Dickens that have since appeared in the Clarendon edition. On the other hand, I have not found it necessary to reproduce the bibliography, inasmuch as the titles included are all familiar to those likely to read this study.

This book owes a great deal to the assistance and encouragement of family, friends and colleagues. I am particularly indebted to Margaret Tomarchio, Alison Wilcockson and Terence McCarthy for their linguistic help and suggestions, and to Sylvère Monod for supporting this enterprise.

Dijon, January 1993

Abbreviations and references

References are to

The Clarendon Edition (General editors, John Butt, Kathleen Tillotson, James Kinsley) for:

DC	*David Copperfield*, Nina Burgis (ed.), 1981
D&S	*Dombey and Son*, Alan Horsman (ed.), 1974
ED	*Edwin Drood*, Margaret Cardwell (ed.), 1972
LD	*Little Dorrit*, Harvey Peter Sucksmith (ed.), 1979
MC	*Martin Chuzzlewit*, Margaret Cardwell (ed.), 1982
OT	*Oliver Twist*, Kathleen Tillotson (ed.), 1966
PP	*Pickwick Papers*, James Kinsley (ed.), 1986

The Norton Critical Edition for:

BH	*Bleak House*, George Ford and Sylvère Monod (eds.), 1977
HT	*Hard Times*, George Ford and Sylvère Monod (eds.), 1966

The Oxford Illustrated Edition for:

CS	*Christmas Stories*
GE	*Great Expectations*
NN	*Nicholas Nickelby*
OCS	*Old Curiosity Shop*
OMF	*Our Mutual Friend*
SB	*Sketches by Boz*
TTC	*A Tale of Two Cities*

For the correspondence up to 1852, references are to The Pilgrim Edition of the *Letters* (Oxford: The Clarendon Press, in progress), General editors: Madeline House, Graham Storey and Kathleen Tillotson:

Vol. I: 1820–1839, Madeline House and Graham Storey (eds.), 1965
Vol. II: 1840–1841, Madeline House and Graham Storey (eds.), 1969
Vol. III: 1842–1843, Madeline House, Graham Storey and Kathleen Tillotson (eds.), 1974
Vol. IV: 1844–1846, Kathleen Tillotson (ed.), 1977
Vol. V: 1847–1849, Graham Storey and K. J. Fielding (eds.), 1981

Vol. VI: 1850–1852, Graham Storey, Kathleen Tillotson and Nina Burgis (eds.), 1988

For the correspondence after 1852, references are to the Nonesuch *Letters*, Walter Dexter (ed.), 3 volumes, 1938:
Vol. II: 1847–1857
Vol. III: 1858–1870

Introduction: to have or not to be

> A pleasant evenin' ... though warm, which, bless you, Mr Chuzzlewit, we must expect when cowcumbers is three for twopence.
>
> Mrs Gamp

Dickens's plots were not always taken very seriously – not even by himself. At least, he could be playful on serious matters and pretend levity when at heart he was in earnest. The following dialogue, occurring right in the middle of *Little Dorrit*, is a good example of his humorous and self-parodic detachment:

> 'Pray', asked Lord Decimus, casting his eyes around the table, 'what is this story I have heard of a gentleman long confined in a debtors' prison, proving to be of a wealthy family, and having come into the inheritance of a large sum of money? I have met with a variety of allusions to it. Do you know anything of it, Ferdinand?' ...
>
> 'Oh, it's a good story, as a story,' returned that gentleman; 'as good a thing of its kind, as need be. This Mr Dorrit (his name is Dorrit) has incurred a responsibility to us, ages before the fairy came out of the Bank and gave him his fortune ...' (*LD*, II, xii, 546–7)

Such tongue-in-cheek allusions to his narrative methods within the novels themselves are indeed far from infrequent. Here is another instance, taken from *David Copperfield*. An inexperienced investor, Betsey Trotwood has sustained heavy losses and thinks it her duty to inform David, her nephew and heir-to-be, of her financial setbacks. In the presence of Agnes Wickfield, she tells the tale of her misfortunes:

> 'Betsey Trotwood,' ... '– I don't mean your sister, Trot, my dear, but myself – had a certain property. It don't matter how much; enough to live on. More; for she had saved a little, and added to it. Betsey funded her property for some time, and then, by the advice of her man of business, laid it out on landed security. That did very well, and returned very good interest, till Betsey was paid off. I am talking of Betsey as if she was a man-of-war. Well! Then, Betsey had to look about her, for a new investment. She thought she was wiser, now, than her man of business, who was not such a good man of business by this time, as he used to be – I am alluding to your father, Agnes – and she took it into her head to lay it out for herself. So she took her pigs ... to a foreign market; and a very bad market it turned out to be. First, she lost

in the mining way, and then she lost in the diving way – fishing up treasure, or some
such Tom Tiddler nonsense, . . . and then she lost in the mining way again, and, last
of all, to set the thing entirely to rights, she lost in the banking way. I don't know
what the Bank shares were worth for a little while, . . . cent per cent was the lowest of
it, I believe; but the Bank was at the other end of the world, and tumbled into space,
for what I know; anyhow, it fell to pieces, and never will and never can pay sixpence;
and Betsey's sixpences were all there, and there's an end of them. Least said, soonest
mended!' (*DC*, xxxv, 437–8)

The incongruous use of the third-person pronoun in this 'autobiographi-
cal fragment' might, of course, be interpreted as just one more sign of the
old lady's eccentricity or as a proof of her fortitude. The pronoun could be a
mask for her, behind which to hide her tears. But to limit oneself to a
psychological reading of the text would mean giving short shrift to the
delightfully subtle irony of a novel which is, as everybody knows, the
fictionalized biography of Charles Dickens, which is also, as one tends to
forget, the fictionalized biography of Dickens the novelist. The scribblings
of Mr Dick (short for Dickens?), the lexicographic compilations of Dr
Strong still 'laboring at his Dictionary (somewhere about the letter D)' in
the final chapter (lxiv, 749), the verbosity and stylishness of Mr Micawber's
letters, the early fascination of the budding novelist with works of fiction,
his identifications with Tom Jones or Roderick Random, his gifts as a
story-teller that transformed the long evenings at Salem House into 'regular
Arabian Nights' (vii, 79), the premonitory signs of his literary career, then
that career itself, in short all the references to reading and writing that crop
up throughout the book are so many reminders that at two different levels
this is the novel of a professional novelist. And what indeed is Betsey doing
here if not also trying her hand at novel-writing? Her pronominal choice
clearly places her remarks beyond the pale of confidences in the world of
fiction. Rather than a character, she appears in this scene as a story-teller.
Her mode of expression is that of narrative discourse.

Hers is, to be sure, a rather compendious tale, the type of account one
would expect to find in some *Companion to English Literature*, but it bears
the stamp of her creator. The style, metaphoric, redundant, facetious, is
easily recognizable: Dickens disguises his voice the better to offer us a
pleasant parody of his own mannerisms.

'Dear Miss Trotwood, is that all the history?' asks Agnes, cleverly joining
the game of interpolated fiction. Aunt Betsey's answer confirms the sharp-
ness of her interlocutor: 'I hope it's enough, child . . . If there had been more
money to lose, it wouldn't have been all, I dare say. Betsey would have
contrived to throw that after the rest, and make another chapter, I have little
doubt. But, there was no more money, and there's no more story' (xxxv,
438). By substituting 'story', which connotes fiction and entertainment, to

Agnes's tentative 'history', which connoted truth and real-life experience, by adding the word 'chapter', she now leaves no doubt as to her own and her author's intentions: what is at stake is no other than the art of story-telling.

In this new retort, however, it is no longer Betsey the novelist but Betsey the critic who is expressing herself, providing, in one sentence, a definition of that well-known literary genre, the Dickens novel, which she parodied beforehand in her narrative, and the definition goes: no money, no story.

The association has gained currency among the critics and, over the years, commentators have improved on Betsey's definition: 'The ugly, disfiguring effect of money as a social force is the central or organizing concern of this novel', Monroe Engel writes of *Martin Chuzzlewit*.[1] '*Our Mutual Friend* is about "money, money, money, and what money can make of life"', writes J. Hillis Miller.[2] And Humphry House defines the mechanism of Dickens's plots and characterization as follows: 'Money is the main theme of nearly every book that Dickens wrote: getting, keeping, spending, owing, bequeathing provide the intricacies of his plots; character after character is constructed round an attitude to money.'[3]

This definition rightly focuses on two major notions: mobility and behaviour. The circulation of money – sales, thefts, debts, bankruptcies, godsends, legacies – is essential to Dickens. What matters is not so much what his characters possess as what they lose or acquire and, still more urgently, the way they lose and acquire it. Unlike so many of his contemporaries, he never specifies the annual income of his characters to a nicety: in the world of his novels, the rich are *too* rich, the poor are *too* poor, and if we are told the exact price of Mrs Gamp's 'cowcumbers' we will never know what the 'immense' fortune of the Chuzzlewits amounted to.

The 'attitude to money', however, should not merely be seen in terms of social injustice, greed or generosity, moral ugliness or altruism. Those who lose money in Dickens's novels lose more than just shillings or pounds: they lose pounds of flesh, they lose the sterling mark of their social status. And 'it don't matter how much' to them: 'it's not the sum,' Bounderby explains after the bank robbery, 'it's the fact. It's the fact of the Bank being robbed, that's the important circumstance. I am surprised you don't see it' (*HT*, II, viii, 138).

I am surprised that the remark has never struck the critics as one of Dickens's most crucial pronouncements on the significance and power of money. The author, who had experienced deprivation in early life and had been so humiliated by his father's financial predicament and ensuing social comedown, had first-hand and lasting knowledge of the helplessness that even a banker – and a coarse man to boot – describes as essential, as more important than figures. He knew the intimate, almost vital connection between the visible token and the fiction of the self. He knew that money was not, never was, never would be an end in itself, not even for the most miserly of misers, that the Golden Calf was never worshipped but as a substitute for the unnameable object of human desire – eternity, perfection, almightiness, the inaccessible attributes of the gods. When he came to write books, he certainly proved capable of creating ridiculous, despicable money-grubbers, but there was always the redeeming vulnerability, the awareness that the acquisitive tendency of man, even in its meanest forms, is the next best to his quest for an absolute. Obsessed as he was with origins and the burden of the past, he always conceived the relationship between man and property as the secular manifestation of some ontological pilgrimage. Experience had taught him that if essence and existence are to be reconciled in a worldly society, man must 'have' in order to 'be'.

The literary tradition that he liked best – that of Fielding's *Tom Jones* and of Smollett's *Peregrine Pickle* – had further persuaded him that the heroes of fiction must 'inherit' in order to be, and, from *Oliver Twist* to *Our Mutual Friend*, the interrelation of parentage and inheritance is central to most of his plots. So much so that in his last and most brilliant dramatization of story-telling , the equation is clearly between story and inheritance, not just story and money: the looking-glass reflections of plot in the dining-room of the Veneerings show us glimpses of the adventures of a will and of a story that turns short when the heir is suddenly reported to have drowned. Mortimer Lightwood, the deputy story-teller, informs us by instalments of the dust contractor's testamentary whims. A first batch of information tells us about legatees: 'His will is found ... It is dated very soon after the son's flight. It leaves the lowest of the range of dust-mountains, with some sort of a dwelling-house at its foot, to an old servant who is sole executor, and all the rest of the property – which is very considerable – to the son' (*OMF*, I, ii, 15). Ending on a suspensive clause – 'and that's all – except –' – which wrongly induces the narrator to conclude that 'this ends the story', Mortimer's narrative is resumed a moment later and specifies the conditions made to the son's inheritance: '– Except that the son's inheritance is made conditional on his marrying a girl, who at the date of the will, was a child of four or five years old, and who is now a marriageable young woman' (*OMF*, I, ii, 16). This raises questions: Mrs Podsnap enquires 'whether the young person is a young person of personal charms?' but Mortimer 'is unable to report'. Mr Podsnap enquires 'what would become of the very large fortune, in the event of the marriage condition not being fulfilled?' and Mortimer replies that, 'by special testamentary clause', the very large fortune 'would then go to the old servant above mentioned, passing over and excluding the son; also, that if the son had not been living, the same old servant would have been sole residuary legatee' (*OMF*, I, ii, 16). But concerning the fortune itself, Mortimer is as vague as Aunt Betsey, and ostentatiously so:

the testator, he explains, had 'made his money by Dust ... Coal-dust, vegetable-dust, bone-dust, crockery-dust, rough dust, and sifted dust – all manner of Dust', but no figures, he warns, will be specified: 'I don't know how much Dust, but something immense' (*OMF*, I, ii, 13). And as soon as the news of the son's death is known, the story is brought to its conclusion and the listeners stop asking questions. They do not show the least interest in the old servant who will now succeed to the whole property, do not even bother to enquire about his name. Romance is over, even for Podsnaps and Veneerings. Like Lady Tippins and the four Buffers, these wealthy businessmen want stories to be odd, exciting and dramatic: they are romantic listeners as we all should be and as Dickens wants us to be.

1   Parentage and inheritance

<blockquote>
Notre Père qui êtes aux cieux
Restez-y
Our Father which art in Heaven
Stay there
Jacques Prévert
</blockquote>

In the name of the father

'Bequeathing', the last word on his list of activities providing 'the intricacies' of Dickens's plots, is also, surprisingly, the least of House's preoccupations. The two chapters of his *Dickens World* which are devoted to 'Economy: Domestic and Political'[1] deal with all manner of questions concerning social and personal attitudes to money such as business, profit, thrift, extravagance, bankruptcy, pauperism, laissez-faire or philanthropy; not a single word is to be found relating to bequests or testamentary gifts.

The same reticence is observable in the works of all the Dickens critics who have specialized in financial matters. They talk of 'capitalism' (Arnold Kettle),[2] of 'supply and demand' (Monroe Engel),[3] of 'love and property' (Ross H. Dabney),[4] of 'money and society' (Grahame Smith),[5] never of inheritance. The omission is too recurrent, too systematic to pass unnoticed, though it would be going too far to speak of deliberate exclusion. The impression one gets reading these studies is that wills and legacies are assumed to be no more than a literary convention, a fit subject for analysis bearing on writing technique but not particularly suitable for a specifically sociological approach. Thus, Grahame Smith describes *Bleak House* as a book that enabled Dickens to return to earlier practices by enlarging on 'one of the elements of popular melodrama, the mystery surrounding a will, which [he] had used a great deal in his early novels'[6] and leaves the question at that.

Earle Davis, being concerned with artistry and composition, feels for his part entitled to go into the details and complexities of the Dickens plot. But he too stresses the artificial and conventional character of the stories. His telegraphese summary of *Oliver Twist*, a sensational novel as he sees it, full of improbable coincidences and developments, shows his blatant disrespect for such a rigmarole:

> The plot ... went something like this: man separated from wife – loves girl – has illegitimate child – mother dies giving birth – father dies soon after – will leaving fortune to bastard son is suppressed – legitimate son pursues brother in relentless hatred – boy raised in Poor House – runs off to city – adopted by criminal gang – attempts made to teach him the art of crime – resists – finds relatives and friends of his parents – is saved – villainous half brother exposed and inheritance restored.

'The way in which Dickens worked out this plot', he goes on, 'is not entirely successful'; there are far too many inconsistencies: 'After all,' he maintains, 'the will was suppressed; Monks and his mother already have the fortune', so why should the legitimate son and heir evince such 'psychotic obsession' with money and such eagerness to persecute a poor, nameless outcast? 'The means of getting to the plot climax', he further argues, 'are also devious. We are asked to believe that the old midwife would have kept up interest on a pawn ticket for years and that Mr Bumble's wife would have redeemed the pledge. The pawn ticket contains the evidence for Oliver's parentage and inheritance.'[7]

Davis's views are widely shared. Edgar Johnson speaks of 'a luridly melodramatic plot ... involving the rightful inheritance of an estate and destroyed proofs of identity'.[8] Arnold Kettle insists that 'we do not care who Oliver's father was and, though we sympathize with Oliver's struggles, we do not mind whether or not he gets his fortune'.[9] Many more scornful dismissals might be quoted, though there is no need to lengthen the list. The disparaging remarks, besides, are not limited to that single novel. Here again is Davis writing about *Martin Chuzzlewit*:

> The second sequence sustains most of the action. It introduces young Martin, whose love for Mary is opposed by his grandfather, this opposition leading to his being disinherited. There is no compelling reason for delaying his marriage to Mary, since he has lost his inheritance anyway. But Dickens motivates the delay reasonably. Young Martin is selfish; he needs a lot of money in order to be happy; therefore he goes off to make his fortune. The Peregrine Pickle type of hero would have returned with his pot of gold or would have found a wealthy inheritance elsewhere, but Martin discovers spiritual regeneration in America, in spite of the people and conditions he encounters. He does not make his fortune, and it is the self-sacrificing spirit of Mark which finally changes his character. When he comes back to Mary he is worthy of her, and the reader feels pleased when Martin's grandfather finally gives him the money he wanted all the time.[10]

One could easily reverse the argument: if, braving the laws of verisimilitude, Dickens always sees to it that his heroes should come into their inheritance, if he devises endings obviously at variance with the purport of his tales, no doubt there is some compelling, inner motivation, stronger than reason or consistency, that urges him to do so. His own rise to fame, in perfect conformity with the Victorian ideal of success, his desire to promote talent and to see merit rewarded understandably prompted him to choose his heroes among the deserving class of self-helping young men of the David Copperfield type. A committed disciple of Carlyle, he had little patience with idleness and incompetence and, barring Oliver Twist, who is trained to no profession, all his heroes and blue-eyed boys can pride themselves on some proficiency: they are book-keepers or book-writers, or clerks, or managers. Like true *Bildungsroman* heroes, they have passed through various ordeals and come out triumphantly, deserving at the end the usual rewards of the narrative agencies: competence, status, requited love. This ought to be enough; but it is not quite enough. Besides getting recognition and asserting themselves as good citizens, they must, of necessity, assert themselves as rightful heirs. Even if the profit is nothing to speak of (which it usually is), inheriting is all too clearly the major event of their lives, coinciding with the happy ending. Many critics, as we have seen, find this conventional. But, after *Oliver Twist*, where is the convention? Is it so very conventional to go to such lengths to secure so little?

More disturbing still, the phenomenon, which in the early novels could be ascribed to the influence of the old masters, outlasts the years of apprenticeship. As late a novel as *Our Mutual Friend* follows the same pattern and displays the same inconsistencies, with the added difficulty of the hero's ideological waverings and reluctance to accept himself as his father's son.

An easy way out of the difficulty is to run down the very notion of plot, as does Grahame Smith, who writes:

The organization of a novel can operate on two levels: that of plot and that of significance. By plot I mean the complications of the detective story, introduced merely to mystify or thrill the reader, or, on a slightly higher plane, the bringing of characters into relationship in a purely external way, through the workings of chance or accident. By significance I mean something very different: that of ordering of people or events which stems inevitably from the inner meaning of character or circumstance.[11]

I personally fail to see the difference. To me, plot *is* significance. But the 'inner meaning' of Dickens's plots cannot be found in the psychological make-up of the characters, where Smith seeks them to no avail. It is inherent in the nature of the hero, in the sonhood of the son, fated to replace the father on his death; it is inherent in the ritual of bequeathing and inheriting, a ceremony imperatively involving two actors appointed by destiny to the exclusion of all the others. Anybody can be a party to ordinary financial transactions: customers, shopkeepers, thieves, beggars, gamblers, money-lenders need not have a special relationship to their partners; in matters of inheritance, donor and receiver are co-substantial, tied by bonds stronger than their wills. The father's money as much as the father's name, the patrimony as much as the patronymic, must be handed over at the appointed hour; it is the son's viaticum, the father's parting gift to the new pilgrim on the brink of his journey.

Mothers and daughters

As tradition will have it, the ritual of succession concerns men and men only. Women are no more than life-givers; they have nothing but their offspring to hand down to posterity. The vocabulary itself is most significant; a brief look at the dictionary reveals that there is no exact equivalence between certain words derived from 'mother' and 'father', although apparently formed following the same rules of derivation. Thus, 'matrimony' refers only to 'the rite of marriage' or to 'the state' of wedlock, never to 'property inherited from' the mother, as one would expect by analogy with 'patrimony'. And 'matronymic' (hardly ever used) is defined in the *Oxford English Dictionary* as 'derived from the name of a mother or other female ancestor, esp. *by the addition of a suffix or prefix* indicating descent' (my italics).

Similar definitions are admittedly given of 'matriarchy' and 'patriarchy', but the words have acquired different connotations in modern societies. Matriarchy, according to Freud, is a primitive social system and the patriarchal order that came to prevail in the course of history represents for him no less than 'a victory of intellectuality over sensuality – that is, an advance in civilization, since maternity is proved by the evidence of the senses while paternity is a hypothesis'.[12] Paradoxically, this very uncertainty lends the father his prestige. 'An advance in intellectuality', Freud maintains, consists 'in deciding that paternity is more important than maternity, although it cannot, like the latter, be established by the evidence of the senses, and that for that reason, the child should bear his father's name and be his heir'.[13] 'Child', of course, means 'boy' for Freud as it does for Mr Dombey. Mothers do exist of necessity in his writings – the mothers of sons – but daughters do not. Nor, for that matter, do girls figure much in the foundation or restoration myths. Sons are the ones who have to hate, fear, murder and honour their fathers before they can settle down in life, father their own children and impose their law. It is their privilege and it is their curse.

Nineteenth-century England is a fundamentally patriarchal society which the Dickens novel faithfully mirrors. His female characters have little power and even less autonomy. As Ralph Nickleby reminds Mrs Mantalini, a 'married woman has no property' (*NN*, xliv, 579), a remark which held true throughout Dickens's lifetime since it was not until 1870 that the *Married Women's Property Act* granted Eve's daughters their financial emancipation.

Even their dowry was not *theirs* strictly speaking; it was passed on to the bridegroom through the agency of the bride's father or guardian, a 'portion given *with* the wife', the dictionary tells us (my italics), if not *as* the wife to be 'husbanded': 'Mr Podsnap', we are told, 'had married a good inheritance' (*OMF* I, xi, 128). On the other hand, all married women, including the portionless, were allowed to spend freely, even to squander their husbands' money, thus running the risk of being termed 'expensive': 'You are too expensive, Madam', Dombey complains to Edith, 'you are extravagant' (*D&S*, xl, 541). Even the best-hated wives had good reasons in those days to be dearly treasured!

Financial autonomy was the prerogative of the unwedded, the sentimentally deprived. Miss Havisham and 'Miss' Trotwood are good instances of this. Being husbandless, the two ladies can do what they like with their money, even stake it on the wrong horse; more important still, they can bestow their property like any man on their protégés: 'The ground belongs to me', Estella tells Pip when they meet in the ruined garden (*GE*, lix, 459).

They can also transmit their name though, at a symbolic level, this power is more limited than it is in the case of men. We learn that Estella's name is that of her adoptive mother almost by accident. The information comes to us through Jaggers when Pip enquires into the past, disturbed as he is by Molly's face and already surmising, because of the likeness, the dreaded relationship:

'Pray, sir,' said I, 'may I ask you a question?
  'You may,' said he, 'and I may decline to answer it. Put your question.'
  'Estella's name, is it Havisham or —?' I had nothing to add.
  'Or what?' said he.
  'Is it Havisham?'
  'It is Havisham.' (*GE*, xxix, 228)

But Jaggers's answer comes as a disappointment, providing no clue to the mystery of the girl's origins which was Pip's real preoccupation. The name of 'Havisham' had only been proffered as a – supposedly – wrong allegation in order to get at the truth, to get at another truth.

Is it not actually rather astonishing that Pip at this stage should still be ignorant of the identity of the girl he loves? But who cares? Does anyone ever refer to her as 'Estella Havisham'? Significantly, on the list of *dramatis personae* placed at the beginning of most editions, she is just 'Estella'. The adoptive mother's name has been omitted, signifying nothing.

Betsey Trotwood's power as name-transmitter is more complex, presumably owing to her ambivalent nature. There is about her something of a transvestite, which justifies Arthur L. Hayward's provocative remark that she is 'a remarkable figure of a masculine woman':[14] energetic, authoritative, self-willed, she certainly has the qualities which are usually said to be proper to the male sex. Her nephew, David the Elder, trusting, improvident, lackadaisical and impractical, was decidedly short of them, it seems, judging especially from her own strictures. No wonder that, when she decides to adopt his doubly orphaned son and has to play the part of the two missing parents, she becomes, as George Ford puts it, 'really more of a father to David than a mother',[15] feeling it her duty to make up for the errors the real father, her blood relation, would have committed as an educator if he had lived to rear his child.

Her functions too are various and somewhat contradictory. She begins her career as a fairy godmother, ready to give her first name to Clara's daughter who unfortunately proves to be a son. Unable to bear such a vexation, she hurriedly leaves the place of the child's disgraceful birth 'like a discontented fairy' (*DC*, i, 11) and is heard of no more. Not until, ten years later, David runs to her for help in Dover and she becomes his 'second mother' (*DC*, xxiii, 296): nursed, coddled, bathed, tied up 'in two or three great shawls' (*DC*, xiii, 167), swaddled like a new-born babe, he enters the world for the second time. To make official this rebirth and the new relationship, the fatherly mother decides that henceforth 'Trotwood' will be added to the boy's family name: 'Thus', David writes, 'I began my new life, in a new name' (*DC*, xiv, 184).

It would be more accurate, however, to speak of an 'extra' name since David never becomes 'David Trotwood'. We are even warned against the mistake:

'. . . I have been thinking, do you know, Mr Dick, that I might call him Trotwood?'

'Certainly, certainly. Call him Trotwood, certainly,' said Mr Dick. 'David's son's Trotwood'.

'Trotwood Copperfield, you mean,' returned my aunt.

'Yes, to be sure. Yes. Trotwood Copperfield,' said Mr Dick, a little abashed. (*DC*, xiv, 184)

Betsey always makes it very clear that the boy is 'David's son' and if he is 'Trot' for many of his close friends, it is as his father's son, David Copperfield the Younger, that he himself chooses to be immortalized. Even a 'masculine woman' would not tread too far on forbidden ground and Betsey knows her place as she dearly wishes trespassing donkeys did.

Daughters, for their part, are little concerned with matters of inheritance. Why should they be, being destined to be married from their very birth and indoctrinated at an early age with notions of female dependence and submissiveness? The most disinherited have no reason to complain of being 'moneyless' or 'propertyless' as young men would be entitled to do: 'portionless' is the word they invariably use to express their predicament, knowing only too well that they have no existence except in relation to a future husband. Even a love story like *Nicholas Nickleby* ends on a superb and significant zeugma, 'Madeline gave her hand and fortune to Nicholas' (*NN*, lxv, 829), which was not meant at all to be ironic, however much doubt it would throw on the bridegroom's intentions today.

A girl's very family name testifies to her state of subordination: it is given her provisionally as a 'maiden name' until a husband stamps on her his own trademark: 'I have made you my wife. You bear my name' (*D&S*, xl, 541), Dombey reminds his untamed wife. 'Do you know your mistress's name?' Murdstone enquires reproachfully of Peggotty after marrying Copperfield's widow, 'I thought I heard you, as I came upstairs, address her by a name that is not hers. She has taken mine, you know. Will you remember that?' (*DC*, iv, 39). One of Dickens's standing jokes is that some people will not remember the married names of ill-matched wives or remarried women: Mrs Skewton calls Edith 'either "Grangeby," or "Domber," or indifferently, both' (*D&S*, xl, 546); Mrs Sparsit addresses Louisa as either 'Mrs Gradgrind' or 'Miss Bounderby', never knowing which is which. It is as if a woman's name was a disposable object, some piece of clothing that is thrown away when it becomes outmoded or does not fit any more.

Bastardy and the ensuing, albeit transient, namelessness or pseudonymity are none the less experienced as an almost unbearable sign of disgrace by marriageable maidens – 'such a wound', says Esther who, until the discovery of her parentage, feels as if she had no right to live: 'So strangely did I hold my place in this world, that, until within a short time back, I had never, to my own mother's knowledge, breathed – had been buried – had never been endowed with life – had never borne a name' (*BH*, xxxvi, 452). But, paradoxically, the humiliation is felt even more sharply when a suitor offers his name in place of this assumed identity. On receiving Guppy's proposal of marriage, unwelcome though it is, Esther is deeply upset as the offer cruelly reminds her of her 'inheritance of shame' (*BH*, xliv, 538), and Rose Maylie rejects Harry's love because of the stain on her name: 'Yes, Harry; I owe it to myself, that I, a friendless, portionless girl, with a blight upon my name, should not give your friends reason to suspect that I had sordidly yielded to your first passion, and fastened myself, a clog, on all your hopes and projects' (*OT*, xxxv, 233–4).

It comes therefore as no surprise that in Dickens's plots of inheritance, daughters should be confined to secondary roles. Little Dorrit, his only eponymous heroine, certainly embodies the moral values of the book, but Arthur Clennam plays the leading part. Florence Dombey, for all her charisma, is no more than a substitute for the missing son and heir. Esther Summerson, if she asserts herself as the main character of her narrative, goes on pretending right up to the end that she is relating Rick Carstone's tragic story and puts a full stop to her account immediately after recording his death. Officially, at least, *Bleak House* is the story of a deprived heir and of an endless judgement. This, of course, cannot blind us to the fact that Rick cuts a poor figure as a hero and that Esther is the true heroine of the book, but then, she is the heroine of a novel which has grown out of the one she had been appointed to write and which focuses on her parentage, not on money expectations. Is it not, besides, as Summer's *son* that she is eventually allowed to play such a prominent part and outshine the male hero? By choosing such a name for her, does Dickens not unconsciously justify her unusual progress into another's story and her right to hold the pen, which is, as a rule, a man's privilege?

Fathers in heaven, sons on earth

All financial transactions – selling/buying, lending/borrowing, bequeathing/inheriting – are polarized between a giver and a receiver, and the dictionary is not extravagant in offering two words for one deal since the same act is perceived very differently depending on whether you are placed at the giving or at the receiving end: bequeathing is made in the name of the father, inheriting in that of the son. The Dickens critics, however, do not make the distinction and use the two words indifferently. The stress in their studies is, as we have seen, on the notion of suspense, on 'the mystery surrounding a will', not on the relationship between the partners of the transaction. But 'will', their favourite term, unfairly, if not intentionally, gives pride of place to the father as donor.

Undeniably, a father's last will is the device that in most novels triggers off the Dickens plot, but Dickens, in whose opinion 'fathers are invariably great nuisances on the stage' (*SB*, 109), always spares us the grating comedy of conventional death-bed scenes showing temperamental old sires bent to the last on exerting their tyranny over beloved or disowned sons. Testamentary deeds always take place behind the scenes, often long before the rise of the curtain. What the novels themselves are really about is the problems raised in the sons' lives by the burden of inheriting, the difficulty in recovering what is lost, the increasing reluctance to accept what is assigned. And it is therefore a matter of the utmost urgency that all the heroes' fathers should be put back where they belong: in heaven, where Dickens placed them.

All of them? Not quite. One exception confirms and justifies the rule: Dombey and son coexist. For a while, at any rate. But the coexistence soon proves dangerous and it will cost little Paul his life not to have been fortunate enough to be, like David, a 'posthumous child' (*DC*, i, 2). Elsewhere, with unerring wisdom, Dickens makes sure to orphan his heroes before the story gets started if they are to survive. And he orphans them all, one after the other: Oliver Twist, Nicholas Nickleby, Martin Chuzzlewit, David Copperfield, Richard Carstone, Arthur Clennam, Charles Darnay, Philip Pirrip, John Harmon, Edwin Drood. All of them, from first to last. Even Barnaby Rudge is an orphan of a sort, the son of a ghost who haunts his mother but of whose existence he himself has no knowledge until he reappears to be sentenced to death. A most timely reappearance: the rope will be spared this half-witted son of a murderer after the hanging of his guilty parent, which somehow clears him of charges, restores him to his former, original innocence. Such is the rule: fathers must die that their sons shall live.

The father's death is vital, necessary to the self-fulfilment of the son whose bereavement is his true birth. He can now take his stand in the order of succession, in the great chain of being, an innocent heir at long last, cleansed of sinful desires, delivered from temptation.

For, as long as the father lives, how can the son be entirely free from expectations and parricidal yearnings? In the acquisitive society of nineteenth-century England that Dickens depicts, some fathers even breed and educate their own murderers. Anthony Chuzzlewit, himself a monster of covetousness, has turned his son Jonas into 'a greedy expectant' (*MC*, xxiv, 385) who, 'from his early habit of considering everything as a question of property, . . . had gradually come to look, with impatience, on his parent as a certain amount of personal estate, which had no right whatever to be going at large, but ought to be secured in that particular description of iron safe which is commonly called a coffin, and banked in the grave' (*MC*, viii, 121). Tired of waiting, of cursing the old man's 'tardy progress on that dismal road' (*MC*, xxiv, 386) or of drinking toasts to his 'quicker journey' with his creditors (*MC*, xlviii, 738), Jonas eventually takes it upon himself to shorten the days of his testator and tries to poison him. The father certainly dies, but he turns out to have died his natural death, which makes the murderous attempt superfluous in terms of narrative sequence. But the son remains none the less guilty and commits suicide, the lack of connection between the deed and the decease thus emphasizing the symbolism of the episode.

This case of parricide is of course unique of its kind in all the works of Dickens. One more would be one too many: very few people, for one thing, can be expected to go to such extremes of behaviour, and by repeating himself the novelist would have been deservedly taxed with sensationalism. He would, besides, have missed his target: it is important indeed that the event should seem at once monstrous and paradigmatic, a grim fable told once for all to illustrate the workings both of society and of the sub-conscious.

In the following novels, the question of parricide is recurrently touched on, but always indirectly, if not casually or unseasonably as in Mr Toots's

apologetic and ludicrous outburst in the presence of Florence Dombey: 'If I
could by any means wash out the remembrance of that day at Brighton,
when I conducted myself – much more like a Parricide than a person of
independent property' (*D&S*, 1, 673). Coming from a simpleton, the remark
could even be easily dismissed as irrelevant; but, in spite or rather because
of its harmless character, does it not betray, on the part of the writer, an
unconscious tendency to associate inheritance and parricide? Another
telling misnomer is when William Dorrit accuses his son of being 'parricidal' (*LD*, I, xxxi, 369) for not showing him due respect and lacking filial
piety. It is as if the threat was always there, the lurking danger that,
paradoxically, only death will put an end to.

By sacrificing the heroes' fathers, Dickens fortunately protects them from
the violence of their sons and bloodshed is avoided … But the laws of the
subconscious cannot be so easily disposed of and the oedipal conflict out-
lives separation. Short of real ones, symbolic murders are performed:
legacies are turned down, kinship is obliterated, false names are assumed.
Even for those who were orphaned from birth, the parricidal impulse seems
to be the only possible form of filial acknowledgement. Significantly, *Great
Expectations*, whose hero has never set eyes on his father and has no reason
to bear him any grudge, is Dickens's drama of parricide *par excellence*. An
unwilling Oedipus, Pip is from childhood overburdened with guilt for the
improbable murder of some parental figure endlessly re-enacted on the
inner stage of his subconscious; the numerous references to the ingratitude
of prodigal sons, the grim performances of *Hamlet* and *George Barnwell*, in
the course of which he is forced into painful identifications with the
murderers of fatherly uncles, further foster his guilty feelings; yet, of all
Dickens's heroes he is the one who should feel the least inclined to harbour
thoughts of revenge or expectations and his oedipal dreams and dreads are
not grounded on fact. His story is actually closer to myth than any of the
novels: a universal fable like Sophocles', it tells us that the murder of the
father is the son's original sin, the deadly sin of origins.

Usually, however, posthumous rebelliousness is also justified by what we
know of the heroes' dead fathers, their tyranny, their intolerance, their
selfish selflessness even. The living fathers of secondary characters who, by
way of compensation, crowd the subplots and run the entire gamut of
parental inefficiency would seem to have survived, some of them at any rate,
merely to substantiate the charges made against those who are not there any
longer.

The Chesterfieldian Chester of *Barnaby Rudge* who, ironically, is the least
fatherly of all the Dickens fathers might stand as an emblem of parental
egoism. He has fathered a bastard, squandered the family wealth, ruined the

prospects of his legitimate son and rightful heir. Unused to living in straitened circumstances, he even comes to toy with the unnatural idea of eventually reversing the roles, marrying his son to some rich heiress and getting thus handsomely provided for in his old age in return for what he has done. When he shamelessly imparts his project to Haredale, we think we can hear the professions of faith of the whole species of unworthy fathers:

> If there is anything real in this world, it is those amazingly fine feelings and those natural obligations which must subsist between father and son. I shall put it to him on every ground of moral and religious feeling. I shall represent to him that we cannot possibly afford it – that I have always looked forward to his marrying well, for a genteel provision for myself in the autumn of life – that there are a great many clamorous dogs to pay, whose claims are perfectly just and right, and who must be paid out of his wife's fortune. In short, that the very highest and most honourable feelings of our nature, with every consideration of filial duty and affection, and all that sort of thing, imperatively demand that he should run away with an heiress. (*BR*, xii, 94)

The text is very cunningly satirical, reminding us of Dickens's most emphatic outpourings, approximating to his rhetoric. We recognize the symmetrical structure of the sentences, the familiar binary rhythm, the lyrical superlatives, even the key words of the moral philosophy to which the novelist normally gives his endorsement, 'nature' and 'duty'. Only one or two slight anomalies – 'for myself', 'all that sort of thing' – pit Chester's values against those of his creator, thus pointing even more derisively to the hypocrisy of the speaker. The last word, however, is unambiguously undickensian and sounds like 'heresy'.

Next in selfishness to this aristocratic paradigm of cynicism come snobbish fathers like William Dorrit, this 'great moral Lord Chesterfield' (*LD*, I, xix, 223), who relies on his children for subsistence, or Turveydrop, 'the Model of Deportment' of whom we are told that, if he dared, he would deprive his son of his very name after taking the bread out of his mouth: 'Yet would you believe that it's *his* name on the door-plate?' a lady asks Esther during her first visit to the academy. 'His son's name is the same, you know', she replies. 'He wouldn't let his son have any name, if he could take it from him' is the lady's clinching retort (*BH*, xiv, 173). Patriarchalism, paternalism and paternity are very ill-assorted words.

But bourgeois generosity can be just as harmful as upper-class stinginess. 'Giving . . . in all of Dickens, is dangerously close to taking', John Kucich writes very perceptively.[16] The narrator of *Dombey and Son* tells us no less when he describes Dombey's fatherly prospects as 'a partial scheme of parental interest and ambition' (*D&S*, v, 49). 'Some philosophers', he again writes, 'tell us that selfishness is at the root of our best loves and affections. Mr Dombey's young child was, from the beginning, so distinctly important to him as a part of his own greatness ... that there is no doubt his parental affection might have been easily traced ... to a very low foundation' (*D&S*, viii, 92). Dickens himself once confided to his friend T. J. Thompson that 'the greater part of [his] observation of Parents [sic] and children' had shown 'selfishness in the first, almost invariably'.[17] Such pronouncements leave no doubt as to his leanings and account for his choice of adopting the sons' point of view in his family romances. The novels of Dickens are very patently, very ostentatiously, the novels of sons and heirs.

2 Domestic and national

... as I often say, I think his disappointment a great thing for him, because if he hadn't been disappointed he couldn't have written about blighted hopes and all that ...

Dickens, *Nicholas Nickleby*

Third revelation: *Inheritance* and *private property* are and *must* be inviolable and sacred

Karl Marx, *The Holy Family*

Dickens and son

Dickens is all too obviously the great father-killer of the Dickens novel. But he is also the great peacemaker who, after estranging the sons from their fathers, invariably engineers their ultimate, symbolic reconciliation, no matter what incredible plot complexities it requires.

Such obstinacy, such persistent self-contradictions might be traced down to the biography of the novelist himself. If we turn to the so often quoted episode of his childhood when his father was imprisoned at the Marshalsea and he had to leave school for the shoe-blacking factory of Hungerford Stairs, if we consider the loneliness and dejection of the young boy of twelve so poignantly recorded many years later in his fragment of autobiography, we realize that, 'utterly neglected and hopeless',[1] left to himself in the London streets, he was then no better than a little orphan. The experience of solitude taught him to rely on no one but himself for survival or social promotion, and his perseverance was quickly rewarded: at the age of twenty-three, Boz had made a name for himself. The widely acclaimed author of the *Sketches*, the compiler and editor of Pickwick's *Posthumous Papers* had risen to the pinnacle of fame under a name which was not his father's. He had turned the tables on those who had let him down, severed the link with the shameful past and might well have stuck to his new signature for life as did so many other writers who, even when their true identity was no longer a mystery, retained the pen-name that had made them famous. Why, we wonder, did he drop the mask? Why did he choose to be remembered as the son of John Dickens? Did the elation of success obliterate the memories of hard times? Did it get the better of ill-feeling and resentment? *Oliver Twist*, the first novel published under his real name, would seem to suggest no less: it is, significantly, the story of a son whose pilgrimage to origins is overshadowed with no misgivings about his unknown (therefore easily idealized) father, a pure story of lost and regained identity. But it was the only one. Exhilaration was short-lived and family relationships soon began to deteriorate: up to his old tricks again, John Dickens not only ran into new debts but began to take advantage of his name to extort substantial loans of money from the unsuspecting publishers of his son. This lasted for a while, until, unable to stand the importunities of his unscrupulous father any longer, Charles had to bring himself to make a public protest: in March 1841, a notice was inserted by Thomas Mitton, his solicitor, in the London newspapers to the effect that certain persons, 'having or purporting to have the surname' of his client, had 'put into circulation, with a view of more readily obtaining credit thereon, certain acceptances made payable at his private residence or at the offices of his business agents' but that the 'said client' was not prepared to pay debts except those contracted by himself or his wife.[2] The young novelist must have felt sorry for himself on realizing that his now celebrated surname had somehow become his father's pseudonym!

Whether there was a strict cause and effect relationship between personal concerns and literary inspiration is of course conjectural, but the idyllic pattern of *Oliver Twist* was not repeated. After this song of innocence came the songs of experience, after the fairy tale the *Bildungsromane*. Fathers were known for what they were, or for what they had been rather, which precluded idolatry. Sons were now placed in ordinarily 'adverse circumstance[s]'[3] and condemned to the 'stern and even cold isolation of self-reliance'[4] that, according to Forster, characterized their creator. The success stories that this 'parvenu' – in the noble, Smilesian acceptation of the word – imagined for his henceforth unprotected heroes were a far cry from the blissful tale of the parish boy's progress.

And yet, the old dream was still there, a dream that the 'very small and not over-particularly-taken-care-of-boy'[5] must have had more often than not to compensate for the frustrating reality of his moral orphanhood, a regressive dream that took him back to the happy days when material comfort and security were quite naturally dispensed by a loving, protecting, almighty father, the family provider, the banker, the donor-to-be.

In *Oliver Twist* it was not Oliver who had dreamed the dream but his helpers[6] and his creator. Now, it was the turn of the heroes themselves to fantasize, the way all day-dreamers do: 'The motive forces of phantasies', Freud writes, 'are unsatisfied wishes, and every single phantasy is the fulfilment of a wish, a correction of unsatisfying reality ... ' The 'mental work' of the dreamer, he goes on, 'is linked to some current impression, some occasion in the present which has been able to arouse one of the subject's major wishes. From there it harks back to a memory of an earlier experience (usually an infantile one) in which this wish was fulfilled.'[7] To illustrate his theory, Freud imagines the following story:

Let us take the case of a poor orphan boy to whom you have given the address of some employer where he may perhaps find a job. On his way there he may indulge in a day-dream appropriate to the situation from which it arises. The content of his phantasy will perhaps be something like this. He is given a job, finds favour with his new employer, makes himself indispensable in the business, is taken into his employer's family, marries the charming young daughter of the house, and then himself becomes a director of the business, first as his employer's partner and then as his successor. In his phantasy, the dreamer has regained what he possessed in his happy childhood – the protecting house, the loving parents and the first objects of his affectionate feelings.[8]

The stories that Dickens's heroes make up for themselves are all shaped after this pattern. Here is, for instance, Nicholas Nickleby, about to leave for the school in Yorkshire and dreaming aloud in his uncle's presence:

'To be sure, I see it all', said poor Nicholas, delighted with a thousand visionary ideas, that his good spirits and his inexperience were conjuring up before him. 'Or suppose some young nobleman who is being educated at the Hall, were to take a fancy to me, and get his father to appoint me his travelling tutor when he left, and when we come back from the continent, procured me some handsome appointment. Eh! uncle?'
'Ah, to be sure!' sneered Ralph.
'And who knows, but when he came to see me when I was settled (as he would of course), he might fall in love with Kate, who would be keeping my house, and – and – marry her, eh! uncle? Who knows?' (*NN*, iii, 27)

Here also is David, building castles in the air: 'I picture Mr Larkins ... saying, "My dear Copperfield, my daughter has told me all. Youth is no objection. Here are twenty thousand pounds. Be happy!"' (*DC*, xviii, 231).

These idle wish-fulfilment dreams, relying on the intervention of some parental or tutelary figure – father, father-in-law, patron, fairy godmother, *deus ex machina* – were no doubt prompted by the author's real-life experience but, interestingly, they are none of them slavish imitations of reality. The dream of little Charles had actually come true when, on the death of his mother, John Dickens had inherited a lump of money that freed him from his debts and from his gaol, and the family had been reunited,[9] but no grandmother ever played the part of Grandma Dickens in her grandson's books. His heroes' constructions should rather be related to the fairy or folk tales that from first to last were his great favourites, like the legend of Dick

Whittington which in *Dombey and Son* is the standard of reference whenever Uncle Sol and Captain Cuttle take up the subject of Walter's prospects: 'We'll finish the bottle, to the House, Ned – Walter's House. Why it may be his House one of these days, in part. Who knows? Sir Richard Whittington married his master's daughter' (*D&S*, iv, 45). The power of fiction is stronger, by far, than reality, verifying Northrop Frye's remark that 'literature shapes itself, and is not shaped externally'.[10] Freud himself had been intrigued by the phenomenon. Case histories, he noticed, were none other than short stories, just as romances and short stories were akin to the fantasies of ordinary day-dreamers: placed 'under the protection of a special Providence', the invulnerable hero of unpretentious fiction was to him, recognizably, 'His Majesty the Ego, the hero alike of every day-dream and of every story'.[11] 'Nature, not art, makes us all story-tellers', writes Barbara Hardy,[12] but art may be second nature.

The tenor of these tales is anyway too unsophisticated and repetitive to engage our attention very much longer. More important is the ambivalent attitude of the novelist, a disturbing mixture of irony and wistfulness. His dreamers are far too naïve and inexperienced for us to believe that he sets great store by their wild imaginings, and we can almost picture him sneering like Uncle Ralph at 'visionary ideas' like those of 'poor Nicholas'; yet, strangely enough, the dreamers' wishes are invariably fulfilled towards the end of the novels with, in most cases, only slight alterations: Nicholas meets the unaristocratic but noble-minded Cheeryble brothers and Kate marries their nephew, David wins Dora and forgets about the twenty thousand pounds, Walter marries 'his master's daughter'. Dickens seems unable to disappoint his heroes and, by so doing, to disappoint himself.

Nor are his readers, who have come to take these rewarding ends for granted, prepared to face disappointment. But suddenly, with *Bleak House*, the east wind blows all hopes away. 'For the love of God, don't found a hope or expectation on the family curse! Whatever you do on this side the grave, never give one lingering glance towards the horrible phantom that has haunted us so many years. Better to borrow, better to beg, better to die!' (*BH*, xxiv, 302) exclaims Jarndyce on one occasion, desperately trying to warn Rick Carstone against his useless fantasies, and the warning is not merely rhetorical, as we would like it to be: 'poor' Rick expects *and* dies. A death-blow has been dealt to both dream and dreamer. Possibly to dream*s* and dreamer*s*.

The author's biography here again helps us to understand this unprecedented relentlessness of plot. *Bleak House* began to shape itself in the mind of Dickens during one of the most gloomy periods of his life. A few months before he wrote the first number of his new story, on the last day of March 1851, his father died rather suddenly, followed to the grave only two weeks later by his ninth and at the time youngest child, one-year-old Dora. Badly affected by this double bereavement, he went on in the daytime with his usual activities, but he spent his sleepless nights walking through the London slums or past gaols or mental homes, obsessed, Robert Newsom tells us, with the sense of his own 'houselessness' and dereliction.[13] There was enough in his mental distress and nightmarish visions to feed his imagination with lonesome places, friendless people and morbid scenes – Tom All Alone's, Jo the street waif, Nemo, the death of Jenny's baby, Tulkinghorn's murder, Esther's night wanderings in search of her mother ending at the churchyard gates – but there was no room for wish-fulfilment dreams and even the basic inheritance plot was like a stillborn child.

The death of the father, less unnatural though it was than that of the infant child, had probably more lasting effects on Dickens's inner life and creative activity. 'John Dickens's death', Newsom remarks, 'coincides with a pivotal moment in his son's career – the inauguration of the "Dark Period".'[14] The dominant gloom of the last novels may well be ascribed, in part at least, to this irretrievable loss that left Dickens for life with an acute sense of his own mortality and with the burden of the 'debt to the father', his – ironically – only legacy.

More surprising, however, is the post-mortem transmutation of Wilkins Micawber into William Dorrit. John Dickens had been a most engaging man, warm-hearted, exuberant, theatrical, and his son admired and loved him as much as he resented his extravagance and irresponsibility. His death had naturally reopened old sores and stirred up old grievances, but after four years one would have expected more dispassionateness: time is supposed to soothe our wounds and appease our resentment, tears come first, laughter follows. Why did only the gloomy side remain, as if the 'damnable shadow'[15] that John Dickens had cast at times over his son's life now prevented sunny interludes? Is it because the sky was clouding over with other shadows, with this 'something missed' in life that was to culminate three years later in the break-up of Charles and Kate's marriage and of the family cell? Did these new sores make the old ones rankle?

And what should we make of all those bad fathers, Arthur Clennam's or John Harmon's, or Casby, or even Magwitch, whose different kinds of badness are quite alien to the incompetence of the novelist's 'prodigal parent'?[16] The prospect of inheriting is darkened in the late novels by the guilty past or the waywardness of tyrannical fathers who cannot by any stretch of the imagination be likened to the original of the Father of the Marshalsea. Dorrit himself has actually been spoiled of his inheritance by one of them, sinned against as much as sinning. Is it not then Dickens's view of society at large that is darkening?

Yet one more question over which we may puzzle our heads: when the sons themselves have grown suspicious and are reluctant to come into their own, when the old dream has turned into a nightmare, why must their obviously disillusioned creator go on contriving his mock happy endings? Should we interpret this as the sign of his unshakeable faith in the traditional domestic values? Or as the desperate attempt of an ageing man to sort out his own problems as a father and a testator? The failure of his sons – especially his two favourites, Sydney and Plorn, who was also the youngest and whose dilettantism and extravagance reminded him only too cruelly of his own father's – embittered his closing years. Two years before his death, this father of ten went so far as to wonder: 'Why was I ever a father! Why was my father ever a father!'[17] The pronominal shift from 'I' to 'he' dramatically suggests that there is no way out of the vicious circle. Except through the old dream constantly revisited.

The holy family

Too many unanswered questions clearly indicate that 'biographical excursions'[18] cannot be expected to provide clues to all our perplexities. But why should our reading of the novels limit itself to the reading of their author's life? By writing books, Dickens was of course not merely trying to come to terms with the painful past or with the doubtful future; very much bound up with the present, very susceptible to change, whether social, moral or artistic, this 'enfant du siècle' is a writer whose inner contradictions were largely those of his times, and who, had he lived at another period, would no doubt have been just as great, but differently 'inimitable'.

The Dickens novel is a long story, covering a long chapter of social history. The early writings, with their unconditional celebration of ancestral values, fireside lives, household words, Dingley Dell Christmas gatherings, hark back to the golden age of pre-industrial England. The novels of the 'dark period', picturing the domestic bliss of Smallweeds, Vholeses, Merdles, Clennams, Podsnaps or Bounderbys, have a grim modernity. The family cell, which was a refuge from the wide world, has become a faithful, unaccommodating mirror of society, the sanctuary of private property reflecting the acquisitive spirit of the age. The cash nexus is perceived with Carlylean bitterness to be the sole link between relatives, and the exposure of Mammonism in the gloomiest sagas, *Little Dorrit*, *Hard Times*, *Our Mutual Friend*, has a ring of Marxism.

But Karl Dickens is not Charles Marx[19] and reprobation, however vigorous, never amounts to downright rejection. The cricket on the hearth no longer chirps very loudly but its small voice is still heard occasionally. Even in *Little Dorrit*, this formidable 'Families, I hate you!',[20] the indictment is not aimed at the 'holy family', the still revered institution, and the novel has its redeeming Plornishes with their die-hard optimism, their make-believe thatched cottage, sunflower and hollyhock painted on the parlour walls, 'a most wonderful deception' (*LD*, II, xiii, 556) inviting us to hope against hope.

The need to belong is crucially felt to the last, and the most rebellious sons eventually return to the fold. Significantly, the only instance of irreversible severance occurs outside England in the fairly distant past and has the sanction of history: Charles d'Evrémonde, the French hero of *A Tale of Two Cities*, an aristocrat by birth, a democrat by choice, gives up for ever his fortune and his title to express his loathing of his despicable father, but it is the whole patriarchal system (embodied in the man) that he has chosen to disown, and his gesture is even more political than personal: 'I believe our name to be more detested than any name in France', he tells his uncle, '. . . we have done wrong, and are reaping the fruits of wrong . . . This property and France are lost to me . . .; I renounce them' (*TTC*, II, ix, 116–18). Similar cases indeed are known to have existed during the unruly days of the French Revolution, justifying the irrevocable character of the decision. What's more, sweet England will be the new fatherland of Charles Darnay, as the exile now calls himself, and of his pretty children: 'it is my Refuge' (*TTC*, II, ix, 119), he declares with enough emphasis for the word to be capitalized in the written transcription of the English 'editor' and 'translator'. But the John Harmons of contemporary England cannot end their days abroad, even in such a place as the Cape of Good Hope, or at home as John Rokesmiths. Nor can young Jacksons remain Barbox Brothers for too long. There comes a time when the hero who has broken loose from the family cell and cast off his name cannot bear any more the 'bitter sense of his namelessness' (*CS, Mugby Junction*, 477); at the crossroads of life, the man from nowhere, who is also a man 'for Nowhere' (*CS*, 491), must needs become a man from somewhere if he is to know where to go or where to settle. He must be able to face his own self in the glass, acknowledge his true identity and celebrate his birthday:

As he put up his watch again, his eyes met those of his reflection in the chimney-glass.

'Why, it's your birthday already,' he said, smiling. 'You are looking very well. I wish you many happy returns of the day.'

He had never before bestowed that wish upon himself. 'By Jupiter! . . . it alters the whole case of running away from one's birthday! . . . I'll go back, instead of going on.' (*CS*, 514)

Back to origins, such ought to be the drive of any man's journey if it is to be a journey towards happiness and self-fulfilment.

Modern literature is not concerned with such matters any more. Families have been banished from most works of fiction, except from the novels of

Ivy Compton-Burnett and some few other belated Victorians. Houses have no heads and stories have no plots. The generation gap is food for journalists, the revolt against the father a fit subject for psychiatrists, educators and autobiographers, whereas novelists and playwrights have, with Beckett,[21] put the parents in the dustbin.

The modern hero is a solitary man, an 'outsider',[22] a 'Mr K',[23] a man with no past, no name, no family, even a first man like Le Clézio's Adam.[24] His anniversary can be celebrated on any day of the year and his identity can change on requirement. In reply to the question 'Webber, what were you doing yesterday?' Stanley, in *The Birthday Party*, proffers another question, 'Yesterday?' The word makes no sense to him. In reply to the question 'Webber! Why did you change your name?' he merely says, 'I forgot the other one.'[25] Hatred like Gide's is outdated; indifference, whether genuine or assumed, has long since taken over.

But, unlike their characters, modern authors have a keen sense of 'yesterday'. Some look back in anger, others look forward to more drastic changes. Others still, more subtly, take the luggage of modern theories in their 'travels back to the nineteenth century' as does John Fowles in *The French Lieutenant's Woman*, this latter-day Victorian novel: 'I am writing ... in a convention universally accepted at the time of my story ... But I live in the age of Alain Robbe-Grillet and Roland Barthes',[26] he explains in one of those analytical digressions that highlight the interrelatedness of past and present and give his fiction its historical perspective.

In such a perspective, which to some extent will be mine here, the domestic novel of the nineteenth century, paradoxical though it may sound, will appear as a more immediate forerunner of our modern novels of solitude than it is usually supposed to have been, paving the way for disruption and estrangement.

That the domestic novel should have come to assert itself at a time when the traditional structures of home and society were undergoing unprecedented changes is in itself astonishing. That it should have superseded, among other things, the picaresque novel in a period of intense geographical and social mobility is no less paradoxical. Unless we consider the omnipresence of the family in Victorian fiction as a sign of its very vulnerability, an anti-nomadic wish-fulfilment dream?

A brief historical survey would seem to confirm the hypothesis. Far from heralding an age of stability, the Industrial Revolution put an end to the old rural domestic system with its closely knit family groups and parishes. One of the first victims was the unmarried aunt or the unmarried sister, the precious spinner who, almost overnight, became the unwanted spinster, sold off at a low price on the marriage market or turning to prostitution or menial work for survival. The desertion of villages, the slow disappearance of squirearchy, the disintegration of patriarchal households led to new forms of cohabitation corresponding for the poorest to unorganized gatherings of strangers under the same roof in the overcrowded slums of hastily built industrial cities and for the less unprivileged to a more modern family unit limited to a couple and their possible offspring.

The massive upsurge of the urban proletariat marked the end of feudalism and contained the germ of emancipation. Under the old system, 'everyone belonged in a group, a family group' and 'tension', Peter Laslett writes in *The World We Have Lost*, was 'incapable of release except in crisis'.[27] Now, the 'father-figure master' was replaced by a boss or a limited company and the personal relationship was making way for class struggles. Now, the town labourer, even if he slaved away for the benefit of others, belonged to a class of free men: factory workers were not liveried servants. Proletarians were not domestics.

Working-class emancipation was a slow process, but occasional rocket-like ascensions disturbed the traditional balance of society and raised new hopes for the talented, the clever, the unscrupulous and the go-getters. The age of proletarians was also the age of upstarts. At mid-century, the gospel of success, popularized by Samuel Smiles, altered ways of thinking:[28] the parvenu became a model allegedly within reach of all and the man who had suddenly risen to wealth, power or celebrity thanks to his sole merit or resourcefulness was a new type of hero, solitary, self-reliant. Fortune now favoured the brave, not only the high-born, and the very foundations of the old patriarchal system resting on the inheritance of family property were badly shaken by this new race of men. Spontaneously generated, parvenus were fatherless.

Scientific discoveries also perturbed the world order. After 1859, the genealogy of the human species had to be reconsidered and God the Father, Creator of Heaven and Earth, began to be suspected of having botched his work on the sixth day of creation or of being a construction of man's imagination. Humanity was being orphaned through the cleverness of its scientists.

Until then the Platonic conception of the universe and the biblical version of its creation had been widely accepted. In *The Great Chain of Being*, Arthur Lovejoy sums up the general assumption:

the conception of the plan and structure of the world which, through the Middle Ages and down to the late eighteenth century, many philosophers, most men of science, and, indeed, most educated men, were to accept without question – the conception of the universe as a 'Great Chain of Being', composed of an immense, or – by the strict but seldom rigorously applied logic of the principle of continuity – of an infinite number of links ranging in hierarchical order from the meagerest kind of existents, which barely escape non-existence, through 'every possible' grade up to the *ens perfectissimum* – or, in a somewhat more orthodox version, to the highest possible kind of creature, between which and the Absolute Being the disparity was assumed to be infinite – every one of them differing from that immediately above and that immediately below it by the 'least possible' degree of difference.[29]

This age-old belief in cosmic determinism, hierarchy and fixism long justified social conservatism and man's acceptance of his condition. Everyone knew his place on the social ladder and, at all levels, society was organized after the pattern of the world itself: the State was dominated by the Prince, the Catholic Church by the Pope, the Family by the Father. Voltaire, in his *Dictionnaire philosophique*, memorably pulled the theory to pieces:

The gradation of beings which ascends from the lightest atom to the supreme being, this ladder of the infinite, strikes one with wonder. But when one looks at it attentively this great phantasm vanishes, as formerly all apparitions fled at the crowing of the cock.

At first the imagination is gratified by the imperceptible passage from brute matter to organized matter, from plants to zoophytes, from these zoophytes to animals, from these to man, from man to spirits, from these spirits, dressed in little aerial bodies, to immaterial substances, and finally a thousand different orders of these substances which ascend from beauty to perfection and finally to god himself. This hierarchy much pleases decent folk, who liken it to the pope and his cardinals followed by the archbishops and the bishops, after whom come rectors, vicars, simple priests, deacons, sub-deacons; then appear the monks, and the march-past ends with the capuchins.[30]

But Voltaire's lampoon was inefficient and determined few conversions. Far into the next century, long after Darwin's theory of evolution had made it obsolete and difficult 'to reconcile with the known facts of nature',[31] a large majority of people still held to the creed. It satisfied man's natural love of order and stability and enabled him to remain at the centre of the universe, safely enjoying the comfortable giddiness of contemplating the two infinites.[32] The thousand or so English families who between them owned the land and ruled the country had every reason to go on believing that 'the earth was made for [them] to trade in, and the sun and moon ... to give them light', that 'Rivers and seas were formed to float their ships', that 'rainbows gave them promise of fair weather', that 'winds blew for or against their enterprises', that 'stars and planets circled in their orbits, to preserve inviolate a system of which they were the centre' (*D&S*, i, 2). And 'decent folk' were easily persuaded for their part that what had been was what would be, that generations came and went whereas the earth remained for ever: their aspirations were at variance with their convictions but daily experience cruelly confirmed that there was nothing new under the sun of England and little to be expected.

The upstart himself, *homo novus* though he was, did not break with traditions. A worthy follower of those early capitalists whose puritanism and worldly wisdom have been admirably described and analysed by Max Weber and Richard Tawney,[33] he had to reconcile success and virtue, ambition and election to justify his position and legitimize his fortune; he needed a God to be one of the chosen few. But his elitism did not exclude legitimism: the *nouveau riche* rarely boasted of his low origins, he needed a crest, 'in gold and eke in silver', and some 'Crusading ancestor' (*OMF*, I, ii, 10) to assert himself in society. 'In the battle between the self-made man and the gentleman', writes Asa Briggs, 'the self-made man won in England only if he became a gentleman himself, or tried to turn his son into one';[34] but it was even better if he succeeded in finding out a gentlemanly father for himself.

This polarization between the need for change and the comfort of habit, the desire to be freed from the fetters of the family group and the yearning for kinship have energizing virtues. Dialectical couples such as faith and doubt, order and disorder, tradition and innovation provide the specific dynamism of the nineteenth century which is, somewhat like the Renaissance, an age of transition between two totally different eras in the history of the world.

Similar couples give the novels of the period, and those of Dickens in particular, their disturbing ambivalence. On three major points, the parvenu, money and the father-figure, ideological indeterminacies entail narrative inconsistencies: we are made to understand that the kingdom of God is intended for the poorest, but moneyed villains are ruined whereas virtuous heroes are rewarded with well-lined purses and credited bank accounts, as if the bane of society was also its panacea; we are made to detest fussy, wilful fathers, but their last wills are accomplished, no matter how repellent or eccentric they had seemed to be at first. Such inconsistencies, however, are less unacceptable when we realize that the real nature of the debate is moral rather than purely ideological and when we agree to draw the line between deserving and undeserving new men, between good and bad money, between fathers and paternity.

For paternity is revered to the last in the name of 'the great father of us all in Heaven' (*LD*, I, ii, 17), 'the Father of one family' (*D&S*, xlvii, 620) in whose clemency Dickens, 'the great Christian',[35] never ceased to believe. Worldly fathers hardly ever come up to the ideal, but the ideal remains and brings comfort to those whom their fathers on earth have unfairly or unwillingly forsaken: 'It was ... so gracious in that Father who had not forgotten me, to have made my orphan way so smooth and easy' (*BH*, iii, 27), Esther Summerson writes, in one of her many outbursts of gratitude. And Florence Dombey, when most cruelly repulsed by her father, is helped on by the thought of 'that higher Father who does not reject his children's love, or spurn their tried and broken hearts' (*D&S*, xliii, 580): 'She only knew that she had no Father upon earth, and she said so, many times, with her suppliant head hidden from all, but her Father who was in Heaven' (*D&S*, xlix, 650).

A realist or an atheist like George Eliot would invite us to accept people as they are and educate us to more leniency and a better understanding of our fellow creatures. Dickens, the idealist, prefers to darken the picture the better to enhance the alternative, as do some of his 'escape artists'[36] like Dick Swiveller or Fanny Cleaver. His fairy-tale endings are akin to prayers, which is Maurice Blanchot's definition of writing: 'Ecrire, forme de prière'.[37]

3 The parish boy's progress: a pilgrimage to origins

... this Piljian's Projiss of a mortal wale

Mrs Gamp

If Oliver Twist was Oliver Twist, there would not be any story. Doomed to the untimely death of neglected children, like little Dick, or to delinquency and to penal servitude, like the Dodger, or, still more mundanely, to the obscure life of the poor and wretched, the boy would not belong to the race of heroes: his life would be too short, too humble or too narrow to be worth recounting at greater length than that of his fellow-sufferers. Who would even care to call him by name? To those condemned to death or to destitution a nickname or a short version of a name is quite enough to live by until they go to their grave. Aware of the precariousness of their existence and of their extreme fragility of being and appearance, the Dicks and Dodgers easily make do with these shadows of identity which are in fact nothing else than a watered-down form of their tragic anonymity. In the 'name' of them all, Jo, the crossing sweeper of *Bleak House*, will express this memorably:

Name, Jo. Nothing else that he knows on. Don't know that everybody has two names. Never heerd of sich a think. Don't know that Jo is short for a longer name. Thinks it long enough for *him*. *He* don't find fault with it. Spell it? No. *He* can't spell it. No father, no mother, no friends. Never been to school. What's home? Knows a broom's a broom ... (*BH*, xi, 134)

Oliver, however, is never anonymous. None of the nicknames – 'Ned' (xxi, 137), 'Nolly' (xx, 131), 'Work'us' (v, 27, vi, 36) – that, in order to spite him, some try to inflict on him ever thrust themselves on our minds or succeed in destroying the promising effect of eponymy, an indisputable sign of his chosen status, survival and heroism. It is a waste of wicked intentions to call him 'nameless' (v, 28) as does Noah Claypole. It is a waste of sympathy to pity him along with Steven Marcus on the grounds of his being 'introduced as an "item of mortality"' for lack of a proper name: 'no hero's designation has ever been more touching in its anonymity',[1] is this critic's comment on the opening lines, in spite of the fact that a fuller quotation would invalidate the remark since, on the contrary, the narrator makes a point of telling us that the child was given a name before being given life, and actually introduces him as 'the item of mortality *whose name is prefixed to the head of this chapter*' (i, 1, my italics).

This is, to be sure, a mere parody of a baptism, as the inventor of the name will himself tell us in the next chapter: 'The child that was half-baptized Oliver Twist, is nine year old to-day' (ii, 6). But this chance name due to a beadle's literary whim – 'I inwented it ... Twist, I named *him*' (ii, 7) – will have its own career alongside our hero. The false identity, which from the start allows the narrator to designate his protégé and so guarantee his future, will never be obliterated by the genuine one even though the plot has no other function than to help us discover the child's parentage.

Thus, Oliver Twist is strangely a hero whose heroism depends on the mystery of his birth, but whose eponymy is based on a falsehood that will survive the revelation. The phenomenon is admittedly as conventional as it is paradoxical, based as it is on a convention firmly established by the eighteenth-century novelists who inspired the young Dickens. In the tradition of *Tom Jones* and *Roderick Random*, *Oliver Twist* is a novel whose title deceives as much as it informs us. It has to lie so as to preserve the central mystery of the narrative while, by assuring a future for the hero, it is also the harbinger of expectations that will not remain unfulfilled.

The subtitle, 'The Parish Boy's Progress', which underscores the exceptional nature of the hero's career has, like the title, the double function of informing and deceiving us. By presenting Oliver as a child in care, it rightly underlines the distance covered between obscurity and fame, but it also implicitly establishes a cause and effect relationship between the two poles of the boy's journey that will be refuted by the narrative. Oliver, as it happens, will not be promoted as a Parish Boy any more than he will be the instigator of his own success, as the deliberately enigmatic reference to Hogarth and Bunyan would have us believe. He will not succeed through vice or through virtue either.

Dickens, who in his prefaces refers back to Hogarth 'whose unique realism he wishes to emulate',[2] as Sylvère Monod points out, should have, in all logic, allowed his hero to be corrupted. Thus, in chapter 8, when Oliver meets the Dodger on reaching London, a reader convinced of the novelist's good faith would be entitled to make the most gloomy forecast about forthcoming events: Michael Slater is among those who think that, after the experience at the workhouse and Sowerberry's, the worst should be expected:

Oliver escapes from this society in chapter 8 only to be decoyed into the criminal underworld of London. A direct cause-and-effect link between social injustice and neglect and crime was always central to Dickens's thinking and the novel's

Hogarthian sub-title, 'The Parish Boy's Progress', gives a clear enough hint of the way in which the novel will move. We might recall again the gentleman in the white waistcoat who so perseveringly proclaims his belief that Oliver will come to be hanged; society, Dickens is saying, is a great maker of such self-fulfilling prophecies.[3]

But the plot develops a twist that will refute the prophets of doom: Oliver will be neither corrupted nor hanged. The one would entail the other almost inevitably, but the novelist who knows full well that delinquency leads to the gallows (as the fate of many characters demonstrates) must, if he wants to spare his hero's life, spare his virtue in the first place. It is not therefore, in spite of appearances, under the threatening auspices of Hogarth that Dickens places Oliver's departure but under the less risky patronage of Bunyan: 'The Young Pilgrim's Progress', the descriptive headline corresponding to the episode in the Charles Dickens edition of 1867,[4] confirm this reading, if necessary.

The double cultural reference thus illustrates the ideological dialectic of a novel in which realism and idealism are constantly at variance. The implicit allusion to the Rake's Progress is misleadingly premonitory; purely antiphrastic, it acts as a foil to the exemplary career of the hero, itself modelled, at least in broad outlines, on the ascent of Bunyan's Pilgrim. At the end of his trials, Oliver, like Christian, will be admitted into Paradise, an earthly paradise indeed, as is proper in an overtly secularized version of the earlier story, but a paradise none the less, 'a little society, whose condition approached as nearly to one of perfect happiness as can ever be known in this changing world' (liii, 365).

As much as the resonance of the titles and broad similarities between the heroes' careers, Dickens's proclaimed intentions, 'I wished to show, in little Oliver, the principle of Good surviving through every adverse circumstance, and triumphing at last',[5] allow us to establish a close connection between the two works: 'Primarily,' Steven Marcus writes, '*Oliver Twist* is a story in the tradition of Bunyan, the morality play, and the homiletic tale'.[6] Strange as it may be, the novelist's 'homiletic tale' is even more utopian than the theologian's. So much so indeed that, although it was meant to 'be a service to society',[7] the story of Oliver can hardly be expected to be as efficiently edifying as was the story of Christian. Edification rests on the assumption that those who set an example will have followers and disciples. But Oliver is at once too perfect and too protected to be really imitated. To whom could he serve as an example when his success depends entirely on chance and grace? Bunyan's own hero does not possess such inhuman perfection: he succumbs to temptation, falls asleep on the way, lets himself be distracted and turned from his path, and even gives way to despair. He is also, as Marcus rightly points out, a man of action and combat: 'He is an active, positive heroic figure whose behavior, though a necessity of Bunyan's art, contradicted Bunyan's predeterminist theology.'[8] Strict adherence to the doctrine of predestination would certainly render utterly pointless the question he asks before starting on his journey, '*What shall I do to be saved?*'[9] But what does Oliver *do*? By what brilliant action does he win fame? What demons must he fight? And, on a more down-to-earth level, what passion urges him on, what eagerness has he to be promoted?

In Sowerberry's service, his only proficiency is the expression on his face: 'There's an expression of melancholy in his face, my dear,' the undertaker says to his wife, 'which is very interesting. He would make a delightful mute, my love' (v, 29). The promotion 'to the black stick and hat-band' (vi, 35) which comes to reward this poor achievement understandably arouses the jealousy of a less gifted and less well thought of apprentice whose persecutions will drive him away from his master's house, ironically compelling him to act and, for once, exert his free will. But, the episode over, Oliver will do nothing worth recording any longer. Nor will he be encouraged to become self-reliant and acquire some competence. None of his benefactors will take the trouble to train him for a job: at Brownlow's house, he will be taught cribbage by Mrs Bedwin, whereas at the Maylies', his musical ear will be developed and his mind improved to better prepare him for the leisured life. Given the ideological context of the age and the importance attached to the concepts of work, effort and perseverance, we would have expected Oliver's career to have conformed more to the ideals of the times, which were also those of the novelist.

But comparing Dickens to Bunyan ends on a double paradox: it is the puritan who makes his hero triumph through his 'works', it is the meritocrat who makes his hero triumph through grace abounding. A totally secular grace, however, since Oliver is not a saint any more than he is a rake: the grace that is granted him is to be his father's son and the chosen one of his creator.

Right from the start of the game, it is obvious that the cards are stacked. We do not fear for Oliver's life when at birth he is said to be 'unequally poised between this world and the next' (i, 1), knowing that the novel would be nipped in the bud, which the laws of the genre forbid:

For a long time after it was ushered into this world of sorrow and trouble, by the parish surgeon, it remained a matter of considerable doubt whether the child would survive to bear any name at all; in which case it is somewhat more than probable that these memoirs would never have appeared; or, if they had, that being comprised within a couple of pages, they would have possessed the inestimable merit of being the most concise and faithful specimen of biography, extant in the literature of any age or country. (i, 1)

The narrator, in fact, is more concerned here with describing his literary enterprise than with creating suspense. There is no question but that we are in for a fully fledged biography and, for the second time in fewer than five lines, eponymy is put forward in this paragraph as the surest guarantee of the hero's survival. But even more promising is the playful nature of the text which trifles with the truth, opts for the conditional rather than the indicative, and by so doing bids us not take too seriously its purely rhetorical threats.

When, a few years later, the short straw is drawn and the narrator informs us that 'it fell to Oliver Twist' (ii, 11), we have no reason to be worried or surprised: if it fell to another, then we would start wondering! Far from being a new danger, the magic ritual of the drawing of lots simply imparts a lastingly heroic quality to one who, guided by 'a stronger hand than chance' (xlix, 335), is destined for a life of exceptional promise. And when, on hearing the report of his insolence, the 'prophetic gentleman' in the white waistcoat swears by the great gods that he will end on the gallows, only the very credulous would feel uneasy and fail to perceive the feigned uncertainty of the narrator whose omniscience it contradicts: 'As I purpose to show in the sequel whether the white-waistcoated gentleman was right or not, I should perhaps mar the interest of this narrative (supposing it to possess any at all), if I ventured to hint, just yet, whether the life of Oliver Twist had this violent termination or no' (ii, 12). Surely, this carefree manner of delaying the answer until the next instalment is the happiest of omens.

Even the final outcome of these adventures is easily predictable. We can imagine from the questions raised as early as chapter 1 – 'where did she come from? ... no wedding-ring ... he might have been the child of a nobleman or a beggar ...' – that the mystery of the child's origins will eventually come to be resolved and that the father will prove no beggar. We do not read *Oliver Twist* as a detective story, with the simple aim of finding out what happens at the end: we read it to the end to verify our guesses and to have the satisfaction of seeing in black and white that what, from time immemorial, was intended to happen has come to pass in actual fact.

People, like facts, are predetermined. As the embodiment of good, Oliver is, of course, incorruptible and the predictions of his evil-wishers are, equally of course, never borne out. Ill-usage at the workhouse fails to turn him into the 'hardened young rascal' that 'by common consent' he is pronounced to be and, although it threatens to reduce him 'for life, to a state of brutal stupidity and sullenness' (iv, 22–3), the narrator's fears will not be verified. Nor will Fagin succeed, however hard he may try, in 'instilling into his soul the poison' which he thinks will 'blacken it, and change its hue for ever' (xviii, 120); nothing will alter the candour of the child who, rather than

'Twist', ought to be called 'White' (xi, 64) and go by the name which, symbolically, proclaims his innocence at the very moment when he is charged with crime. The man who, in Fang's office, baptizes him for the second time, guesses more correctly than his predecessor: Oliver does not have the twisted soul that his current name would suggest.

But every rose has its thorn. The immaculate conception of the hero that frees him from original sin also deprives him of moral freedom. As a chosen one, Oliver is not free to do evil or, for that matter, to do right either. He is absent from his destiny. Readers soon perceive it and never wonder 'What is he going to do next?' as they normally would with ordinary heroes; the only question that occurs to them, 'What is going to happen to him?', is the one people ask of fairy-tale heroes whose universe is ruled by the ethics of 'passion' rather than of action as in genuinely realistic novels.[10]

A fairy-tale hero never interferes with his fate. He does not choose, he waits. He does not act, he endures. Oliver is such a hero. He has, as a rule, no initiative and leaves it to others to dispose of his life. Major decisions concerning his lot are even taken when he is not there. In fifty-three chapters, no fewer than twenty-one take place in his absence, many of which will none the less determine the course of his life. And in the scenes where he does show up, he often behaves as a perfect 'mute' in conformity with Sowerberry's early predictions, an attitude which is, indeed, all the more remarkable as it occurs in a novel where dialogue is so important. His interventions are in fact so rare (fewer than one hundred and fifty in all) and, what is more, so very brief that they scarcely make up more than one hundredth of the text (a little fewer than four out of the three hundred and sixty-eight pages in the Clarendon edition). It should be added that, like a good child, he scarcely speaks unless spoken to and gives the tersest of answers: 'Yes, sir', 'No, sir', 'Certainly, sir', make up nearly a third of his replies, agreement coming top as in duty bound. Several interventions are dictated by others, including the famous 'Please, sir, I want some more' (ii,11) that he utters under duress and that will seal his destiny. There are fewer than ten sentences of as many as three lines, while those giving the illusion of genuine emotion can be counted on the fingers of one hand. And if, by chance, he is asked to speak for himself or recount his adventures, he is immediately cut short. On two occasions, exhaustion condemns him to silence when he would most need words to exonerate himself: in Fang's presence, he is too weak to hear the questions he is asked and when he knocks at the Maylies' door he is 'speechless and exhausted' (xxviii, 185). And if – rarely! – circumstances allow him to express himself freely, the narrator, acting as if he could not bear such sudden volubility and with the excuse of sparing the reader the well-rehearsed story of the boy's adventures, either sums up his narrative in indirect speech or ostentatiously omits to report it, as in the following instance: '*The conference was a long one*; for Oliver told them all his simple history: and was often compelled to stop, by pain and want of strength. It was a solemn thing, to hear, in the darkened room, the feeble voice of the sick child *recounting a weary catalogue of evils and calamities* which hard men had brought upon him' (xxx, 193, my italics). Even stylistically, he is under supervision . . .

But what is the point of speaking if others do it for you? What is the point of struggling if the game is already played? Oliver's passivity – 'the passivity of waiting, of expectation, of "great expectations"', says Hillis Miller[11] – is only wisdom after all, the wisdom, it would seem, of one who knows the end . . . It is difficult in these conditions to agree with Chesterton that 'Oliver Twist is pathetic because he is an optimist':[12] Oliver has the faith that preaches to the converted and the optimism that buoys up the elect.

The reader's early acquired conviction that the hero has received grace in advance of his virtue is, however, shared by few of the characters who cross the boy's path and must form an opinion without the benefit of the narrator's rhetoric: the worst anxieties are usually displayed concerning this newcomer.

Such reluctance to accept him has the dramatic advantage of delaying for the long term the happy conclusion of his adventures. It furthermore offers a fair illustration of bourgeois exclusiveness since distrust usually comes from people in authority and worthy representatives of social or moral order. Even at his birth, on realizing that he is a bastard, the doctor wagers that the child '*will* be troublesome' (i, 2). On hearing the news of his asking for more, the members of the board do not hesitate to predict that he 'will be hung' (ii, 11). On merely setting eyes on him, Grimwig expresses barely concealed accusations, demanding 'with a sneer, whether the housekeeper was in the habit of counting the plate at night; because, if she didn't find a table-spoon or two missing some sunshiny morning, why, he would be content to – and so forth' (xiv, 89), whereas Dr Losberne, knowing from experience that an angel's face can hide an evil soul, 'mourningly' shakes his head as he warns Rose and Mrs Maylie that 'Vice . . . takes up her abode in many temples', and that 'crime, like death, is not confined to the old and withered alone' (xxx, 191). Whenever he enters a new section of middle-class society, including the workhouse – financially and morally dependent on the well-off and the well-bred – Oliver appears as an intruder, and the same anxiety is invariably expressed, the same fear of harbouring a black sheep by trusting to deceitful appearances, the same reflex of self-defence. Asking for more gruel or just looking miserable is felt to be as dangerous to society as spiriting away the silver, a threat alike to property, stability and establishment. The moral criteria of the middle class are hardly distinguishable from their economic tenets: they must protect themselves from those who are 'poor or otherwise criminal', as Boz had put it in *The Mudfog Papers* (*SB*, 653).

Undeniably, the narrator of *Oliver Twist* has no more patience than Boz with the redressors of wrong, and shows, on the whole, more compassion than suspicion towards the underprivileged. It is none the less striking that the very criteria which he turns to ridicule are those that he himself uses to persuade us that his protégé deserves help and sympathy. His hero, the story will show, has not been chosen indiscriminately and all the tests he undergoes are there to convince us of his innate goodness, of his honesty, of his adaptability, of his perfect docility.

The story of the happy days that Oliver spends in the country in the company of his benefactors is in this respect very revealing. Everything there happens under the sign of conformity, immobility and imitation. Often the child remains sitting: he listens, he observes and never says a word. If he moves, if by any chance he takes the risk of running, it is to do an errand, to obey a request, to make himself useful to the two ladies, 'so happy if they wanted a flower that he could climb to reach, or had forgotten anything he could run to fetch'. In this so-called 'new existence', time stretches forth and repeats itself and archaisms prevail as do verbal forms expressing routine: 'Oliver', we are told, '*would* sometimes *sit him down*', he '*would* walk', he '*would* work hard', there '*would* be no candles lighted at such times as these; and Oliver *would* sit by one of the windows, listening to sweet music, in a perfect rapture'. The binary rhythm of well-balanced sentences pleasantly lulls us into day-dreaming and the easy comfort of intellectual sloth: 'pleasure and delight', 'peace and tranquillity', 'hills and woods', 'close and noisy', 'brick and stone', 'pains and pleasure', 'dim and feeble', 'enmity and hatred', 'vague and half-formed', 'remote and distant', 'pride and worldliness', 'noise and brawling', 'turf and moss', 'peaceful and serene', 'pleasant and happy', 'neat and clean', 'proud and pleased', 'spruce and smart' – like well-behaved school children, the words quietly file past in twos so as not to disturb such unearthly tranquillity. The scenery itself is prim and proper, flanked by purring adjectives, a countryside where the hill is 'green' and the air 'balmy', a magnified cliché. Ideal and idyllic, nature is an abstraction: like the 'the ivy and honeysuckle', '*the* rose' grows there in the singular (xxxii, 210–11, my italics). In this paradise regained, fashioned in the image of his 'white-headed' master, Oliver already seems like an old man or, worse, like an old child. As Dickens so charmingly and ingenuously puts it, 'it is no wonder that, by the end of that short time, Oliver had become completely domesticated' (xxxii, 212): nowhere in the novel is the use of the passive voice so well attuned to its subject.

There should be at this stage no further obstacle to the child's integration into the cosy world where he fits so well. Dickens could easily summon Brownlow back from the West Indies and bring his novel to a conclusion. If he does not do so, it is because he has a number of problems to solve, punishments to inflict, accounts to settle. He must bring Bumble to book, track down Monks, kill off Nancy, execute Sikes and make sure that Fagin is tried and sentenced to death. The result is that, meanwhile, Oliver is removed from the foreground. During a sequence of as many as fourteen chapters (from chapter 37 to chapter 50), he puts in an appearance on one occasion only. Should we infer that he is no longer the main character of the novel that bears his name? Of course we should not when, all too obviously, accounts are settled with the sole aim of avenging his past and of securing his future. The blood of the guilty will not be shed in vain or for pure morality's sake: Oliver will gain a father and an inheritance into the bargain. A paltry success, one might object, since the father is dead and the inheritance partially squandered, but 'signs and tokens'[13] matter more to Dickens than living fathers or ready money.

The discovery of the child's origins has, besides, the immense merit of reassuring old Mr Grimwig. Reassuring Mr Grimwig may not appear indispensable if we only see him as an old eccentric or a second-rate character. But, no matter how ludicrous and episodic he may seem to be, the man plays a vital role in what he himself calls, like the novelist he is, 'the life and adventures of Oliver Twist' (xiv, 89). For we must bear in mind that he is the one who in chapter 14 gets the action going again: it is following his visit to Brownlow and the bet which ends their talk that the boy is put to the test, sent on an errand to the bookseller's and thus exposed to the dangers of the London streets where he will once again fall a victim to Fagin's schemings. Had not Grimwig challenged his friend, Oliver would have stayed put and been spared a lot of trouble! Nor would this have happened, it should be noted, if Brownlow himself, rather than disprove his friend's suspicions, had chosen to ignore them. And as Brownlow is no eccentric, his reaction raises a number of questions: does not the good man's imprudence betray his own prejudices? And, under the cover of eccentricity, is not Grimwig after all the spokesman of a whole class of men brought up to mistrust? Is he not expressing the unacknowledged fears of his own interlocutor and would not their dialogue be better described as a monologue in two parts? Their parallel replies, ' "We shall see" ... "We will" ' (xiv, 89), would invite us to think so.

The conflict that opposes them is in fact no more than a friendly tiff. The two friends simply agree to differ, waywardly sticking to surmises that only the test of time will prove. But, when it comes to the means of getting at the truth, they are no longer at variance. Grimwig, to justify his distrust of the boy, asks a series of questions, 'Where does he come from? Who is he? What is he?', which would sound provocative to many modern interlocutors but which raise no objection on the part of Brownlow. He merely concedes that he is ill-informed: 'Mr Brownlow admitted that on no point of inquiry could he yet return a satisfactory answer; and that he had postponed any investigation into Oliver's previous history until he thought the boy was strong enough to bear it' (xiv, 88). How indeed could he react otherwise when his deep-seated worries coincide exactly with his friend's questions. Right from the first moment of meeting Oliver, he has been obsessed with the child's looks and possible connections, confusedly associating character and pedigree: 'There is something in that boy's face,' he says to himself, 'something that touches and interests me. *Can* he be innocent? He looked like – ... Bless my soul! – where have I seen something like that look before?' (xi, 61). And to confirm his favourable prejudices, he will henceforth devote himself to proving the boy's origins, being as convinced as his opponent that essence precedes existence.

Should Brownlow fail to find a father for his protégé, we may even wonder if it is not Grimwig who would win the wager. For the questions that the two friends have at the back of their minds are precisely those that Dickens's novel is bent on answering: origins, identity, status or character (Where? Who? What?) are too closely interrelated throughout for us to dissociate the purpose of the novelist from the enquiries of his fussy old men. And when Brownlow tells Dr Losberne of the 'object' he has in view, namely 'the discovery of Oliver's parentage, and regaining for him the inheritance of which, if this story be true, he has been fraudulently deprived' (xli, 281), it is almost like hearing the voice of the author describing his own enterprise as well as his methods and his reservations. As it turns out, the story *is* true and the boy's parentage is discovered and proved. A novel of origins, *Oliver Twist*, like *Tom Jones*, ends on the celebration of the hero's merit and birth, which for Dickens as for Fielding are two sides of the same coin.[14] Oliver's merit, like Tom's, was not a means but a sign; it never favoured his ascent, but simply justified it.

The 'ifs' of the story-teller, false quarrels, feigned suspicions, mere stratagems intended to delay the happy ending ('if the story be true'), are quite acceptable in terms of narrative technique, and we certainly cannot condemn the novelist for resorting to such well-tried devices to keep us interested. But when we consider the social message of the book, we come up against too many inconsistencies to find the method entirely satisfactory. The constraints of realism that should normally determine his fate carry no weight with Oliver, and this is all the more remarkable and disturbing as all the other characters in this novel are conditioned from childhood by the world in which they grew up: 'Thank Heaven upon your knees, dear lady,' Nancy says to Rose, 'that you had friends to care for and keep you in your childhood, and that you were never in the midst of cold and hunger, and riot and drunkenness, and – and something worse than all – as I have been from my cradle; I may use the word, for the alley and the gutter were mine, as they will be my death-bed' (xl, 271). The future will prove her right: no one will be spared, neither the guilty nor even the innocent. No one except Oliver whose fate blatantly contradicts authorial pronouncements on social determinism and narratorial warnings. To give just one example: at the end of the first chapter, the newly born child 'enveloped in the old calico robes' of the workhouse is 'badged and ticketed' for life, we are told, 'a parish child – the orphan of a workhouse – the humble half-starved drudge – to be cuffed and buffeted through the world – despised by all, and pitied by none' (i, 3); but 'the power of dress' soon proves less irreversible than we were first led to believe: no sooner does he re-enter the world to which he truly belongs than Mrs Bedwin exclaims very perceptively, 'How well he looks, and how like a gentleman's son he is dressed again!' (xli, 280). Any other parish boy in similar circumstances would have seemed decked out in someone else's Sunday best. Dressed in borrowed robes, Oliver on the contrary looked from the very first 'like a gentleman's son' disguised as a beggar. He is the exception that confirms the rule, the waif that goes through life uncontaminated by evil influences, speaks the king's English almost in his cradle, has an innate knowledge of the decalogue and goes by its rules in the midst of criminals: he is the fairy-tale hero of a realistic novel.

Some critics offer a different reading of the book: 'There is nothing of the fairy-tale in *Oliver Twist*' asserts Q. D. Leavis,[15] while Arnold Kettle puts the stress on the social implications of the novel's topicality: 'For when he walks up to the master of the workhouse and asks for more gruel,' he writes, 'issues are at stake which make the world of Jane Austen tremble.'[16] But the social satire that Dickens provides does not make the world of Jane Austen shake as violently as Kettle would have us believe, since it is precisely the world of Jane Austen into which the hero is eventually repatriated. The picture that, meanwhile, the novelist gives us of the underworld serves first and foremost to exalt the hero's exceptional progress, the workhouse and the thieves' dens being obstacles to be overcome rather than worlds to be reformed, temporary shelters for a gentle *picaro*.

Nor can it be convincingly maintained that Oliver is turned overnight into the son of a gentleman: 'Until he wakes up in Mr Brownlow's house', Kettle writes, 'he is a poor boy struggling against the inhumanity of the state. After he has slept himself into the Brownlow world he is a young bourgeois who has been done out of his property.'[17] Surely, there is no such metamorphosis. Oliver *was* a 'young bourgeois' from the very moment of his conception both in the genetic and in the literary sense. His awakening at Brownlow's house is a symbolic rebirth following upon a state of lethargy which acts as a reminder of his embryonic life. The narrator's musings on prenatal life in chapter 32 (devoted to 'the happy life Oliver began to lead with his kind friends') will have a similar function:

The memories which peaceful country scenes call up, are not of this world, nor its thoughts and hopes. ... but beneath all this, there lingers, in the least reflective mind, a vague and half-formed consciousness of having held such feelings long before, in some remote and distant time; which calls up solemn thoughts of distant times to come. (xxxii, 210)

Through this allegory of the *déjà vu* and of the relation between past and present, we are invited to read the boy's integration into the world of the middle class as a *re*integration, a 'domestication' in the literal sense, the homecoming of the lost child whose virtuous behaviour must have been, all things considered, the spontaneous manifestation of subliminal memory.

Oliver, as we see, is a false parvenu whose progress was in fact a pilgrimage to origins and who had arrived long before he had left. If therefore we read the novel as the story of Oliver Twist, rather than as a document on crime and poverty, we must acknowledge that the social fable is far from subversive; it does not disturb order, it is a return to order, and the two nations, once the curtain has dropped, will remain mutually exclusive worlds whose sole connections will be those of cops and robbers.

But, as a family romance, the story is more disturbing, for it ends with the enthronement of a bastard son and heir, which implies an unusual and unorthodox reversal of parts.[18] Oliver, the love-child, has for his creators (author and father) the 'true legitimacy' (*BH*, lxiv, 753) that John Jarndyce will recognize some years later in Esther, whereas his half-brother, the fruit of a sordid marriage, bears the mark of 'true bastardy', a birthmark, the scarlet letter of his parents' loveless union, 'A broad red mark, like a burn or scald' (xlvi, 315) which is also the sign of his moral degeneracy. The testament of Edwin Leeford, the father who has come to curse his legitimate son, officially confirms this anomaly:

'The will,' said Mr. Brownlow, ... 'was in the same spirit as the letter. He talked of miseries which his wife had brought upon him; of the rebellious disposition, vice, malice, and premature bad passions of you, his only son, who had been trained to hate him; and left you, and your mother, each an annuity of eight hundred pounds. The bulk of his property he divided into two equal portions – one for Agnes Fleming, and the other for their child, if it should be born alive and ever come of age. If it were a girl, it was to inherit the money unconditionally; but if a boy, only on the stipulation that in his minority he should never have stained his name with any public act of dishonour, meanness, cowardice, or wrong. He did this, he said, to mark his confidence in the mother, and his conviction – only strengthened by approaching death – that the child would share her gentle heart, and noble nature. If he were disappointed in this expectation, then the money was to come to you; for then, and not till then, when both children were equal, would he recognise your prior claim upon his purse, who had none upon his heart, but had, from an infant, repulsed him with coldness and aversion.' (li, 351)

Owing to his spiritual bastardy, Monks thus loses in a single blow his rights as first born and his patrimony. He is still entitled to bear the name of his father, though he does not deserve it: 'Edward Leeford,' Brownlow says to him, 'blush for your unworthiness who bear the name' (xlix, 332). But he will not often be given a chance of blushing since he has of his own accord estranged himself from his father and opted for a pseudonym, 'that assumed name' (liii, 365) that he will take with him right to the New World.

Baseness is Monks's true inheritance. Dickens through this creation stigmatizes the damaging effects of a society which has proved capable of engendering monsters by its greed and selfishness, a subject that fore-shadows more vehement attacks in the later novels. But it would be wrong to read in *Oliver Twist* the same indictment of bourgeois society as in, say, *Martin Chuzzlewit* or *Little Dorrit*. Dickens in this novel treats the middle class very tactfully and shows more consideration for the monstrous off-spring of a bourgeois couple than for monsters born from the scum of society. Monks will be spared the fate of Fagin and his companions although he is no better than any of them. He will even be given a new chance together with a portion of his brother's inheritance though he has no claim to it: 'By the provisions of his father's will, Oliver would have been entitled to the whole; but Mr Brownlow, unwilling to deprive the elder son of the opportunity of retrieving his former vices and pursuing an honest career, proposed this mode of distribution, to which his young charge joyfully acceded' (liii, 365). Then, for justice sake, he will eventually be made to die; he will die 'in prison' after squandering his money and 'undergoing a long confinement for some fresh act of fraud and knavery' (liii, 365), but this will be a natural death and it will take place offstage and abroad, far from Brownlows and Maylies whose serenity should henceforth go undisturbed. Surely, these are attentions that cannot go unnoticed . . .

At the end of his trials, as he has not stained his name, Oliver for his part becomes his father's genuine legatee and this inheritance at once sanctions his birth and rewards his merit. All is well that ends well, we are first inclined to think. Yet, to be perfectly satisfactory the inheritance should also include the family name, but who ever heard of Oliver Leeford? The father, alas, when he drew up his last wishes, did not suspect that the child would enter the world in clandestine circumstances and be deprived at birth of his other parent so that for many years there would be 'a blank left for

[his] surname' (xxxviii, 254) on the civil register as there was on his mother's partly engraved 'wedding-ring'. The orphan will pay dearly for the sins of his parents, so dearly indeed that he will never come to be called by his father's surname. His identity comes too late to gain him acceptability even from the pen of his biographer. When the novel comes to a close, our hero has a father, but it is as if he had no forebears.

4 The sons of Dombey

Tout le monde ne peut pas être orphelin

Not everybody can be an orphan

Jules Renard

A daughter after all?

Dombey and Son is, notoriously, a novel that does not keep the promises of its title. With the death of little Paul in chapter 16, we realize that the henceforth superfluous 'and son' had been misleadingly ironic from the very start and we feel invited to interpret the structural and dramatic irony of the story as a welcome form of poetic justice, the well-deserved punishment of a proud and selfish father whom we have been educated to dislike for his cruelty to his daughter, his overbearing attitude to his domestics, his chilling affection for his son and heir, his businessman's vision of private life.

This retributive strategy is none the less very cruel on the hero, suddenly cheated of expectations that he had been encouraged to take for granted. It is all the more so as the encouragement had come after much frustration: no fewer than ten years had elapsed before Dombey had been blessed with the birth of a male child, ten full years of 'hope deferred'.[1] Then another six or seven years of wishful thinking had preceded this bereavement that readers themselves find it hard to bear. Dickens in this novel has dramatized the fulfilment of his hero's dream so as to dash it spectacularly. Never before had he behaved so cynically, never had he dealt so harshly with a character, not even with Grandfather Trent: the death of little Nell had been tragic, not ironic.

Fulfilling his hero's dream and then thwarting it actually goes against the grain of Dickens's usual manner. The process will be repeated only once, some fifteen years later, in *Great Expectations*, his treacherous 'tale of lost illusions'[2] aiming, rather unsuccessfully, at the destruction of his own favourite myth, the providential myth so well illustrated in *Oliver Twist*. Here, more understandably, it is a father's myth that he sets out to challenge.

But, on close examination, Dombey's fatherly myth proves to be very similar to the basic myth, the sons' myth of expectations, that informs the

44

other novels; it is the negative image of the photograph somehow, a dream of continuity, or, to stick to the metaphor of photography, a dream of re-production. Dombey has been Son, and Son will be Dombey; it is in the nature of things that it should be so, it is written in the compelling 'and' that links them together as it must link future and past generations for ever and ever: 'He had risen, as his father had before him, in the course of life and death, from Son to Dombey' (*D&S*, i, 2), the narrator says of the present head of firm and family. Like father, like son: Son will be his *alter ego*, his biological and social replica, 'the little image by inheritance, and in unconscious imitation' (viii, 93) whose likeness must be confirmed at the Registrar's office: 'He will be christened Paul, ... of course,' Dombey says to his dying wife. 'Of course,' she 'feebly' echoes (i, 1).

The 'of course' sounds ironic and is clearly intended to be so. But the irony is not consistent with Dickens's allegiances both as a novelist and as a family man: first sons in his novels are all baptized in the name of the father when they are legitimate, and his own first born was named 'Charles' in perfect accordance with bourgeois tradition. The ultimate development of this story will in fact illustrate the symbolism of the father/son identity so dear to his heart and contradict this hasty and, all things considered, unjustified criticism. His real disapproval concerns the use of the word 'son' itself, the Dombeyan connotations attached to the common noun, not the choice of a Christian name:

But he loved his son with all the love he had. If there were a warm place in his frosty heart, his son occupied it; if its very hard surface could receive the impression of any image, the image of that son was there; though not so much as an infant, or as a boy, but as a grown man – the 'Son' of the Firm. (*D&S*, viii, 92)

What is wrong about Dombey is his confusion of family and business relationships. The 'Son' of his dream has been capitalized in the financial as much as in the typographical sense of the term, turned into an emblem, an advertisement, a trademark. A link in the chain, 'Son' is destined to become, like his father, a transient 'representative of the firm' (i, 2) and of the 'name' (x, 127), a creature of Dombeyism; and Dombeyism rather than Dombey is the target of the moralist.

Dombey himself actually appears to be the first, though acquiescent victim of the system. As long as a new link with the future was missing, he has uncomplainingly played the double part of 'Dombey and Son', and, the eponymous hero of the book on these two accounts, he goes on playing it during the first quarter of the novel while his little boy is 'qualifying for a man' (xii, 170). Little Paul knows that much: 'He's Dombey and Son', he says to Mr Toots with inadvertent insolence in reply to a question concerning his father's affluent position. But still more inadvertently subversive is Toots's reaction on his failing to catch the meaning of the phrase: 'And which?' he asks (xii, 153). 'And Son, Sir', replies Paul. During this brief verbal exchange, the two innocent ironists thus offer us a sharp and grotesque parody of the book's title and of the values at stake.

The reifying 'which' of Toots sums up the situation and justifies the plot or what should rather be called the counterplot of *Dombey and Son*. For the book actually reads as if two novelists were writing it simultaneously though at cross-purposes, or as if it was the sum of two novels with one title: *Dombey and Son* by Paul Dombey the Elder, and *Dombey and Son* by Charles Dickens.

Dombey is a narrative artist of a compulsive, unimaginative type, making no allowances for unforeseen contingencies, 'impatient to advance into the future, and to hurry over the intervening passages of his [son's] history' (viii, 92). Dickens, the master novelist, is in no such hurry, knowing that he will have the last word anyway, watching his dupe from a distance, warning the reader and preparing him for further developments:

Often after dark, one other figure walked alone before the Doctor's house. He rarely joined them on the Saturdays now. He could not bear it. He would rather come unrecognised, and look up at the windows where his son was qualifying for a man; and wait, and watch, and plan, and hope.

Oh! could he but have seen, or seen as others did, the slight spare boy above, watching the waves and clouds at twilight, with his earnest eyes, and breasting the window of his solitary cage when birds flew by, as if he would have emulated them, and soared away! (xii, 170)

Those two paragraphs well show the two novelists at work, but the second's knowledge of the first is not reciprocated and one narrator has been delegated to tell the two stories. Dombey's waiting, and watching, and planning, and hoping is a small Russian doll in the big belly of Dickens's novel.

In his famous letter of 25 July 1846, Dickens had clearly imparted to Forster his intention to foil the plot of his hero:

I will now go on to give you an outline of my immediate intentions in reference to *Dombey*. I design to show Mr D. with that one idea of the Son taking firmer and firmer possession of him, and swelling and bloating his pride to a prodigious extent. As the boy begins to grow up, I shall show him quite impatient for his getting on, and urging his masters to set him great tasks, and the like ... When the boy is about ten years old (in the fourth number), he will be taken ill, and will die ... The death of the boy is a death-blow, of course, to all the father's schemes and cherished hopes ...[3]

Nothing could be plainer, except the first note of the Memoranda, '*Boy born, to die*',[4] or the trenchant remark in the letter of 6 December informing Forster of a slight change of schedule, 'Paul, I shall slaughter at the end of number five.'[5] But there is no need for the ordinary reader to have an intimate knowledge of the correspondence or of the number plans to perceive the author's purpose. How indeed could he miss the hints when they are so many and when they so early stare him in the face? The child's fate is heralded when he is still in his cradle: long before he begins to wither and sicken, long before he becomes 'a living skeleton' (viii, 97), Paul is pronounced to be 'a temporary' (iii, 27), baptized 'into [his] grave' (v, 58), doomed to an untimely death. It is easy to surmise that his will be a fast journey from the cradle to the grave.

The flippancy of Susan Nipper's – or the narrator's – remarks tends, however, to make the child less pitiable than he might be under other stylistic circumstances. Paul is too little, of course, to repeat Hamlet's joke himself during the dismal scene of his baptism, but he will soon behave as if he was in the know, the author's accomplice enjoying the game and cheekily handling the 'ifs' of suspense: 'That's what I mean to do, when I— . . . If I grow up' (xiv, 190), he declares to Mrs Pipchin whose 'grey eye' scans his 'thoughtful face' in vain for explanations. 'If you had to die', he enquires from the 'much disturbed' Mr Toots, ' – Don't you think you would rather die on a moonlight night . . .?' (xii, 168–9). Informed, it would seem, of what the future of the novel has in store for him, he rather perversely tries the unhappy ending on his listeners whereas, in the meantime, his blind and far more pitiable father goes on hoping against the odds.

The use of modals subtly opposes the son's awareness of his creator's intentions ('If you *had to* die') and the father's mistaken certitudes which, ironically, outlast even the end of the dream. On the train to Leamington, when hopes have turned into regrets, Dombey, pathetically, sticks to the auxiliary that deceitfully helped him take his dreams for granted, establishing a lasting and irrational confusion between destiny and expectations: 'To think that this lost child, who *was to* have divided with him his riches, and his projects, and his power, and allied with whom he *was to* have shut out all the world as with a double door of gold, should have let in such a herd to insult him with their knowledge of his defeated hopes' (xx, 275, my italics). The hopes are defeated, but not the hoping. Being introduced in the next chapter to the beautiful widow of Mr Granger, one of the first questions he will think of asking will be related to his obsession: 'Was there any family?' 'There was a boy', he will be told, which will set him thinking backward – 'a shade came over his face' – and forward: '"Indeed?" said Mr Dombey, raising his head' (xxi, 286). The new hope, inevitably, will meet another defeat.

The narrator, for his part, has no need of modals to predict the future. In plain indicative the opening description of Dombey and his new-born son already contradicts the pledges of the title. The well-advertised 'and' that seemed to bind them together for ever is given pride of place in the very first sentence that pompously hinges on it, but it is abruptly dropped and made conspicuous by its absence in the following paragraphs:

Dombey was about eight-and-forty years of age. Son about eight-and-forty minutes. Dombey was rather bald ... Son was very bald ...

Dombey, exulting in the long-looked-for event, jingled and jingled the heavy gold watch-chain that depended from below his trim blue coat ... Son with his little fists curled up and clenched, seemed, in his feeble way, to be squaring at existence for having come upon him so unexpectedly. (i, 1)

Deconstruction and construction are seen to be paradoxically connected from the first in Dickens's narrative grammar. The undermining of the father's plot is already at work in the narrator's syntax, weakening the foundations of the dream. Its full stops are like dead ends, preventing co-ordination.

Estranged from the outset, father and son will remain strangers right up to the end. When they are last seen together, the dying child is unable to identify the 'still and solemn' figure at the bottom of his bed; he only sees an 'it', an unnameable, almost frightening 'that', a 'figure with its head upon its hand ...', rarely lifting up its face', and he hardly trusts his eyes:

Paul began to wonder languidly, if it were real; and in the night-time saw it sitting there, with fear.

'Floy!' he said. 'What *is* that?'

'Where, dearest?'

'There! at the bottom of the bed.'

'There's nothing there, except Papa!'

The figure lifted up its head, and rose, and coming to the bedside, said:

'My own boy! Don't you know me?' (xvi, 222)

Dombey, the reifier, is reified in his turn. Though it would be more accurate to say that he was reified in the first place and that his sharpsighted son has perceived what grown-ups are unable to see.

'The design affecting Paul and his father', Forster tells us, 'had been planned from the opening, and was carried without real alteration to the close.'[6] The letter of 25 July is indeed quite explicit on this point and on what was to follow:

When the boy ... is ill, and when he is dying, I mean to make him turn always for refuge to the sister still, and keep the stern affection of the father at a distance. So Mr Dombey – for all his greatness, and for all his devotion to the child – will find himself at arms' length from him even then; and will see that his love and confidence are all bestowed upon his sister, whom Mr Dombey has used – and so has the boy himself too, for that matter – as a mere convenience and handle to him. The death of the boy is a death-blow, of course, to all the father's schemes and cherished hopes; and 'Dombey and Son,' as Miss Tox will say at the end of the number, 'is a Daughter after all.' ... From that time, I purpose changing his feeling of indifference and uneasiness towards his daughter into a positive hatred ... At the same time I shall change *her* feeling towards *him* for one of a greater desire to love him, and to be loved by him ... So I mean to carry the story on, through all the branches and off-shoots and meanderings that come up; and through the decay and downfall of the house, and the bankruptcy of Dombey, and all the rest of it; when his only staff and treasure, and his unknown Good Genius always, will be this rejected daughter, who will come out better than any son at last, and whose love for him, when discovered and understood, will be his bitterest reproach.[7]

This summary, however, does not provide the whole story. 'All kinds of things will be added to it, of course', Dickens actually warned his friend at the end of his letter. It seems that at this stage, he had no knowledge of what 'all' these 'things' would be: no mention is made of another wife, and no name-dropping tells us about Mrs Skewton and Major Bagstock's circle; but these people were soon to play a prominent part and push Florence into the background, while Dombey's second marriage was to become, as John Butt and Kathleen Tillotson remark, 'the real storm-centre of the novel'.[8]

Admittedly, we never forget about Florence, but her path and her father's do not cross very often and Miss Tox's observation does not correspond to what we get after the fifth instalment or even, in spite of Dickens's professed intentions, to what we get at the end of the novel when the remark is repeated with good emphasis on its early pertinence: '"And so, Dombey and Son, as I observed upon a certain sad occasion," said Miss Tox, winding up a host of recollections, "is indeed a daughter, Polly, after all"' (lix, 803). Father and daughter are reunited at long last, but this is not enough to justify the idea that 'Dombey and Daughter' would have been a more suitable title: *Dombey and Son*, as I read it, is *Dombey and Son* 'after all'.

This, I am aware, is not the way people read the novel as a rule. It is usually assumed that 'the central interest is sustained on the relationship between Florence and her father',[9] that their reconciliation is what the novel has been driving at from the first, that the power of love and unfailing faithfulness is the message of the moral fable. My own contention is that this is what Dickens sincerely meant to do but that he betrayed himself into doing something different.

It has even been suggested that Dombey was a new King Lear.[10] But this comparison is totally unfounded: Lear craves the affection of his daughter as early as Act I, scene i, and their tragedy is based on a misunderstanding, whereas Dombey in turn ignores and hates Florence until his last minute change of heart. Lear, who has no son, has no reason to behave like a sexist father and is actually taken in by the flattery of two unscrupulous daughters. It is, besides, a dead Cordelia that is brought back to him, with no hope on which to build the future, whereas in Dickens's drama Florence is alive and well when she returns to her father and the epilogue confirms expectations of long-lasting happiness. If we want a reference to Shakespeare we would be better advised to seek it in other plays than in the tragedy of Lear. In the *Winter's Tale* for instance: lost and banished like Perdita, stared into stone by the Gorgon like Hermione, Florence impersonates the spirit of the tale, a tale of return and rebirth; like Mamilius, Paul has been sacrificed, the victim of a father's misdirected feelings, but a son-in-law is expected to replace him in the house of Dombey as Florizel will do at the court of Leontes; Susan Nipper, when she admonishes her wrong-headed master and speaks her mind – 'respectful and without offence, but out, and how I dare I know not but I do!' (xliv, 588) – well deserves Butt and Tillotson's comparison with Paulina.[11]

But *Cymbeline* would be even closer to the mark. The situation is indeed very similar in the novel and the romance. At the beginning of the play we are told that Imogen has secretly married Leonatus Posthumus with whom she was brought up and who had long been like a brother to her. 'Her husband banished', and 'she imprison'd',[12] the Princess complains that, 'like the tyrannous breathing of the north', the King, her father, has chosen to shake all 'buds from growing'.[13] So well might Florence when her own father, urged on by Cloten-like Carker, exiles Walter, her dear 'brother', to the West Indies and she remains a prisoner 'in the great dreary house' with the 'blank walls' staring at her. Her filial devotion prevents her from being as outspoken as Shakespeare's heroine, but Dickens uses the same kind of imagery to describe her predicament: 'above the archway of the door, there was a monstrous fantasy of rusty iron curling and twisting like a petrification of an arbour over the threshold, budding in spikes and corkscrew points' (xxiii, 311); and he constantly refers to Dombey as an ice-cold man, a man with a 'frosty heart' (viii, 92), so stiff and unbending that he 'might have been hung up for sale at a Russian fair as a specimen of a frozen gentleman' (v, 61).[14] Left alone, Cymbeline's daughter runs away from her father's home, is rescued by friendly men, believes for a while that Posthumus is dead, and eventually returns to the King to whom she brings the two sons and heirs who had in childhood been stolen from him. Florence's story follows the same pattern: self-banished from home where she has been unfairly treated, she seeks sanctuary at Uncle Gills's place where Captain Cuttle becomes her protector, soon hears the sad news that Walter has been shipwrecked and believes him to have drowned, marries him when he returns (having miraculously survived the shipwreck), follows him to China, gives birth to a boy, and then returns to her father to whom she offers this new little Paul as if she were restoring the lost one. The scene of her return, related in a chapter ambiguously entitled 'Retribution', dramatizes this symbolic restitution: 'Papa, love, I am a mother. I have a child ... A boy, Papa. His name is Paul' (lix, 802).

Dickens had a good knowledge of Shakespeare and, leaving details aside, we may perceive in this novel the influence of the last plays, tragedies that end well, marked like the Greek romances after which they were modelled by the separation of lovers and close relatives, false reports of death, shipwrecks, chance meetings and 'miraculous reunions of parents and children, or lovers, long believed dead'.[15]

Very Shakespearian too is the theme of restoration that dominates the last pages. Miss Tox thought she was clever when she declared that 'Dombey and Son' was 'a Daughter after all', but Mrs Toots is even more shrewd in her commentary of the happy dénouement: '"Thus," said my wife,' her husband reports, '"from his daughter, after all, another Dombey and Son will ascend" – no "rise;" that was Mrs Toots's word – "triumphant!"' (xlii, 832). The 'after all', which is very noticeably a verbal echo of Tox's famous remark, underscores Dickens's awareness of the deeper, long-hidden meaning of his fable. Less subversive or feminist than he is often said to have been in this novel, the novelist has been very thoughtfully working at this restoration of the rightful heir to the throne of the Dombeys. The self-referential 'after all' shows how carefully structured and thought out the whole story was: 'after all', Dombey's dream is fulfilled; 'after all', the title of the novel was less misleading than we first believed.

Susan's expression, 'another Dombey and Son', it will be objected, is not quite appropriate: as Mrs Chick early prophesied, 'Florence will never, never, never, be a Dombey' (v, 50) and her baby, whether we like it or not, is not a Dombey either. Dickens was, of course, well aware of that and had to devise a means of making the message sound acceptable. The only solution was to turn Walter, the genetic father, into a symbolic representative of the House of Dombey. This was, to be sure, a challenging enterprise, difficult to reconcile with the Whittingtonian aspirations of the moneyless young clerk which, in the early chapters, have a grossly suspicious ring: the stereotyped wish-fulfilment dream of marrying one's master's daughter, however naïve and innocent it may be made to appear, suggests misplaced expectations, and if the dream comes true the gratified dreamer runs the risk of being taken for a usurper. The danger here was all the greater as the dream throughout is very crudely formulated by Uncle Sol and Captain Cuttle. No sooner has Walter entered the firm as a junior clerk than the two men begin fantasizing and drink a toast to 'Walter's House': 'We'll finish the bottle, to the House, Ned – Walter's House. Why it may be his House one of these days, in part. Who knows? Sir Richard Whittington married his master's daughter' (iv, 45). And the fiction is shamelessly repeated whenever Walter's future is discussed or Florence's name mentioned. In chapter 17, relating Cuttle's first visit to the firm after the death of the rightful son and heir, the subject is again tackled by the Captain with offensive disregard for the memory of the dead child:

'Gay has brilliant prospects,' observed Mr Carker, stretching his mouth wider yet: 'all the world before him.'
    'All the world and his wife too, as the saying is,' returned the delighted Captain.
    At the word 'wife' (which he had uttered without design), the Captain stopped, cocked his eye again ...
        ...
    'There's a general in-draught that way,' observed the happy Captain. 'Wind and water sets in that direction, you see. Look at his being present t'other day!'
    'Most favourable to his hopes,' said Mr Carker.
    'Look at his being towed along in the wake of that day!' pursued the Captain, 'Why what can cut him adrift now?'
    'Nothing,' replied Mr Carker.
    'You're right again,' returned the Captain, giving his hand another squeeze. 'Nothing it is. So! steady! There's a son gone: pretty little creetur. Ain't there?'
    'Yes, there's a son gone,' said the acquiescent Carker.
    'Pass the word, and there's another ready for you,' quoth the Captain. 'Nevy of a scientific uncle! Nevy of Sol Gills! Wal'r! Wal'r, as is already in your business! And' – said the Captain, rising gradually to a quotation he was preparing for a final burst, 'who – comes from Sol Gills daily, *to* your business, and your buzzums.' (xvii, 231–2)

If Carker was not Cuttle's interlocutor, if we were not aware of his own base designs on Florence, the scene would be unbearable and we would wish 'Wal'r' to the devil.

Another reason why we tolerate the Captain's pushful clumsiness is that we know him to be a kind-hearted, well-intentioned man, speaking in favour of a sincere lover. Dickens has, besides, always seen to it that Walter's aspirations should be dissociated from the vicarious hopes of his protectors. When he drinks to the House and to his master's daughter with them for the first time, he does it very tactfully, almost apologetically: 'Since you have introduced the mention of her, and have connected me with her, and have said that I know all about her, I shall make bold to amend the toast. So here's to Dombey – and Son – and Daughter!' (iv, 46). And after meeting Florence and falling in love with her, he complacently nurses his infatu-ation, yet reasonably considers his dreams as hopeless fancies:

In this way, Walter, so far from forgetting or losing sight of his acquaintance with Florence, only remembered it better and better. As to its adventurous beginning, and all those little circumstances which gave it a distinctive character and relish, he took them into account, more as a pleasant story very agreeable to his imagination, and not to be dismissed from it, than as a part of any matter of fact with which *he* was concerned. They set off Florence very much, to his fancy; but not himself. Some-times he thought (and then he walked very fast) what a grand thing it would have been for him to have been going to sea on the day after that first meeting, and to have gone, and to have done wonders there, and to have stopped away a long time, and to have come back an Admiral of all the colours of the dolphin, or at least a Post-Captain with epaulettes of insupportable brightness, and to have married Florence (then a beautiful young woman) in spite of Mr Dombey's teeth, cravat, and watch-chain, and borne her away to the blue shores of somewhere or other, triumphantly. But these flights of fancy seldom burnished the brass plate of Dombey and Son's Offices into a tablet of golden hope, or shed a brilliant lustre on their dirty skylights; and when the Captain and Uncle Sol talked about Richard Whittington and masters' daughters, Walter felt that he understood his true position in Dombey and Son's, much better than they did. (ix, 113)

Walter's 'would have been' is more promising than it seems. The expression of his natural sense of the proprieties and of his self-effacing respect for his social betters, it was clearly intended to win the Victorian readers over to a cause that was by no means felt to be a lost one: few are those who, knowing Dickens, would have failed to guess that, no less eager than Uncle Sol and Captain Ned to favour the boy's prospects, the avuncular novelist was secretly planning the happy fulfilment of those 'flights of fancy'. Unlike the 'was to have been' of Dombey that betrayed the incurable arrogance of the defeated dreamer and doomed him to further defeat, this past conditional is the future of the novel.

It had not always been so. When Dickens first conceived the general design of his new story, he had intended the boy to go wrong after a while and enter a life of dissipation. In his letter of 25 July, he had told Forster:

About the boy, who appears in the last chapter of the first number, I think it would be a good thing to disappoint all the expectations that chapter seems to raise of his happy connection with the story and the heroine, and to show him gradually and naturally trailing away, from that love of adventure and boyish light-heartedness, into negligence, idleness, dissipation, dishonesty, and ruin. To show, in short, that common, every-day, miserable declension of which we know so much in our ordinary life; to exhibit something of the philosophy of it, in great temptations and an easy nature; and to show how the good turns into bad, by degrees ... Do you think it may be done, without making people angry? ... The question of the boy is very important ... Let me hear all you think about it.[16]

Forster obviously expressed his disapproval and, by November, Dickens had made up his mind to follow his friend's advice: 'I see it will be best as you advise', he wrote, 'to give that idea up; and indeed I don't feel it would be reasonable to carry it out now ... But when I have disposed of Paul (poor boy!) I will consider the subject farther.'[17]

When he considered the subject further, Dickens shaped Walter into the hero of romance he had first promised to become, 'a gallant lad' (xlix, 658) that was to travel the stormy seas, brave all kinds of dangers and return gloriously to marry the heroine. But making Walter worthy of Florence and of the readers' romantic expectations was not sufficient to promote him to the Dombeys' chain of being and did not entitle him to replace the missing link. The laws of romance are not those of fairy tales, and novelists cannot perform ontological miracles. But they can engineer transference rituals and, short of being transformed overnight into a new Paul Dombey, Walter could well be invested with the attributes of the son and heir and officially proclaimed his rightful successor.

Two such ceremonies, with Paul duly officiating, had early paved the way for the ultimate symbolic investiture. The first one had taken place in Brighton, when Walter had travelled there all the way down from London to seek his master's or 'governor''s[18] financial help on behalf of his ruined uncle, and Dombey's son, for the first and, as it turned out, last time in his life, was invited to play his part as partner in the firm. 'Would you like to begin to be Dombey and Son, now, and lend this money to young Gay's uncle?' Dombey had asked Paul, giving solemnity and grandeur to the event. 'You will consider that this is done for you by Master Paul' (x, 134–5), he had then insisted. Walter, to whom 'Master Paul' had meant to *give*, not lend, the money, had thus returned home invested with the boy's fortune thanks to the father's dramatically ironic remark.

The second memorable gesture had been Paul's dying words, 'Remember Walter, dear Papa' (xvi, 224). The exhortation of a dying child is bound to be loaded with meaning, and Paul's was felt to be so both by those who were present and by those who had heard of it. Captain Cuttle had at once declared that Walter would henceforth be 'towed along in the wake of that day' (xvii, 232). Carker had malignantly acquiesced, secretly hoping that the well-named 'Son and Heir' would literally tow away his rival in the wake of death, which had been his intention already in choosing young Gay as the 'successor' of the 'junior' reported to be dead in the Barbados agency (xiii, 174). Florence had been more explicit in her interpretation of her brother's words: 'he liked you very much, and said before he died that he was fond of you, and said "Remember Walter!" and if you'll be a brother to me Walter, ... I'll be your sister all my life' (xix, 261), she had told Walter when he was about to leave, and her parting gift, a little purse with money in it, had first been intended for Paul: 'I made this little gift for Paul. Pray take it with my love, and do not look at it until you are gone away. And now, God bless you, Walter! never forget me. You are my brother, dear' (xix, 263).

The transference is so heavily proclaimed in the scenes preceding Walter's departure that we may wonder whether Dickens is not actually repeating the pattern of raised then dashed expectations already used about Paul. And the news of the shipwreck seems to confirm such apprehensions: had not Paul's last journey been described as a voyage out, a fatal response to the irresistible attraction of the sea? The waves that had beckoned Paul on towards those distant shores from which no one returns might once again sing their sirens' song as they did in chapter 16:

Sister and brother wound their arms around each other, and the golden light came streaming in, and fell upon them, locked together.

'How fast the river runs, between its green banks and the rushes, Floy! But it's very near the sea. I hear the waves! They always said so!'

Presently he told her that the motion of the boat upon the stream was lulling him to rest. How green the banks were now, how bright the flowers growing on them, and how tall the rushes! Now the boat was out at sea, but gliding smoothly on. And now there was a shore before him. Who stood on the bank! –

He put his hands together, as he had been used to do, at his prayers. He did not remove his arms to do it; but they saw him fold them so, behind her neck.

'Mama is like you, Floy. I know her by the face!' (xvi, 224–5)

What the waves did not say, however, was that *Dombey and Son* was not an anticipation of *The Mill on the Floss*. Walter's identification with Paul, his imaginary death by drowning, his miraculous survival were to tell us a different tale altogether from George Eliot's, namely that, 'in their *life*', brother and sister were not to be divided.

But this entailed difficulties. The incestuous embrace of Tom and Maggie in their ultimate reconciliation will be discreetly suggested, short-lived of necessity, and beautified by death. Marrying Walter and Florence is quite another matter and, in chapter 50, Dickens is obviously at great pains to erase the insistently built up allegory of his lovers' relationship. Florence may well insist that they 'can be brother and sister no longer' (1, 677); she fails to convince us. She even fails, for a while, to convince poor Walter whose denegation, 'I have not a brother's right, ... I have not a brother's claim' (1, 678), further stresses the disturbing ambiguity of the new situation.

The task Dickens has set himself is all the more tricky as metaphorical incest is anyway necessary to his fable. If 'another Dombey and Son' is to 'rise' from this union, there must be at some stage a blurring of identities, some confusion perhaps as in that strange dream of Florence's where father, brother and lover are blended with each other and she can hardly separate them in her subconscious:

In her sleep, however, Florence could not lose an undefined impression of what had so recently passed. It formed the subject of her dreams, and haunted her; now in one shape, now in another; but always oppressively; and with a sense of fear. She dreamed of seeking her father in wildernesses, of following his track up fearful heights, and down into deep mines and caverns; of being charged with something that would release him from extraordinary suffering – she knew not what, or why – yet never being able to attain the goal and set him free. Then, she saw him dead, upon that very bed, and in that very room, and knew that he had never loved her to the last, and fell upon his cold breast, passionately weeping. Then, a prospect opened, and a river flowed, and a plaintive voice she knew, cried, 'It is running on,

Floy! It has never stopped! You are moving with it!' And she saw him at a distance stretching out his arms towards her, while a figure such as Walter's used to be, stood near him, awfully serene and still. (xxxv, 487–8)

This is precisely the kind of confusion that the novelist tries to establish in his readers' minds when Florence fondly tells her 'love' that she has a son: 'Papa, love, I am a mother. I have a child ... A boy, Papa. His name is Paul' (lix, 802). The child with a Christian name and no surname appended to it (who ever heard of 'Paul Gay'?) is later mistaken for his own son by Dombey when, in his delirium, he rambles 'through the scenes of his old pursuits' (lxi, 818): 'One time when Walter was in his room, he beckoned him to come near, and to stoop down; and pressing his hand, whispered an assurance to him that he knew he could trust him with *his* child when he was dead' (lxi, 819, my emphasis).[19] The dreaming daughter and the delirious father tell us the same story of transference.

This story, which the dreaming narrator had all the time been telling us between the lines, is both a tale of love's labour that is not lost and an allegory of fatherhood and maternity: Florence who, in her childhood, had mothered her little brother against her father's will (it was, we remember, to be 'wean[ed]' (xi, 141) of her love that Paul had been sent to Dr Blimber's), is rewarded, on reaching womanhood, with the privilege of bearing a new son to her deprived and now repentant father. After replacing her deceased mother, she acts in the place of Dombey's second and unloving wife, the 'new Mama' whose first night in her husband's house had not been spent in her husband's bed but in her step-daughter's bedroom and in her step-daughter's dream, a figure of death-in-life: 'In every vision, Edith came and went, sometimes to her joy, sometimes to her sorrow, until they were alone upon the brink of a dark grave, and Edith pointing down, she looked and saw – what! – another Edith lying at the bottom' (xxxv, 488). Unlike Edith, Florence has never thought of killing and burying her better self; winning her father 'to a better knowledge of his only child' has been 'the purpose of her life' (xxiii, 314) and on succeeding she can bring the loved one the token of her love. The unwanted daughter, the 'bad Boy' (i, 3), long despised, has been entrusted with the part of surrogate mother, the part that Bilhah had performed for Rachel in order that Jacob[20] should not die without issue, a role which, all things considered, was not unsuited to the heroine of a Book of Genesis.

The sons of Dombeyism

The novel that had threatened to be the story of 'Dombey and no Son' has now come full circle and with Walter, the emblematic albeit transitory son and heir, and baby Paul, the substitute for the lost one, it has eventually become the chronicle of Dombey's *sons*.

Dombeyism, in the meantime, has generated offspring of its own. Rob the Grinder, the rebellious son, James Carker, the spiritual son, Carker the Junior, the prodigal son, illustrate, each in his own way, the relationship of dependence, debt and duty that the patriarchal system establishes between men.

Hardly connected with the plot (anyone else could do the spying for him), unimportant as an actant, Rob is brought in artificially. With him we move from the personal and novelistic to the topical and journalistic. Dickens had something to say about Charity Schools and the damage wrought on children by an educational system that he judged inadequate and he gave the boy a role that his story did not require in itself or fully justify.[21]

If the approach had been purely novelistic, it would have been more appropriate to have focused our attention on Rob's youngest brother, Paul's contemporary, the child deprived of his mother's milk because the son of a rich man needed it more urgently. But this young Toodle is not even given a first name. After a brief intrusion into the novel and into Mr Dombey's drawing-room in his mother's arms, the six-week-old infant is carried away by his aunt Jemima and heard of no more. Having banished him out of his house, Dombey will have to banish him from his thoughts which, at the time of Polly's appointment, have been running on the gloomy possibility of some treacherous substitution:

it occurred to him – and it is an instance of the strong attraction with which his hopes and fears and all his thoughts were tending to one centre – that a great temptation was being placed in this woman's way. Her infant was a boy too. Now, would it be possible for her to change them?

Though he was soon satisfied that he had dismissed the idea as romantic and unlikely – though possible, there was no denying – he could not help pursuing it so far as to entertain within himself a picture of what his condition would be if he should discover such an imposture when he was grown old. Whether a man so situated, would be able to pluck away the result of so many years of usage, confidence, and belief, from the impostor, and endow a stranger with it? (ii, 20–1)

In the last paragraph quoted it is in fact the novelist as much as his character that can be heard entertaining and dismissing the 'romantic' idea of the changeling. The hesitant syntax, with its 'thoughs', 'ifs' and 'whethers', betrays the author's reluctance to give up a subject that strongly appeals to his imagination but would lead him nowhere, being totally unsuited to his plot. Once this 'idle speculating'[22] is over, Dickens will discard all thought of giving a role to the last born of the Toodles. The child from now on will be no more a threat to the Dombey dynasty than any of his 'apple-faced' brothers, though no less likely than any of the brood to prove a nuisance 'some day' by 'claiming a sort of relationship to Paul' (ii, 17).

Rob, the eldest, as it turns out, will become such a claimant, unwittingly selected or 'nominated' for the part by Dombey himself when he enrols him with the Grinders: 'Having the power of nominating a child on the foundation of an ancient establishment, called ... the Charitable Grinders,' he tells Polly some six months after her arrival, 'I have ... nominated your eldest son to an existing vacancy' (v, 62). Precedence being due to seniority in Dombey's, and for that matter Dickens's, patriarchal view of society, the choice of the eldest son is no accident. It has the further advantage of rendering the boy's progress immediately operative and of easily following it through within the time-scheme of the main story, which would not be possible with a child of Paul's age. In all other respects, Rob is just one Toodle among many, a representative of the lower classes promoted, within limits, by their social betters.

The limits imposed on the promotion are crudely stated: 'I am far from being friendly,' Dombey explains to the boy's mother, 'to what is called by persons of levelling sentiments, general education. But it is necessary that the inferior classes should continue to be taught to know their position, and to conduct themselves properly. So far I approve of schools' (v, 62). Such a declaration, as a matter of fact, sounds improbably emphatic and cynical and the choice of direct speech is not very felicitous: in the text that Dombey is given to utter as an employer it is the narrator's voice at his satirical best that we at once recognize and we regret that the author should not have opted here for narratorial discourse or interior monologue, either of which would have been more cleverly and more broadly satirical. For, all too obviously, exclusion is considered here as a class attitude, the ruling principle that determines conservative legislation and even social action, and not merely as a father's obsession. It may well have been to drive home these no-trespassing notions into the heads of the poor that such things as Charity Schools had been imagined but, surely, Dombey cannot be held responsible for the educational system of the whole country and his narrow paternal dreams are but a poor reflection of paternalism at large, which is the real subject of the author's disapproval.

The Grinders, not surprisingly, have disastrous effects on Rob who, by dint of being 'huffed and cuffed, and flogged and badged, and taught, as parrots are, by a brute jobbed into his place of schoolmaster with as much fitness for it as a hound' (xx, 274), becomes morally stunted, acquires underhand manners and gets 'into bad ways', even living for a time by sneaking and petty crime. 'The usual return!' Dombey laments on hearing the news, 'The usual return!' (xx, 274).

Much of the irony of the Grinders' episode rests on this notion of return. Dombey, even as he professed to widen the gap between young Paul and his foster-brothers by having Rob thus educated, acknowledged his debt to

Polly's family and established with them the very relationship that he most wanted to prevent, so that his disappointment is to some extent that of a father, or, if we prefer, of a paternalist master. When Rob goes wrong, significantly, his degeneration is expressed in terms of filial impiety; a 'prodigal son' (xxii, 301) for the narrator, he is a 'bad son' for Carker:

'This fellow,' said Mr Carker to Polly, giving him a gentle shake, 'is your son, eh Ma'am?'
    'Yes, Sir,' sobbed Polly, with a curtsey; 'yes, Sir.'
    'A bad son, I am afraid?' said Mr Carker.
    'Not a bad son to me Sir,' returned Polly.
    'To whom then?' demanded Mr Carker. (xxii, 301–2)

To whom indeed? The question is left pending as if, getting no answer from Polly, and expecting none, Carker knowingly turns to us now: 'to whom *then*,' he seems to say, 'if not to Dombey and Dombeyism?'

Ungrateful, refractory and idle, the boy who, instead of letting himself be ground into shape by his teachers, has taken to 'wagging from school', 'walking-matching' and 'bird-catching' (xxii, 297–8) is unquestionably a bad son to Dombeyism. But what else could be expected of this little outcast? Rob is a bad son to a bad father. When, looking for a job, he knocks at the door of the firm and claims 'a sort of relationship' to his mother's 'dear boy' (xvi, 224), he is received as an intruder, denied the welcome he thinks he deserves: 'it's hardly to be bore Sir', Mr Perch complains to Carker, 'that a common lad like that should come a-prowling here, and saying that his mother nursed our House's young gentleman, and that he hopes our House will give him a chance on that account' (xxii, 295–6). Especially now that 'the House's young gentleman' is dead, the claim of the Toodles' living 'son and heir' (xxiii, 318) is felt as an impertinence. Perch, who has imbibed the values of Dombeyism after many years in office at the firm, reacts almost like his master, reminding us of the scene at the railway station, when Dombey had received Toodle's marks of sympathy with 'an angry sense of humiliation' (xx, 273) and the feeling that 'every one set up some claim or other to a share in his dead boy' (xx, 275). There is no sharing in Dombey's system: unloved, unwanted, driven away, 'chivied through the streets', bullied and 'pounded' (xxii, 298), Rob, like Adam's first born, is doomed to be a wanderer: 'young Cain that you are', Carker says to him, 'an't you the idlest vagabond in London?' (xxii, 297).

The story of Rob, 'Rob the Grinder', reads like a fable of social exclusion. But for those who have read Dickens's fragment of autobiography, it has a more personal ring. The words used by Carker, 'Cain', 'vagabond', are the very same words that came to the author's mind when he recorded his own loneliness at the time of his father's imprisonment and desertion: 'The key of the house was sent back to the landlord . . .; and I (small Cain that I was, except that I had never done harm to anyone) was handed over as a lodger to a reduced old lady ..., who, with a few alterations and embellishments, unconsciously began to sit for Mrs Pipchin in *Dombey*, when she took in me', he writes.[23] Slightly further down comes the often quoted remark: 'I know that I have lounged about the streets, insufficiently and unsatisfactorily fed. I know that, but for the mercy of God, I might easily have been, for any care that was taken of me, a little robber or a little vagabond.'[24] Rob is the bad boy young Charles might have been.

But, if he understands juvenile delinquency, Dickens does not excuse it. A most unpleasant character, the Grinder is the creation of a self-righteous man who always remembered that, in adversity, *he* had withstood temptation and kept himself above crime. His social fable is written for the benefit of fathers and patriarchal masters, not as a plea for young criminals or rebellious sons.

A true son of Dombeyism, Carker the Manager, with his 'arrogance of manner, either natural to him, or imitated from a pattern not far off' (xiii, 173), might almost be mistaken for Dombey's younger brother. Almost, but not quite: 'Though always somewhat formal, in his dress, in imitation of the great man whom he served, he stopped short of the extent of Mr Dombey's stiffness: at once perhaps because he knew it to be ludicrous, and because in doing so he found another means of expressing his sense of the difference and distance between them' (xxvii, 369). By thus differentiating himself from the man on whom he models his dress and his behaviour, Carker turns imitation into mimicry, admiration into insolence. This attitude betrays the man's wounded pride, his sense of humiliation at being no more than a 'paid servant' (xlv, 602). He has the ability to manage the great man's business, he knows all about the affairs of the House and even thrives on it financially, he is Dombey's 'confidential agent' (xlii, 570),[25] he is his 'ambassador' and his 'go-between' (xlv, 602), but he will never be his equal or his partner, 'a distinction hitherto reserved solely to inheritors of the great name of Dombey' (xlvi, 606). Not to be a Dombey is the man's tragedy. Not to be a son, Dombey's son, rather. For, in spite of the slight difference in years,[26] Carker's reaction to Dombey's tyranny is that of a spiteful son, his frustration that of a bastard, and it is clearly a son's place that he covets as his reaction shows on the death of Paul, the rightful heir: 'alone in his own room he shows his teeth all day', we are told, smiling at his new prospects, 'and it would seem that there is something gone from Mr Carker's path – some obstacle removed – which clears his way before him' (xviii, 236). Walter Gay, another youngster and a potential son-in-law, is also perceived by the Manager as a rival, an obstacle to be removed, and it is at his suggestion that the boy is shipped off to the West Indies on the 'Son and Heir'.

Such rivalries are disturbing, given the man's age. But, when Edith steps into the novel and the servant becomes his master's rival, the situation is no less pathological.

We know Carker to be a voluptuous man, sensitive to female beauty of the Alice/Edith type. His former affair with Mrs Brown's daughter, the comfort, 'refinement and luxury' (xxxiii, 454) of his cottage, the pictures and prints on the walls, the very titles of the books on his shelves, all testify to his sensual nature. But when we see him in his easy chair looking, 'with a musing smile', at a picture representing a 'scornful Nymph' that looks 'like Edith' (xxxiii, 455), his interest, we realize, is of a different order than sexual attraction or artistic emotion:

With a passing gesture of his hand at the picture – what! a menace? No; yet something like it. A wave as if triumph? No; yet more like that. An insolent salute wafted from his lips? No; yet like that too – he resumes his breakfast, and calls to the chafing and imprisoned bird, who, coming down into a pendant gilded hoop within the cage, like a great wedding-ring, swings in it, for his delight. (xxxiii, 455)

The parrot on her wedding-ring has drawn our attention to a more subtle likeness: the picture is first and foremost like Mr Dombey's wife. This likeness becomes even more threateningly ironic on the occasion of Dombey's visit, when Carker looks at the picture 'with a wicked, silent laugh upon his face' (xlii, 567) while his visitor, sitting with his back to it, discusses his wife's refractoriness and watches the bird swinging 'to and fro, in her great wedding-ring' (xlii, 574), utterly unaware of the storm that is brewing. Entrusted with the task of reasoning Mrs Dombey into obedience, Carker will a moment later hypocritically, yet truthfully, reject the idea of being placed in a false position: '*I* in a false position! ... I could have wished, I own, to have given the lady at whose feet I would lay my humble duty and devotion – for is she not your wife! – no new cause of dislike; but a wish from you is, of course, paramount to every other consideration on earth' (xlii, 575). The oedipal relationship could not be more eloquently expressed.

This blend of hatred and fascination for the father-figure, the wish to serve the father and to destroy him, even if it entails (as it will) self-destruction, the desire to sleep with the father's wife, all the characteristics of the oedipal conflict are impersonated by Carker the Manager. From beginning to end, the man is obsessed by the fatherly image, much as believers are with the thought of God at the back of their minds. He wants to be acknowledged, even as a sinner, by the man whose 'will is law' (xlii, 570). He wants to exist as a son.

The only way for him to exist is to rebel against the father, to be caught in the act, punished, cursed, crushed to death. The long chapter describing his return home from Dijon, his flight away from Dombey's revenge and towards Dombey's last judgement, provides an admirable metaphor of the ambiguous love–hate relationship that binds him to his employer. During his interminable journey towards the green land of childhood and innocence, Carker is haunted by the image of the man 'who had been true and generous to him' (lv, 736) and whom he has wronged and betrayed, an image much more present than that of the woman who has rejected him and used him for her own revenge. The 'villain' (lv, 731) in this chapter becomes a tragic villain, hating Dombey, hating himself, rehearsing the past, remembering 'how jealous he had been of the boy, how jealous he had been of the girl' (lv, 736), a prey to 'fear, regret, and passion' (lv, 737). On reaching the station where he stops for the night, he knows that death is impending: 'How goes the time?' he asks, in almost Shakespearian accents, 'My watch is unwound' (lv, 740). 'Death [is] on him' (lv, 743) and the death-wish is in him, compulsive, irresistible. He spends his last night watching the trains, fascinated by 'the cruel power' of those monsters with the 'red eyes', anticipating his fate: 'To see the great wheels slowly turning,' he muses, 'and to think of being run down and crushed!' (lv, 741–2). At long last, the cruel power of the father will exert itself and, on 'the wooden stage' of the railway station, the tragedy will reach its long-awaited conclusion: 'he saw the man from whom he had fled, emerging from the door . . . And their eyes met' (lv, 743). The death-blow is dealt by Dombey's eyes. When, an instant later, the 'red eyes, bleared and dim' (lv, 743), of the engine stare Carker out of the world he is already a dead man: the law of the father has prevailed and the son has deferred to the father's will.

Chapter 55, devoted to Carker's death, is entitled, derisively, 'Rob the Grinder loses his Place'. This is, to be sure, an easy form of irony, but it is also a reminder that these two characters had much in common. The man and the boy had gone wrong for very similar reasons, being the victims of the same exclusion, both unwanted and rebellious sons, and when their roads had crossed they had tacitly conspired against the oppressor. The accident that brings to an end the wicked association further binds their destinies: too far gone into villainy to be now redeemed by his creator, Carker, by losing his life, makes it possible for the youth, in losing his job and his employer, to be removed from bad influence and to be given a new chance in life. The pairing of characters is often used to such moralizing ends in Dickens's novels, and in his economy, the survival of the redeemable often costs the lives of the damned.

Even more explicit is the connection established between these two other figurative sons, Carker the Junior and Walter. It is John himself who describes the boy as his *alter ego* in a conversation with his brother the Manager:

'I have had . . . my whole heart awakened by my observation of that boy, Walter Gay. I saw in him when he first came here, almost my other self.'

'Your other self!' repeated the Manager, disdainfully.

'Not as I am, but as I was when *I* first came here too; as sanguine, giddy, youthful, inexperienced; flushed with the same restless and adventurous fancies; and full of the same qualities, fraught with the same capacity of leading on to good or evil.' (xiii, 178–9)

Knowing Dickens's original plan for young Gay, we can easily imagine what use he first intended to make of the older man: 'We may be sure', Butt and Tillotson write, 'that Carker the Junior's "extraordinary interest" in Walter Gay was an interest in a young man who was to fall as he had fallen.'[27] The confession he makes to Walter about his past errors and the warning he gives him before his departure – 'God bless you, Walter! Keep you, and all dear to you, in honesty, or strike them dead!' (xiii, 180) – do support their assumption. But, when the novelist changed his mind about the boy's future, Carker the Junior threatened to become a loose thread and another part had to be found for him.

It took Dickens some time to reinstate him into the novel. Much in the background after the fourth instalment, the man is no more than a model of meekness and gratitude during the major episodes and does nothing worth recording until, in the closing number, he is given the unexpected role of providential donor. Dombey has been ruined by his former manager's mismanagement and John, the Manager's brother, who in his youth was forgiven and kept in service after robbing the firm, thinks it an 'act of duty' to repay the 'old lost debt' by handing his own inheritance over to his employer: '[his] chief happiness in this act of restitution', Harriet explains to Morfin, 'is to do it secretly, unknown, and unapproved of' (lviii, 779). 'I have no right to mar the great end of a great history', comments Morfin (lviii, 780), emphasizing Dickens's concern with narrative structure: the loose thread, after all, is not left dangling.

By an interesting reversal of parts, the prodigal son thus becomes the ruined father's benefactor. This edifying dénouement should, as we realize, be attributed primarily to the novelist's love of order and purposefulness; but, even if it was devised to meet aesthetic or structural requirements, it conveys a truly Dickensian message of loving-kindness and generosity. In a novel which has social exclusion for its main subject, this episode also carries rather ironic overtones by turning the master into his servant's dependant: 'Nothing has drifted to him from the wreck of his fortunes, but a certain annual sum that comes he knows not how, with an earnest entreaty that he will not seek to discover, and with the assurance that it is a debt, and an act of reparation' (lxii, 829). Dombey's feelings are spared and the irony of the fable is lost on him. It is not lost on the reader for whose benefit and entertainment the book was written.

5   Nemo's daughter and her inheritance of shame

At sight of her painting
 Though she lies cold
 In churchyard mould,
I took its feinting
As real, and kissed it.
             Thomas Hardy

Every meaning is virtual
Charles Sanders Peirce

Nemo's daughter or Summer's son? Who is Esther? Someone with no name
of her own, no expectations, no right even to exist whether as a person
(within the fiction) or as a character (in Dickens's project). 'It would have
been far better, little Esther, . . . that you had never been born!' her aunt
Barbary tells her on a memorable birthday, when she is still a little girl,
'Your mother, Esther, is your disgrace, and you were hers' (iii, 19). This,
her 'inheritance of shame' (xliv, 538), is all she has been endowed with, the
burden she must bear throughout her journey from girlhood to womanhood,
the 'fault' she has to atone for (iii, 20). Convinced as she is of her
unworthiness and insignificance, she has agreed to be no more than a
reporter, an eye and ear witness who has been entrusted with a 'portion' (iii,
17) of the narrative and ought to remain in the background, with no
life-story intruding on the report.

But her life does intrude: 'It seems so curious to me to be obliged to write
all this about myself!' she says. 'As if this narrative were the narrative of *my*
life! But my little body will soon fall into the background now' (iii, 27). Far
from disappearing, however, her little body keeps 'coming into the story
again': 'I don't know how it is, I seem to be always writing about myself',
she apologizes. 'I mean all the time to write about other people, and I try to
think about myself as little as possible, . . . but it is all of no use. I hope any
one who may read what I write, will understand that if these pages contain a
great deal about me, I can only suppose it must be because I have really
something to do with them, and can't be kept out' (ix, 102–3). She certainly
could be kept out if she stuck to her subject (Rick and Ada's tragic fate and

misplaced expectations), but writing in the first person is a dangerous enterprise as the following passage shows:

It touched me then to reflect, and it touches me now, more nearly, to remember (having what I have to tell) how they both thought of me, even at that engrossing time. I was part of all their plans, for the present and the future. I was to write to Richard once a week, making my faithful report of Ada, who was to write to him every alternate day. I was to be informed, under his own hand, of all his labours and successes; I was to observe how resolute and persevering he would be; I was to be Ada's bridesmaid when they were married; I was to live with them afterwards; I was to keep all the keys of their house; I was to be made happy for ever and a day. (xiv, 163–4)

This is a remarkable instance of self-absorbing selflessness. The narrative 'I' has here invaded the narrative syntax and will gradually invade the whole text, ousting the hero from the centre of the story. An unwilling usurper, the pen-holder will surreptitiously assert herself as a heroine, so that, no matter what she was first intended to tell, Esther's book will be 'the book of Esther'.

Esther what, though? The question is well worth asking, were it only because the writing Esther does not go by the same name as the one that is written. When she reaches the end of her narrative, she tells us she has been married for 'Full seven happy years' (lxvii, 767) to Allan Woodcourt whose name therefore is now her own. Yet, in this last chapter, which is devoted to the present time, she provokingly refers to herself as 'the mistress of Bleak House', or 'the doctor's wife', never 'Esther Woodcourt', and her reticence, which cannot be accidental, invites us to wonder: 'Supposing', on her birthday, she started speculating on her identity, the way Mr Bagnet does, examining herself in the catechism, 'What is your name? and Who gave you that name? . . . And how do you like that name' (xlix, 587), what would be the most likely answer? Of course, nobody can tell, for nobody knows how much *she* knows: has she read the other 'portion' of the story or has she merely handed her manuscript over to the editor without enquiring further into the matter? Bred 'in secrecy from her birth' (xvii, 213), has she tried to enter into her mother's secret or has she not rather preferred ignorance out of respect for the dead?

Whichever interpretation we choose to favour, we are bound to realize that Esther must be aware of her lasting namelessness, having never been formally recognized by her father. When Guppy asserts that 'the little girl's name was not Esther Summerson, but Esther Hawdon' (xxix, 362), the truth he is stating has a genetic but no legal backing. Nemo may well be 'English for some one' (x, 122), Esther is the daughter of her Latin father and she will remain so to the end of her life; knowledge of the father's name would certainly alter the degree of her namelessness, but it could not prevent it. Hence perhaps this easy, uncomplaining acceptance of all the names and nicknames – Summerson, Fitz-Jarndyce, Dame Durden, Dame Trot, Mother Hubbard – that are given her as if she were a 'bad boy' or someone in a nursery rhyme. Hence perhaps also the feeling we have that this woman who has been 'starring'[1] is to the end a nobody.

'Summerson', admittedly, is the name that gives the unacknowledged girl the right to be acknowledged by society, something to answer to, a convenient key to social intercourse. 'Miss Summerson, if I don't deceive myself?', the Bleak House maid enquires as a matter of form on greeting her to her new home. 'Yes', she replies. 'That is my name' (vi, 65). But when a straight answer to the question would be a plain 'Yes, I am', the impersonal turn of phrase points to the inadequacy of this so-called 'identity'. 'Summerson' identifies Esther with no one, fails to place her in relation to genitors or forebears and misleads the listeners. The maid does not deceive herself, but she *is* deceived, and Esther has no choice but to take part in the deception.

Deception, including self-deception, is indeed necessary if the bastard child is to exist at all, even, most cruelly, to exist in her mother's eyes. Formally introduced as 'Miss Summerson' to Lady Dedlock, she will bear no other name in her mother's heart once the truth of their relationship is no longer a mystery: significantly, 'Esther Summerson' is the mark embroidered on the handkerchief that the mother will later treasure like a fetish, a poor sign that her dead child has come to life again. After the dramatic scene of mutual recognition and parting for ever, when Esther reads her mother's letter containing revelations about her birth and early education, she rightly underscores the importance of bearing a name so as to have some sort of existence even in the mind of the woman who gave her life: 'So strangely did I hold my place in this world, that, until within a short time back, I had never, to my own mother's knowledge, breathed – had been buried – had never been endowed with life – had never borne a name' (xxxvi, 452). Esther is aware that, in Victor Hugo's words, 'a name is a self',[2] but she also knows that an assumed name is for her the only means of both assuming and concealing the guilt of others.

The guilt, however, will *not* be concealed. The legacy of shame has been made visible by a double inheritance of looks: branded in her very flesh, Esther, as we come to learn, has the unusual privilege of looking exactly like both her parents, of being recognizably the fruit of their sin, the tell-tale image of their forbidden union. Were she not illegitimate, this would be something to wonder at unreservedly, as does Betsey Trotwood when she first sees young David and is only too happy to identify him as the son of her nephew: 'He would be as like his father as it's possible to be, if he was not so like his mother, too' (*DC*, xiii, 164), she proudly tells Mr Dick. But Esther's likeness to her father and mother is hardly ever mentioned straightforwardly. Conspicuous though it is supposed to be, it goes either unnoticed or unformulated, or is pointed out indirectly.

The likeness to the father is indeed so discreetly touched on that a hasty reading of the scene – the only one – in which it is suggested might lead to wrong interpretations. It occurs fairly late (we are almost half way into the novel), some time after George Rouncewell has returned to England and opened his shooting-gallery. Mr George has become Richard's fencing-master and visits Jarndyce to discuss the young man's abilities as a shot and as a swordsman. Esther, who is present, suddenly joins in the conversation and the visitor, puzzled by her looks, changes the subject:

If he had not looked at me before, he looked at me now, in three or four quick successive glances. 'I beg your pardon, sir,' he said to my guardian, with a manly kind of diffidence, 'but you did me the honour to mention the young lady's name —'
'Miss Summerson.'
'Miss Summerson,' he repeated, and looked at me again.
'Do you know the name?' I asked.
'No, miss. To my knowledge, I never heard it. I thought I had seen you somewhere.'
'I think not,' I returned, raising my head from my work to look at him; and there was something so genuine in his speech and manner that I was glad of the oppor-tunity. 'I remember faces very well.'
'So do I, miss!' he returned, meeting my look with the fulness of his dark eyes and broad forehead. 'Humph! What set me off, now, upon that!' (xxix, 305)

No name is mentioned, and we would no doubt infer that the face the speaker has in mind is the face of Lady Dedlock (whose likeness to Esther is by now a familiar theme) if what we know of the man's life-story did not argue against it, as a brief reckoning will show. Mr George, for one thing, has been away from home for as many as thirty-five years, which means that he left Lincolnshire before being able to set eyes on Sir Leicester's wife or future bride; on the other hand, he has served abroad under Captain Hawdon, has been his close friend, has even letters from him in his posses-sion and is unwittingly involved in Tulkinghorn's enquiry into the past of the mysterious copyist; we have therefore every reason to decide that Hawdon's is the face that he associates with Esther's. But we can also under-stand why he abruptly gives up enquiring further into the matter, for, having been informed that Esther's name is Summerson, how could he put into words what must be no more than a passing speculation?

The scene will lead nowhere. Esther asks no questions, gives no expla-nations, and there is no telling whether her reticence is intentional or not. She has made it a rule to recreate the past as she experienced it, without ever trying to enlighten it with more recent knowledge, so that the mystery of George's musings remains unexplained. But all this has not been totally unnecessary as far as *we* are concerned, for it gives the heroine a sort of legitimacy by compelling us to visualize her as her father's daughter in our mind's eye.

Unambiguous though it is, the likeness to the mother is also presented through a curiously oblique strategy. Dickens resorts to a device already used in *Oliver Twist* to trace the hero's parentage: the likeness to a portrait. But in the earlier novel, the trick was justified since the boy's mother was dead. Here, on the contrary, the mother being alive, it will appear to many as a far-fetched means of identification, for, if the likeness is as striking as it is said to be, it ought to be obvious to all those in Esther's circle who are acquainted with the mistress of Chesney Wold. Surprisingly, however, nobody seems to notice it, not even when the two women happen to be placed side by side. Jarndyce himself, attentive though he is to the face of his dear ward, betrays no surprise, no emotion whatever, when he introduces her to Sir Leicester's beautiful wife:

'But present me,' and she turned full upon me, 'to this young lady too!'
  'Miss Summerson really is my ward,' said Mr Jarndyce. 'I am responsible to no Lord Chancellor in her case.'
  'Has Miss Summerson lost both her parents?' said my Lady.
  'Yes.'
  'She is fortunate in her guardian.' (xviii, 229)

Has the man gone blind or is he pretending? Has Miss Barbary told him the full secret of Esther's parentage? Is that the reason why he remains so disturbingly formal?[3] But then, others might blunderingly remark on the likeness, Esther's maid Charley, for instance, or Ada, or even Boythorn, Skimpole, Mademoiselle Hortense. None of them does. Eyes have they, but they see not.

Only Jo, the crossing sweeper, seems able to notice what should normally stare anyone in the face: 'She looks to me the t'other one. It ain't the bonnet, nor yet it ain't the gownd, but she looks to me the t'other one' (xxxi, 381), he says of Esther, undeceived by her disguise. But the street truth-teller has no name to tag on Esther's mysterious double who thus remains anonymous, alienated, 't'othered'. The boy's words are therefore meaningless to his listeners and only the reader can make sense of them thanks to the other narrator's report which has already informed him of Esther's likeness to the portrait of a lady: the face keeps the secret that the portrait betrays.

This portrait, which from first to last is absent from Esther's report, works indeed as a tell-tale sign in the other 'portion' of the book; it is one of the numerous devices used there by the professional narrator to organize, dramatize, give shape and meaning to events that in real life (supposedly the world of the memorialist) remain unexplained or pass unnoticed; so that the reader, who has the privilege of shuttling back and forth between the two narratives, can bring what information he has gleaned from the detective story into his interpretation of the heroine's candid account.

The likeness to a portrait, which we have been tempted to dismiss somewhat hastily as a clumsy device, is therefore more subtle than first meets the eye. In this complex novel which gives pride of place to 'Signs and tokens'[4] and uses as subject-matter the very art of fiction-making, Lady Dedlock's portrait comes to be perceived as an indirect piece of information, a sign in the sense in which any representation is a sign for semioticians. 'A type', Pascal writes, 'conveys absence and presence, pleasure and pain. A cipher has a double meaning, one clear, and one in which it is said that the meaning is hidden ... A portrait conveys absence and presence, pleasure and pain. The reality excludes absence and pain.'[5] This is precisely what Dickens tells us, albeit jokingly: 'Of Mrs Bayham Badger *in esse*, I possess the original, and have no copy' (xiii, 157–8), he has Mr Badger say. 'My Lady is at present represented, near Sir Leicester, by her portrait. She has flitted away to town' (xvi, 197), writes his omniscient narrator, with or, more probably, without the benefit of the French philosopher. It seems fair enough, therefore, to turn to semiotics for a closer study of the lady's portrait if we are to decipher the various messages of this meaningful representation.

'There are', Peirce writes, 'three kinds of representations':

First. Those whose relation to their objects is a mere community in some quality, and these representations may be termed *likenesses*.

Second. Those whose relation to their objects consists in a correspondence in fact, and these may be termed *indices* or *signs*.

Third. Those the ground of whose relation to their objects is an imputed character, which are the same as *general signs*, and they may be termed *symbols*.[6]

The portrait of Lady Dedlock proves to have this triple function, depending on whether we consider it as a mere reproduction, as a piece of evidence or as an emblem of essential sameness.

The first relation is a matter of course and should go almost without saying. Portrait-painting in the nineteenth century still implies the notion of faithful representation, so that, not too surprisingly, the portraits of *Bleak House* are all presented as perfect imitations of the models who sat for them. The walls of Chesney Wold are covered with the 'ghostly likenesses' (lxvi, 766) of 'the pictured Dedlocks' (vii, 81), Professor Dingo's portrait is 'a speaking likeness' (xiii, 157) of Badger's predecessor, Guppy's is 'more like than life' (xxxviii, 477). Lady Dedlock's portrait is also said to be 'a perfect likeness, and the best work of the master' (vii, 82), but iconic faithfulness in this particular case does more than testify to the talent of the artist. If such had been the case, the narrator would have described it as meticulously to enhance artistry or style as he describes some of Sir Leicester's pictures, 'ancient and modern', for satirical purposes, taking stock of all the details, listing them 'like the miscellaneous articles in a sale' (xxix, 357). Here, we must take it on trust that the painting is lifelike and a masterpiece, since no details are given to illustrate skill or accuracy; we are not told whether it is a full-length portrait or a bust, whether the subject is standing or sitting, side-face or full-face, indoors or out of doors, whether the colours are bright or dull, and nothing is said of the lady's features, expression or dress. What really matters is not what the portrait is like but what is said of it and whose unsuspected likeness it betrays:

> But a portrait over the chimney-piece, painted by the fashionable artist of the day, acts upon him like a charm. He recovers in a moment. He stares at it with uncommon interest; he seems to be fixed and fascinated by it.
> 'Dear me!' says Mr Guppy. 'Who's that?'
> 'The picture over the fire-place,' says Rosa, 'is a portrait of the present Lady Dedlock. It is considered a perfect likeness, and the best work of the master.'
> 'Blest!' says Mr Guppy, staring in a kind of dismay at his friend, 'if I can ever have seen her. Yet I know her! Has the picture been engraved, miss?'
> 'The picture has never been engraved. Sir Leicester has always refused permission.'
> 'Well!' says Mr Guppy in a low voice, 'I'll be shot if it ain't very curious how well I know that picture! So that's Lady Dedlock, is it!' (vii, 82)

The picture works, we see, as an index to various things. It indicates talent, it indicates wealth, it indicates a desire to immortalize beauty. But it indicates above all an anomaly, since it represents one person and points to someone else. Guppy looks at the portrait of Lady Dedlock and it is the image of Esther that he sees: there are two 'signifieds' for one 'signifier'. From that moment on the plot is set going: Guppy's attention has been alerted and his discovery will be the starting-point of investigations that will turn this half of the novel into a thriller.

Still, it will be argued, Dickens in this scene could well have done without his device. Lady Dedlock might just as easily have been present on the occasion of Guppy's visit instead of being 'represented' by her picture and there is no reason why the sharp-eyed clerk should have missed the likeness. But Dickens is little concerned with verisimilitude or realistic presentation of his mystery. By focusing the riddle on a representational object, he dramatizes the very notion of sign and creates a distance between a mere story and the art of story-telling.

The Allegory which adorns Tulkinghorn's ceiling fulfils a similar function; with its Roman soldier pointing his index-finger 'with no particular meaning', it is *par excellence* the illustration that 'every meaning is virtual': 'For many years, the persistent Roman has been pointing, with no particular meaning, from that ceiling. It is not likely that he has any new meaning in him to-night. Once pointing, always pointing – like any Roman, or even Briton, with a single idea' (xlviii, 585), writes the narrator who had warned us from the start that making 'the head ache' is 'what would seem to be Allegory's object always, more or less (x, 119). But when we re-enter the realistic world of murderers and policemen, signs have to be made to speak: once placed in charge of the investigation following Tulkinghorn's murder, Inspector Bucket will be seen 'comparing forefingers' (liii, 626) with the enigmatic Roman, thus emphasizing the difference between fiction and reality, and literally 'pointing to' the semiotic role of iconography in his creator's code of communication.

Unlike the Roman who looks 'as if he were a paralysed dumb witness' (xlviii, 585), the portrait of Lady Dedlock has been acting as an informer during Guppy's visit to the Hall. But, within the broader framework of the novel of origins, its symbolic function, 'in which it is said that the meaning is hidden', is of a more secret nature.

'Symbol' is given here the literal meaning of something that 'brings together'.[7] A symbol in ancient Greece was an object that close relatives or close friends would break in two before a long separation. When they met again, after years of absence, aged or physically altered, the two halves proffered by each partner of the former transaction could be put together again and used as a sign of mutual recognition. In a similar way, the portrait at Chesney Wold in which mother and daughter are identified one with the other can be said to be a token that will be stronger than time, outlasting death and disfigurement.

But this symbolism, it should be noted, is a secret shared by novelist and readers only. No one in the novel is ever aware of it. Few people have seen the portrait, fewer even know its double reference. Guppy will never see beyond its 'clear meaning'. Lady Dedlock never looks at it. Esther does not know of its existence. But for us it is the object that will best illustrate the identity of mother and child, perpetuating the recollection of the admirable scene in which Esther, looking at the face of a strange woman, suddenly sees her own as in a broken glass:

But why her face should be, in a confused way, like a broken glass to me, in which I saw scraps of old remembrances; and why I should be so fluttered and troubled ... by having casually met her eyes; I could not think.

... And yet *I – I*, little Esther Summerson, the child who lived a life apart, and on whose birthday there was no rejoicing – seemed to arise before my own eyes, evoked out of the past by some power in this fashionable lady, whom I not only entertained no fancy that I had ever seen, but whom I perfectly well knew I had never seen until that hour. (xviii, 225)

The mirror-image, graphically represented in the text – '*I – I*' – is a perfect symbol in the original sense of the term, and the symbolism is captured here at the very moment when the two halves which had long been severed are being reunited. A moment later, hearing 'the voice' which sounds like her own and yet is another's, Esther is affected 'in the same strange way': 'Again, in a moment, there arose before my mind innumerable *pictures* of myself' (xviii, 228, my italics), she writes.

The mother is also 'startled' at the sight of this strange yet familiar face, the ghost of the woman her dead child might have grown to be like: 'When she had first seen me in the church', Esther reports, 'she had been startled; and had thought of what would have been like me, if it had ever lived, and had lived on' (xxxvi, 452–3).

The revelation, which takes place inside the church during the Sunday service, has a mystic quality. Reading of it is like attending the celebration of some Holy Duality, the mystery of a communion in which two persons are perceived as one and the same and in which absence *is* presence. In the reader's mind, when the two faces are eventually ruined by death and disease and no longer recognizable or mutually identifiable, the symbolic portrait will be the monument of this ceremony in the course of which the 'ontophanic' sameness was celebrated in the house of God, unbeknown to all the other attendants.

This essential likeness, which has placed Esther for ever in the great chain of being, need not remain visible to all. Quite the contrary. When, having recovered from her long illness, Esther meets her mother again, she rejoices at the thought that her 'new face' (xxxvi, 447) will from now on prevent recognition: 'I felt, through all my tumult of emotion, a burst of gratitude to the providence of God that I was so changed as that I never could disgrace her by any trace of likeness; as that nobody could ever now look at me, and look at her, and remotely think of any near tie between us' (xxxvi, 449). The secret is now 'safe' (xxxvi, 450) and Esther Summerson runs no risk any longer of being the 'disgrace ... of a proud family name' (xxxvi, 453).

But the disgrace could have worked both ways and, in disfiguring Esther, in depriving her of her inheritance of looks, the novelist has prevented this further discredit. There was, besides, a greater danger of his heroine being identified with the sinful woman after the scandal of her treachery and flight from home. For we must remember that, whereas Sir Leicester's favourite portrait of his wife has never been engraved – 'Sir Leicester has always refused permission', Rosa explained to the visitors (vii, 82) – there is another portrait of my Lady which has been duplicated and widely circulated. It is one of the items of Weevle's 'choice collection of copper-plate impressions from that truly national work, The Divinities of Albion, or Galaxy Gallery of British Beauty, representing ladies of title and fashion in every variety of smirk that art, combined with capital, is capable of producing' (xx, 256).

Not symbolic by any means but diabolic[8] rather, this portrait contains all the attributes of worldly vanity that the narrator, no longer sparing of details, lavishly enumerates:

Mr Guppy affects to smile; and with the view of changing the conversation, looks with an admiration, real or pretended, round the room at the Galaxy Gallery of British Beauty; terminating his survey with the portrait of Lady Dedlock over the mantel-shelf, in which she is represented on a terrace, with a pedestal upon the terrace, and a vase upon the pedestal, and her shawl upon the vase, and a prodigious piece of fur upon the shawl, and her arm on the prodigious piece of fur, and a bracelet on her arm. (xxxii, 396)

Taking the form of a realistic enumeration, the satiric style, which brings out the preposterous and the contemptible, clearly betrays narratorial and authorial disapproval. The engraving, besides, has been profaned by too many hands and too many eyes, displayed on too many walls (including those of the room in which the lady's unmentionable lover had ended his obscure life) for Dickens not to have feared the gossips of this 'speaking likeness' (xxxii, 396) and their disparaging effects on Esther's reputation. By altering her looks, he has liberated his heroine from the guilt of her genitors and spared her honour.

Esther's 'disfigurement, *and* [her] inheritance of shame' (xliv, 538, my italics) are inseparably linked for worse and for better: at the end of the novel, the deformed has been transformed and the bastard child who has acquired for herself the right to be praised for her 'true legitimacy' (lxiv, 753) can bear her inheritance 'with a better kind of shame' (xvii, 213). Her story certainly does not end like the stories of her male counterparts in Dickens's other novels; no legal document is conjured up at the last minute to authenticate her birth, she inherits no name, no money, 'no nothink'. Even her life as someone's daughter has been a short-lived episode, the rebirth of the child that might have been and is already dead when, on the step of the churchyard, she sees a woman lying cold and dead, 'the mother of the dead child' (lix, 713). And yet Esther exists as few Dickens heroes do: being a woman, with no need to transmit – and therefore inherit – any tokens of her origins, she has the privilege of existing as a heroine in her own right, self-made, self-written, self-t'othered,[9] and when she looks in the glass, she needs only say 'I am I.'

6   'Nobody's Fault' or the inheritance of guilt

Lear: 'Dost thou call me fool, boy?'
Fool: 'All thy other titles thou hast given away; that thou wast born with.'
Shakespeare

Nobody

The father–son relationship in *Oliver Twist* was purely academic. Edwin Leeford, a progenitor rather than a father, was dead before Oliver's birth, and only indirect evidence gave us a vague idea of the sort of man he had been, an image which it was easy for us to embellish. He was not the ideal father, but he could have been. He was weak but well-intentioned. He had suffered bad luck. Rose and Harry's happy marriage could have been, should really have been his. The novel ended without ill-feeling or lasting bitterness, and with a compensatory celebration of marital love, family life, simple joys, rediscovered innocence. Happiness was still possible. Oliver's story was no more than an accident that would soon be forgotten.

When, almost twenty years later, Dickens embarks on *Little Dorrit*, he starts from a situation very similar to that of his first novel. Like Oliver, Arthur Clennam is the illegitimate child of a man early married against his will to a cantankerous, vindictive and grasping woman. This father, like Oliver's, is absent from the novel and the roll call of characters: the plot follows on from his death and his part in it is over when the first chapter begins. Through the sketches of those who happened to know him, he appears as an almost exact copy of Leeford, just as weak and irresolute, just as unfit for the society in which he finds himself. Like him he bowed to parental authority in his youth, like him he later sought refuge from his unhappy marriage in deception and adultery and, again like him, he ended his days in exile, away from his shrewish wife.

Here similarities end and differences begin. The first and major novelty of *Little Dorrit* concerns the relations between the father and the son, which this time are quite real. Arthur is forty when his father dies, he has never left him since he was a child, even following him into his exile. Ignorance has given way to long-standing intimacy.

The new novel, besides, begins exactly where the earlier one ended, at the moment when the son and heir takes over from his father. But where before the problems were solved, difficulties now spring up for, at this solemn hour, the son is seized with misgivings about his inheritance. Attending his father during his last moments, Arthur perceives that some secret overburdens the conscience of his testator, something, he gathers, linked with the family fortune, some past misdemeanour still to be atoned for; but the dying man is too weak to make a proper confession and his secret dies with him. Aware of his father's remorse, but uninformed of the offence, the orphaned son realizes that if the silent message is to be deciphered, the co-operation of his widowed mother, the probable secret-sharer, will have to be sought out. Bent on investigating the family secret, he soon leaves China for his native shores and reaches England, where his mother lives, with his inheritance of guilt.

He also returns home with his share of the property, but only after giving up the family business which he had run with his father. 'You'll have bitter words together to-morrow, Arthur; you and your mother', Jeremiah warns. 'Your having given up the business on your father's death – which she suspects, though we have left it to you to tell her – won't go off smoothly' (I, iii, 37). Nothing indeed will go off smoothly in this novel where succeeding the father is no longer the happy ending of a quest but the starting-point of a painful enquiry:

'I want to ask you, mother, whether it ever occurred to you to suspect –'
At the word Suspect, she turned her eyes momentarily upon her son, with a dark frown . . .
' – that he had any secret remembrance which caused him trouble of mind – remorse? . . .'
. . .
'Is it possible, mother,' . . . 'is it possible, mother, that he had unhappily wronged any one, and made no reparation?'
. . .
'. . . Remember, I was with my father. Remember, I saw his face when he gave the watch into my keeping, and struggled to express that he sent it as a token you would understand, to you. Remember, I saw him to the last with the pencil in his failing hand, trying to write some word for you to read, but to which he could give no shape. The more remote and cruel this vague suspicion that I have, the stronger the circumstances that could give it any semblance of probability to me. For Heaven's sake let us examine sacredly whether there is any wrong entrusted to us to set right.' (I, v, 46–7)

'I want to know, I want to know', he goes on repeating throughout the novel in his tireless though fruitless appeals for information, and his eagerness to know and to knock at every door is what will keep the story going. We thus soon find ourselves reading a detective story of the *Oliver Twist* type where the father's past must once again be probed into; but this time it is the hero who conducts the enquiry, it is the son who spies on the guilty father. Complaining of this to Flintwinch, Mrs Clennam unwittingly provides a good summary of Dickens's new plot pattern:

'In the very hour of his return almost – before the shoe upon his foot is dry – he asperses his father's memory to his mother! Asks his mother to become, with him, a spy upon his father's transactions through a lifetime! Has misgivings that the goods of this world, which we have painfully got together early and late, with wear and tear and toil and self-denial, are so much plunder; and asks to whom they shall be given up, as reparation and restitution!' (I, v, 48)

But the guilty father's spy is also the executor of the repentant man who, on his death-bed, bequeathed the terrible legacy of his guilt and whose very portrait seems, like the ghost of Hamlet's father, to demand reparation and urge the son on to action: 'His picture, dark and gloomy, earnestly speechless on the wall, with the eyes intently looking at his son as they had looked when life departed from them, seemed to urge him awfully to the task he had attempted' (I, v, 54). Never before had Dickens imagined a situation so fundamentally tragic: the enquiry is made in the name of the father, but the name of the father is also the name of the son, a guilt-ridden son whose oedipal contradictions will inevitably become the cause, as in Shakespeare and Sophocles, of much blundering action and much self-castigation.

Self-destruction or self-negation would be even more appropriate words for, although he has set out to accomplish his filial mission and has no thought ever of disclaiming his parentage, Arthur can only describe himself as nameless and purposeless, 'a waif ... liable to be drifted where any current may set' (I, ii, 19), unowned and non-existent: 'Why should he be vexed or sore at heart? It was not his weakness that he had imagined. It was nobody's, nobody's within his knowledge, why should it trouble him?' (I, xvi, 194) '... and such a state of mind was nobody's – nobody's' (I, xxvi, 301). His interior monologues are those of someone who has lost his sense of self and who, in his dereliction, has become a non-entity, as anonymous as a foundling, 'somebody's child – anybody's – nobody's' (II, ix, 524), as Pancks says of Tattycoram.

He will, fortunately, never complete his search: by tacit consent, the novelist and Amy Dorrit will spare him the cruel truth: 'The secret was safe now!' says the narratorial voice in the closing number, speaking on behalf of both author and character, 'She could keep her own part of it from him ... That was all passed, all forgiven, all forgotten' (II, xxxiii, 788). The truth will out none the less, but for the reader's benefit. Thanks to other investigators or conspirators such as Pancks, Rigaud or Flintwinch, the reader will eventually be informed of the double sin which soiled the family name and the hero's inheritance. Harried by Rigaud, the blackmailer, Mrs Clennam will even make a confession that the narrator will duly record; the secret of

Arthur's birth will thus come to be disclosed and we will learn how, from earliest childhood, the boy was removed from his real mother's care so that appearances should be safeguarded; the illegitimacy of the family fortune will also be brought to light and we will learn how, on the death of Gilbert Clennam, a codicil to the will that benefited the Dorrits was fraudulently suppressed, making his nephew, Clennam the Elder, sole heir to the property. This tidying up of the plot is part of the novelist's implicit contract, something he feels he owes his reader, but these revelations are not the real business of the book and it matters little in fact that Arthur should not know all the details of those misdeeds. It is not the knowledge of evil but the discovery of good that will bring about the happy ending. It is not by replacing the missing piece of the jigsaw that, as in *Oliver Twist*, everything will be set to rights, 'forgiven and forgotten'. Forgetfulness now is willing oblivion, the willing suspension of hate and resentment, another word for forgiveness.

'Passed', 'forgiven', 'forgotten', however welcome, are unexpected words at the end of a novel whose great issues were memory, atonement and vindictiveness. 'Do not forget', said the initials 'D.N.F.' which, mysteriously engraved on old Clennam's watch-case, were the mainspring of the action. 'Do not forget' is also the formula that best seems to describe the author's intentions and the narrator's method, that merciless way he has of hoarding up evidence and of recording mischief as clerks at court record the minutes of a trial. *Little Dorrit* is a novel which, from first to almost last, tells us that the past cannot be wiped out, that sins long outlive sinners, that because the fathers have eaten sour grapes the children's teeth are set on edge.

'The transgressions of the parents are visited on their offspring' also declares Mrs Clennam in a dramatic outburst, but the transgressions she has in mind are of a different order from those that the novel condemns. They are sins of origins: 'there was an angry mark upon him at his birth', she says of her husband's illegitimate son in self-justification when she explains to Amy Dorrit why from the first she had to be so 'stern with him' (II, xxxi, 769). The angry mark is certainly there but it has been stamped on him by his educators rather than his begetters: 'I am the only child of parents who weighed, measured, and priced everything', he says to Meagles, and the female parent included in this plural is not the genetic but the adoptive mother. 'Strict people as the phrase is, professors of a stern religion', he goes on explaining, '... Austere faces, inexorable discipline, penance in this world and terror in the next – nothing graceful or gentle anywhere, and the void in my cowed heart everywhere – this was my childhood, if I may so misuse the word as to apply it to such a beginning of life' (I, ii, 20). The inheritor of perverted values, he is weak and irresolute, a fallible man, someone with no roots, no self, no future, no will: 'Will, purpose, hope? All those lights were extinguished before I could sound the words' (I, ii, 20). His illegitimate birth *and* his upbringing, his genetic inheritance *and* his cultural heritage, have together made him what he is, or what he is not rather, a 'Nobody' in search of his true identity.

But Arthur's predicament is by no means unique of its kind. Whichever way we may turn, we see people – Casby's daughter, Tattycoram, William and Amy Dorrit, and indeed many others – who have been wronged and spoiled, deprived of their rights, of their youth, of their wealth, of their liberty, by unscrupulous elders, or social betters, some of them long since dead or self-righteously locked up in their ivory towers. 'Nobody's Fault', the title Dickens first intended to give to his novel, admirably rendered his satirical intentions, and his decision to drop it is therefore difficult to account for. It actually took him as many as five months to discard the idea and return to the tradition, less committing and more popular, of the eponymous title.

   This change of mind as well as the compared merits of 'Nobody's Fault' and *Little Dorrit* have been meticulously analysed by John Butt and Kathleen Tillotson in the last chapter of their *Dickens at Work*. Starting from a remark in one of the novelist's letters according to which '"Nobody's Fault" represents "the one idea and design" of social criticism of which "Society, the Circumlocution Office and Mr Gowan" are "three parts"',[1] they underline the satirical nature of a title which clearly denounced domestic and national irresponsibility. The novel was written, they remind us, at a time when, on the one hand, the scandals of the Crimean War at last came into the open[2] and when, on the other hand, administrative reform was being undertaken with a view to ending the undemocratic system of sinecures that left incompetent aristocrats in high posts of command.[3] On 30 August 1856 (*Little Dorrit* by that time had been running for a full nine months), Dickens was to publish in *Household Words* an article on these questions, 'Nobody, Somebody, Everybody', written in the same vein as the most topical chapters of the novel denouncing 'the whole science of government', the 'How not to do it' Civil Service motto, Barnacleism, and the viciously circular Circumlocution Office. Using the same rhetoric and vocabulary, he violently condemned in his journalistic piece the institutionalized shift of responsibility onto a mythic 'Nobody':

The power of Nobody is becoming so enormous in England, and he alone is responsible for so many proceedings, both in the way of commission and omission; he has so much to answer for, and is so constantly called to account; that a few remarks upon him may not be ill-timed.
   The hand which this surprising person had in the late war is amazing to consider. It was he who left the tents behind, who left the baggage behind, who chose the

worst possible ground for encampments, who provided no means of transport, who killed the horses, who paralysed the commissariat, who knew nothing of the business he professed to know and monopolised, who decimated the English army. It was Nobody who gave out the famous unroasted coffee, it was Nobody who made the hospitals more horrible than language can describe, it was Nobody who occasioned all the dire confusion of Balaklava harbor, it was even Nobody who ordered the fatal Balaklava cavalry charge ...

In civil matters we have Nobody equally active. When a civil office breaks down, the break-down is sure to be in Nobody's department ... The government, with all its mighty means and appliances, is invariably beaten and outstripped by private enterprise; which we all know to be *Nobody's fault*.[4]

The overlapping would, of course, have been more immediately perceptible if the novel had been serialized as 'Nobody's Fault', though few readers of *Little Dorrit* can have failed to notice it, for, in dropping his title, Dickens did not drop his subject. 'Bleeding-Heart Yard', the chapter he wrote immediately after taking his decision, is indeed one of his most virulent attacks on governmental laissez-faire and irresponsibility, as this brief extract will show:

There was pretty well all sorts of trader you could name, all wanting to work, and yet not able to get it. There was old people, after working all their lives, going and being shut up in the Workhouse, much worse fed and lodged and treated altogether, than – Mr Plornish said manufacturers, but appeared to mean malefactors. Why, a man didn't know where to turn himself, for a crumb of comfort. As to who was to blame for it, Mr Plornish didn't know *who was to blame for it*. He could tell you who suffered, but he couldn't tell you *whose fault it was*. (I, xii, 136, my italics)

The *Household Words* article itself appeared only a few weeks after 'A Shoal of Barnacles' (I, xxxiv), a chapter which exposed the corruption, inefficiency and mismanagement of British civil servants. Dickens's journalism, we see, did not fill a gap left open in his fiction but rather came as a complement to it. *Little Dorrit* was the 'J'accuse' that 'Nobody's Fault' had been meant to be. Why, then, had the first title to go?

No explanation was given. Dickens merely wrote to Mrs Watson that '*Little Dorrit*' had 'a pleasanter sound in [his] ears' and that it was 'equally applicable to the same story',[5] which it certainly was not, the stress being now shifted from theme to character and from condemnation to praise. Butt and Tillotson's commentary on the new orientation, '*Little Dorrit* [represents] the optimism about humanity which sets the rest in perspective',[6] is more satisfactory, even though it is difficult to call *Little Dorrit* an optimistic novel.

But there is another possible explanation that the two critics did not envisage. From the fifth instalment onwards, full emphasis, we must remember, was to be placed on Arthur's ontological uneasiness, with chapter headings focusing on his almost clinical depersonalization: 'Nobody's Weakness', 'Nobody's Rival', 'Nobody's State of Mind', 'Nobody's Disappearance'. In retaining 'Nobody's Fault' for his title, Dickens was therefore running the risk of causing a serious and most unfair misunderstanding by pinning onto one man what was intended to be a general accusation, and by charging the hero with all the sins of the world, of which he was innocent though he had taken all the guilt on himself. There was the further danger of fixing him once and for all in his non-being and denying him the right ever to become 'Somebody'. The change of title took place immediately after Dickens had finished writing the first ten chapters, that is to say immediately before starting the serial number in which Arthur's metamorphosis into 'Nobody' would occur. We have therefore every reason to believe that the novelist felt at this stage that he had to decide who 'Nobody' should unambiguously refer to and that he chose to sacrifice his title rather than give up his study in psychopathology.

The change, however, is not entirely satisfactory. It grants Amy more weight than she really has and it is unfair on Arthur, who does not get the eponymy which his messianic role entitled him to. Not that I am suggesting that 'Arthur Clennam' would have been a good title either, for, by stressing character over theme, it would, like *Little Dorrit* for that matter, have failed to advertise the notions of duty and dependence that really inform the novel. Even a title of the 'Clennam and Son' type would have narrowed the perspective, reducing the novel to a single relationship or, as Rigaud would say, to 'the history of a house' (II, xxx, 750), whereas *Little Dorrit* is the history of many houses. As he carries out his investigations, Arthur enters many private and public places, ranging from his mother's home to the Home Office, so many indeed that, gradually, the indictment of a family and of a father turns into the trial of all families and of all fathers. It is the patriarchal system as a whole that is challenged in this novel and a theme-oriented title (why not 'Do Not Forget'?) would certainly have been better suited to its purpose, as it would rightly have subordinated the personal plot to problems of more general interest.

It might also have prevented criticism bearing on the absence of structural unity. For *Little Dorrit* has been accused either of lacking a plot or of having too many. John Wain calls it 'a plotless novel',[7] while Geoffrey Thurley deplores 'a radical indecision, an uncertainty about the true nature of the novel's fundamental concern': 'there are', he says, 'at least two novels here: the story of Arthur Clennam's dread and guilt, and the story of the Dorrit family ... it is as if Dickens actually changed his mind about what the real subject of his novel was to be ... Clennam deserts a stage he never promised to occupy very interestingly anyway, and the Dorrits take over.'[8] But what we do get actually is a self-generating form of creation, with new stories branching out from the 'mother plot' and interconnecting to infinity, forbidding closure, as the last sentence of the book suggests. Far from being inconsequent, this structural complexity of stories within stories is the logical consequence of the novel's 'fundamental concern': responsibility and interdependence. The story of Nobody is in fact the story of Everybody.

Everybody

Little Dorrit is an overcrowded novel. In Dickens's early fiction, characters came in singly, each to perform his allotted part. They now bring in whole families with them, even including dependants, in-laws and poor relations. Amy is a case in point, a little mite of a Dorrit in the Dorrit community, with brother, sister, father, uncle, Plornishes and (later) Merdles, all swarming around her, though special emphasis is clearly placed on her daughterly affection, dutifulness and devotion.

Another major difference should be pointed out here. Dickens's first novel, although entirely centred on the quest for a father, was a novel without fathers, featuring only childless husbands, like Bumble and Sowerberry, or bachelors, like Grimwig and Brownlow. In *Little Dorrit*, on the contrary, there are fathers in plenty. But throughout the twenty years and eight novels that have intervened, the paternal image has been more and more frequently given form and in losing its mystery it has lost much of its prestige. The last six books in particular have all in turn contributed to the illustration of paternal incompetence in various guises – ranging from authoritarian paternalism to infantile abdication – and of its destructive effect on the younger generation. There has been a progressive demystification and the attack now reaches its climax.

The dream of order certainly lingers, together with the belief that knowing one's place in the chain of being is indispensable to human happiness, but, paradoxically, it can only be expressed when there is no such knowledge:

'O dear, dear!' cried Mother, breaking out again, 'when I saw all those children ranged tier above tier, and appealing from the father none of them has ever known on earth, to the great father of us all in Heaven, I thought, does any wretched mother ever come here, and look among those young faces, wondering which is the poor child she brought into this forlorn world, never through all its life to know her love, her kiss, her voice, even her name!' (I, ii, 17)

Mr Meagle's recollection of the visit to the orphanage where he and his wife picked up Tattycoram, with its evocation of the great Father Figure at the top of the pyramid, offers evidence that the author of *Oliver Twist* has not renounced his ideal. But the very same Meagles who was intended to move us when he talked of the neglected becomes utterly ludicrous as soon as he embarks on pernickety investigations into the descent of the high-born and well-connected:

'Aye, aye?' said Meagles. 'A Barnacle is he? *We* know something of that family, eh Dan? By George, they are at the top of the tree, though! Let me see. What relation will this young fellow be to Lord Decimus now? His Lordship married, in seventeen ninety-seven, Lady Jemima Bilberry, who was the second daughter by the third marriage – no! There I am wrong! That was Lady Seraphina – Lady Jemima was the first daughter by the second marriage of the fifteenth Earl of Stiltstalking with the Honourable Clementina Toozellem. Very well. Now this young fellow's father married a Stiltstalking and *his* father married his cousin who was a Barnacle. The father of that father who married a Barnacle, married a Joddleby.—I am getting a little too far back, Gowan; I want to make out what relation this young fellow is to Lord Decimus.'

'That's easily stated. His father is nephew to Lord Decimus.'

'Nephew – to – Lord – Decimus,' Mr Meagles luxuriously repeated with his eyes shut, that he might have nothing to distract him from the full flavor of the genealogical tree. 'By George, you are right, Gowan. So he is.'

'Consequently, Lord Decimus is his great uncle.'

'But stop a bit!' said Mr Meagles, opening his eyes with a fresh discovery. 'Then, on the mother's side, Lady Stiltstalking is his great aunt.'

'Of course she is.' (I, xvii, 199–200)

Nor is the author's satire limited to snobs or aristocrats. All that appertains to family life or family relationships, at whatever level of the social ladder, is now suspect. So is, strikingly, the vocabulary associated with the subject. Household words like 'father' and 'family' have so little to do with paternity and kinship that they have become signifiers without signified. 'Brother' and 'sister' are meaningless terms for which any false synonym will do, 'Niece, nevy, cousin, serwant, young 'ooman, greengrocer. – Dash it! One or other on 'em' (I, vi, 59), to quote the Marshalsea turnkey. Family ties are so universally loose that Gowan's cynicism goes unnoticed when he claims to belong 'to a clan, or a clique, or a family, or a connexion, or whatever you like to call it' (I, xxxiv, 392), and even Mrs General is genteelly subversive:

'Papa is a preferable mode of address,' observed Mrs General. 'Father is rather vulgar, my dear. The word Papa, besides, gives a pretty form to the lips. Papa, potatoes, poultry, prunes, and prism, are all very good words for the lips: especially prunes and prism. You will find it serviceable, in the formation of a demeanour, if you sometimes say to yourself in company – on entering a room, for instance – Papa, potatoes, poultry, prunes and prism, prunes and prism.' (II, v, 461–2)

It is almost like reading Edward Lear or Lewis Carroll. Or Dickens's 'Book of Nonsense'.

Nonsensical indeed are many other linguistic fantasies in which, chal-

lenging the basic laws of semantics, Dickens decrees that words are inter-
changeable, that 'Merdle' and 'Millions' (II, xiii, 557) are new synonyms in
the English language which the school-children of Britain should be duly set
to copy in their exercise-books as spelling or writing drills, or that 'the
country' is 'another word for the Barnacles and the Stiltstalkings' (I, xxvi,
306). Nonsensical is, above all, the description of these 'shoals of Barnacles',
'hungry and adhesive' (I, xxxiv, 396), sticking to the rock of British admin-
istration, yet proliferating all over the place and 'dispatch-boxing the
compass' (I, xxxiv, 390); nonsensical the imagery and the rhetoric of excess
brought into play to make their parasitism hilariously detestable. And all
this is done with gusto. As he conjures up his shoalfuls of Barnacles and
Stiltstalkings into all the nooks and crannies of the British Isles and British
dominions, Dickens the magician revels in his power, like a modern
Prospero whose knowledge of the art would put Shakespeare's Duke to
shame: 'the so-potent art of Prospero himself would have failed in summon-
ing the Barnacles from every speck of ocean and dry land on which there was
nothing (except mischief) to be done' (I, xxxiv, 391), he writes triumphantly.
It is for such extravagant creations that we go to Dickens, for his talent to
flesh out the fantasies of his imagination, for his power to give credibility to
the incredible.

Yet, when we turn to history books, we realize that Dickens's fiction
almost comes short of reality. When seats in Parliament were for sale,
pensions and sinecures were invariably awarded to people connected by
blood or by marriage with important politicians, creating a situation as
caricatural as Dickens's caricature: 'Soon after George III made his chief
favourite, the Scotsman Lord Bute, into the equivalent of Premier',
G. D. H. Cole and Raymond Postgate write, 'the pensions list was found to
contain sixty-three Macs, twenty-five Campbells, an uncertain number of
Hamiltons, and a large number of other Scots names'![9] Dickens's nonsense,
then, makes sense in that it mirrors the nonsense of the age.

Ironically, the image of British society that emerges is not unlike that of
the orphanage described by Meagles: a structure organized in strict hierarchy, with 'the presiding Idols' (I, x, 111) at the very top, 'lesser star[s]' (I,
x, 103) further down, and cyphers on the lower rungs. Little communication
is carried on between the different strata of this very neatly compartmenta-
lized world. Unconcerned with the needs and aspirations of the small fry
underneath, the Almighty Fathers – invisible gods like Lord Decimus or
Tite Barnacle – stand aloof from the rest and exert their power through
intermediaries. Whether in Parliament, Government Offices or private
establishments, the same pattern is repeated: there is ordering from the top,
worshipping and fawning or complying at the bottom. Even within the
Barnacle clan, the second-rank Barnacles stand under orders from 'the

heads of the family', jobbing and toadying, fetching and carrying (I, xxxiv, 396), just as Pancks fetches and carries, and tugs and puffs for the benefit of 'the Patriarch'. The Marshalsea prison itself has its Father and the Marshalsea Father his toadies.

The great paradox of the patriarchal system that Dickens dramatizes here is that it magnifies a relationship that does not exist. The fatherhood of the fathers is exalted everywhere, but the fathers are not fatherly. They ooze benevolence, and they tyrannize.

Among all these fathers, one father-figure stands out, *the* Father, unique, paradigmatic, a god in majesty. But thus capitalized, the word 'Father' is like the Emperor's garment in Andersen's tale: an abstraction, a mere figment of popular imagination. People pay their respects (and their tribute) to the title-holder, attend ceremonies, worship at the shrine of Paternity and remain blind to the fact that the Emperor is naked. Amy alone, like Andersen's child, has this awareness: 'she knew well – no one better – that a man so broken as to be the Father of the Marshalsea, could be no father to his own children' (I, vii, 70). But she is too loving and too devoted to undeceive others, and the deceit worsens with the passing years as Dorrit goes on parading his Fatherliness: 'The more Fatherly he grew as to the Marshalsea, and the more dependant [sic] he became on the contributions of his changing family,' we are told, 'the greater stand he made by his forlorn gentility' (I, vii, 72).

For 'gentility' is the great priority, the fiction that must be preserved. Dorrit is a snob and the public image he wishes to build up is that of a genteel father. But, having lost touch with the world for so long, he has no living examples to go by and models himself on illustrious figures of the past, dispensing advice to the Collegians 'like a great moral Lord Chesterfield' (I, xix, 223), dramatically and ludicrously old-fashioned. Dickens, as we know, detested Chesterfield's aristocratic arrogance[10] and the comparison is not meant as a compliment. But, besides stressing the conceit of the man, it underscores his alienation and makes him truly pathetic.

Pathetic is also Dorrit's comportment towards his last-born daughter when, Lear-like, he proclaims his preference for her as the one of his three children who knows best how to repay his protestations of love: 'Amy, my love,' he says, 'you are by far the best loved of the three' (I, xix, 224). He also calls her 'my favorite child' (II, v, 465), 'my dear and sole remaining daughter' (II, xv, 591), yet proves unable right up to the end to act as a loving, unselfish father. The comparison with Lear is not explicit but it is obviously there: Dorrit has the irrationality, the selfishness, the grandiloquence of Shakespeare's hero; like him he suffers from the ingratitude of two of his children, is obsessed with the sense of his authority in spite of his foolish abdication from responsibility, becomes oracular in his insanity and, when he meets his death, reaches tragic grandeur. There is no evidence, of course, that Dickens wanted his readers to read the tragedy of Lear into that of William Dorrit but Lear is such a familiar figure that the analogy forces itself on us, giving this creation a more tragic dimension.

But the tragic dimension of the Marshalsea Father cannot be dissociated from the personality of his 'favorite child'. What I mean is that Amy's tragic father is not the tragic father of his two other children (which, incidentally, is also true of Shakespeare's hero, for what would Lear be with only Regan and Goneril and no Cordelia?). Fanny and Tip lower Dorrit's literary status from the high to the low 'mimetic mode', tending to integrate him with his society instead of isolating him, compelling us, in Northrop Frye's words, to 'respond to a sense of his common humanity'[11] and see him as a man with ordinary failings: fussy, tyrannical, lachrymose, irresolute, pompous, snobbish and on the whole comic or at best tragicomic.

As a comic father in a domestic comedy, Dorrit also enters that larger fictional category, the comedy of manners, which Frye describes as 'the portrayal of a chattering-monkey society devoted to snobbery and slander',[12] where he is placed almost on a par with the second-rate characters that figure in the subplots. Almost, but not quite. For, judged after the norms of 'the low mimetic mode' – plausibility and normality – he is too much of a caricature to be really convincing. His reaction to his daughter's marriage for instance, similar though it is to that of Meagles, strikes us as stiff and stilted and too cynical to be true:

Mr Dorrit, on being informed by his elder daughter that she had accepted matrimonial overtures from Mr Sparkler, to whom she had plighted her troth, received the communication, at once with great dignity and with a large display of parental pride; his dignity dilating with the widened prospect of advantageous ground from which to make acquaintances, and his parental pride being developed by Miss Fanny's ready sympathy with that great object of his existence. He gave her to understand that her noble ambition found harmonious echoes in his heart; and bestowed his blessing on her, as a child brimful of duty and good principle, self-devoted to the aggrandisement of the family name. (II, xv, 578)

Meagles is just as vain and proud but more credible both as a father and as a suburban snob. His fatherly fondness, his occasional misgivings as to Gowan's ability to make his pet daughter happy, his petty social dreams and petty 'parental pride' give him the credibility that Dorrit lacks from first to last. The fatal consequence is that we tend to judge him more severely than the eccentric egoist who can be easily dismissed as foolish and improbable. Of all the bad fathers pictured in the novel, it is, paradoxically, the most devoted one who best lends himself to criticism, to the criticism, that is, that we normally aim at our next-door neighbours.

During the early stages of Gowan's courtship of Pet, when passing clouds are said to obscure 'Mr Meagles's sunshine' (I, xxvi, 301), the clouds are so easily dispelled by the prospect of high connections that we soon grow allergic to his superficial sentimentalism. When Gowan brings young Barnacle, his distant cousin, to the Twickenham cottage, the narrator himself cannot help expressing his disappointment on seeing the good man look 'as gratified as if his [Barnacle's] whole family were there' and beaming complacently: 'his frank, fine, genuine qualities paled; he was not so easy, he was not so natural, he was striving after something that did not belong to him, he was not himself' (I, xvii, 203), says the narratorial voice, trying to play up his strong points and minimize his weaknesses. It seems, unfortunately, that Meagles *is* himself in this scene, and no less so than when he is shown in a more favourable light: his self-contradictions are simply those of a kindhearted snob, both endearing and despicable. We feel truly sorry for him at the end of the book when his daughter's marriage does not prove the success he had looked forward to, we feel truly irritated to see him incorrigibly blinded by his social prejudices and we feel truly upset by the last remark he makes on his dear Pet and on her husband: 'but she's very fond of him, and hides his faults, and thinks that no one sees them – and he certainly is well connected, and of a very good family', he tells Little Dorrit one day. 'It was the only comfort he had in the loss of his daughter, and if he made the most of it, who would blame him?' the lenient narrator comments (II, xxxiii, 789), and we feel inclined to share this leniency.

Still, it is somewhat disquieting to see this doting parent so easily reconciled to the unhappiness of his beloved child, and we cannot help thinking that, had he remained single, his reputation would have been very different: this 'honest, affectionate, and cordial' man (I, xvi, 189) would have been a perfect avuncular figure, a new Cheeryble or a new Brownlow, and no one would have suspected the latent incompetence. Why the dickens did Meagles marry? Why was Meagles 'ever a father'?

Oppression and lack of concern breed resentment and rebelliousness. And when the authority of the father is questioned, when the son opposes the will of the father, Dickens senses at once the true nature of the danger, a murderous threat that Dorrit also perceives: 'you had no right', he tells his disobedient son, 'to make up your mind to what is monstrous, to what is – ha – immoral, to what is – hum – parricidal' (I, xxxi, 369). To express his reprobation, Dorrit hits on a word that psychoanalysis has now educated us to take almost for granted, but in the middle of the nineteenth century it must have been received by the majority of readers as a sign of the man's precocious senility like all his ' – hums' and ' – has'. Dickens, however, really meant what Dorrit said; he knew that, at a symbolic level, Tip's refusal to obey 'the governor' (I, viii, 84) was, like any act of filial dis-obedience, a parricidal gesture. Meagles, whom no one would suspect of being in his dotage, speaks of Tattycoram, the rebellious child, in terms just as violent and excessive as those of Dorrit: 'I don't like to think of the way in which that unfortunate child, with all that passion and protest in her, feels when she hears the Fifth Commandment on a Sunday' (I, xvi, 192), he confides one day to Arthur. Surely, Tatty's restiveness might have been expressed in milder terms! But Dickens's obsession must betray itself in his characters' remarks.

Far from being limited to the domestic world, the theme of parricide reappears in the broader context of political and social subversion. 'In the eighteenth century,' Barthes writes, 'the word *parricide* meant any attack against authority (Father, Sovereign, State, the Gods).'[13] In Victorian England, this still holds true, as Dickens well knows. Thus, the little revolution that takes place in Bleeding Heart Yard under Pancks's leader-ship at the end of the novel is very clearly intended to appear as a substitute for the murder of the Patriarch. Some time before the event, a conversation between Pancks and Arthur alerts our attention to the symbolism of Casby's impending public exposure:

'Mentioning that, I may tell you, between ourselves, that I am sometimes tempted to do for him myself.'

Arthur started and said, 'Dear me, Pancks, don't say that!'

'Understand me,' said Pancks, extending five cropped coaly finger-nails on Arthur's arm; 'I don't mean, cut his throat. But, by all that's precious, if he goes too far, I'll cut his hair!' (II, ix, 525)

Arthur's misunderstanding is, of course, no accident, but a devious way on the part of the novelist of suggesting the hidden meaning of his character's ambiguous phraseology. Pancks admittedly denies harbouring murderous intentions against his task-master and it would occur to no one to doubt his sincerity, but his denial cannot but be perceived as what we would now call 'Freudian negation'.

The description of Casby's downfall confirms our intuitions. The life of the Patriarch is never threatened but the cropping of his head on the market-place (just under the sign-post of 'the Casby's Head'!), performed as it is in 'a paroxysm of animosity', gives us a foretaste of the scenes of violence that Dickens will describe in his next novel: the shears that Pancks suddenly whips out of his coat pocket snip off 'the sacred locks' (II, xxxii, 780) with as much fierceness and alacrity as the 'National Barber' will chop off the heads of aristocrats in revolutionary France, and the Bleeding Heart Yard tenants watch the scene with as much enthusiasm as the people of Saint-Antoine will watch public executions or dance at the sight of Foulon's head at the end of its pike (*TTC*, II, xxii).

The *Little Dorrit* scene should, admittedly, not be taken more seriously than it deserves. Once all is over, the sound of laughter can be heard 'rippling through the air, and making it ring again' as it would at the end of a Punch and Judy show, which is very different from the bloody scenes of the French Revolution. But the guilt is there none the less and, while the onlookers are clapping their hands and making merry, Pancks is shown recoiling 'in consternation' before 'the frightful result of his desperate action'; he stares at the 'bare-polled ... phantom' that seems to have 'started out of the earth to ask what [has] become of Casby', then runs away to seek shelter 'from the consequences of his crime' (II, xxii, 780). The possible consequences and the nature of the crime in this fantasy will become historical truth in *A Tale of Two Cities* with the murder of Monseigneur: 'Monseigneur was the father of his tenants', the villagers whisper at the fountain, and his murderer 'will be executed as a parricide' (*TTC*, II, xv, 162). Read in the light of Dickens's French Revolution novel, the popular uprising of the 'Bleeding Hearts' appears as more dangerously subversive than its anecdotal and farcical character would at first seem to suggest.

The patriarchal system in this novel is threatened in more ways than one. Omnipotence, as we have just seen, leads to parricidal or castrating gestures, impotence to the danger, be it ever so slight, of women taking over. I use the word 'danger' because I do not think that Dickens can be suspected of very feminist leanings. His thinking women (Mrs Jellyby), his political furies (Madame Defarge and the Vengeance), his self-willed wives (Mrs Merdle, Fanny Sparkler) bear witness to his lack of enthusiasm for a matriarchal order. Even in a literal sense, the man did not like women to wear the trousers: tomboy clothes, bloomers and other forms of sartorial emancipation which became the craze in the eighteen-fifties seemed to him ugly and ridiculous, though probably, as Butt and Tillotson suggest, because of 'his strong distaste, not so much for the change of fashion, as for the state of mind implied in the change and for the proselytizing fervour accompanying it'.[14] If in *Little Dorrit* women dress in men's attire, we must not suppose that Dickens sees it as a form of progress; it is to fill a gap on the stage that the men have deserted. When Flintwinch remarks that Mrs Clennam has 'the head of two men' (I, xxx, 348) it is the anomaly, the monstrosity that is pointed out. When William Dorrit discovers that 'Clennam and Co.' is 'a – hum – a mother' (II, xvii, 601), the remark, which echoes Miss Tox's about 'Dombey and Son' – 'a Daughter, after all' – does not ring a happy bell. And Miss Wade's confessions of a 'self-tormentor' (II, xxi), express the bitterness of a woman who has been the victim of paternalist oppression: her lesbianism, we are made to understand, is a form of 'misandry'.

The only female character whose taking over is not meant to be dreaded

or despised is Little Dorrit herself, the eponymous heroine who is intended
to set an example. But her role as family head is none the less very
disturbing. There is no clash in her case between femininity and masculi-
nity, no feminist protest or usurpation, but a reversal of parts that disturbs
the natural order and the seasons of her life. When she is no older than eight,
on her mother's death, although the youngest of the Dorrit children, she fills
up the vacant place and is promoted 'eldest of the three' (I, vii, 70). More
disturbing still, 'the Child of the Marshalsea' immediately 'beg[ins] her
womanly life' and '[takes] upon herself a new relation towards the Father'
(I, vii, 70), mothering him, nursing him even with the milk of her kindness.
Euphrasia of Syracuse who, according to the legend, had fed her father,
King Evander, 'with the milk of her breasts'[15] when he was in prison, did
not equal her in abnegation:

There was a classical daughter once – perhaps – who ministered to her father in his
prison as her mother had ministered to her. Little Dorrit ... did much more, in
comforting her father's wasted heart upon her innocent breast, and turning to it a
fountain of love and fidelity that never ran dry or waned, through all his years of
famine. (I, xix, 222)

Amy's 'womanly' life is not the life of a woman (a condition to which she
has no claim for most of the novel), but the life of a mother: a daughterly
mother, a sisterly mother, a 'Little Mother', selfless, devoted, catering to
the needs of all the members of the family, a contradiction in terms and in
looks. When she reaches maturity, the anomaly persists because of her
slender build. Arthur, who first meets her when she is twenty-three, sees
'the little creature' (I, ix, 91) as a child who needs protecting, not as a
woman to be loved and courted. During the night when she and Maggy are
locked out of the prison, the Little Mother is mistaken for the child of her
protégée and thus shielded from the dangers that would normally threaten a
girl of her age in 'the cruel streets' of London: 'Though everywhere the
leader and the guide, Little Dorrit, happy for once in her youthful appearance, feigned to cling to and rely upon Maggy. And more than once some
voice ... had called out to the rest, to "let the woman and the child go by!"'
(I, xiv, 169); but a prostitute steps back in horror on realizing that the
street-walking child is in fact an adult female: '"Why, my God!" she said,
recoiling, "you're a woman!"' (I, xiv, 170).
    The prostitute's reaction might well be the reader's, for this dispropor-
tion between age, looks and behaviour is truly monstrous and shocking. Too
much innocence, besides, can be really unhealthy: innocent references to
unlawful or abnormal sexuality, the innocently incestuous relationship with
the father, the innocent walk in the red-light district, create a climate of
uneasiness around the womanly child which is all the more disagreeable as

Little Dorrit herself fosters the ambiguous image of child-wife and child-mother. If, like other female usurpers – say, Betsey Trotwood or Mrs Clennam – she had set out to play a man's part, she would be either comic or detestable, and we would know where to stand; but the trouble with her choosing to replace the mother is that it rouses in us, as in the London passers-by, these mixed feelings of admiration and repulsion that are so very uncomfortable.

Amy, as much as a daughter, is a slave chained to her father by her devotion and even by her name. The title on the picture that Phiz designed for the wrapper of monthly parts well illustrates the situation: the letters that make up the adjective 'L I T T L E' are spaced well apart, whereas those that make up the name of 'Dorrit' are conspicuously tied together by the links of a chain. But the slave likes her chains, much preferring her father's name – 'my right name' she calls it (II, xxix, 736) – to her Christian name that points to her singularity.

It will be argued that 'Little Dorrit', the 'right name' so dear to her, also binds her to another man, Arthur Clennam, who solemnly gave it to her, somehow acting as her new godfather on the night of her visit to his lodgings with Maggy: 'As you just now gave yourself the name they give you at my mother's, and as that is the name by which I always think of you, let me call you Little Dorrit', he had said. 'Thank you, sir,' she had replied, 'I should like it better than any name' (I, xiv, 160). From Rome, months later, she writes to him:

she [Mrs Gowan] speaks to me by my name – I mean, not my Christian name, but the name you gave me. When she began to call me Amy, I told her my short story, and that you had always called me Little Dorrit. I told her that the name was much dearer to me than any other, and so she calls me Little Dorrit too. (II, xi, 536)

But this double bondage increases the ambiguous relationship with the father. We might have hoped that love would free her from her enslavement, and we cannot fail to wonder at the perversity of a destiny that will eventually bind her with the ties of marriage to a man who, when she was no more than a child to him, named her after her father.

Somebody

When Little Dorrit becomes Arthur's wife, her father has been dead and buried for quite a while and all her fortune is gone. 'All lost, and all gained', one of the descriptive headlines to the Charles Dickens edition,[16] well sums up the situation: both the death of her father and the financial crash that deprived her of her inheritance were necessary to the heroine's emancipation. She and her penniless husband are now free to start from scratch, no longer burdened with the guilt and tyranny of their fathers and unhampered by heirlooms, and it is to be hoped that their union will herald happier days.

Whether it will herald a radically new era is quite another matter. The bride who emerges from the church portico on a sunny autumn morning, if she looks 'at the fresh perspective of the street' (II, xxxiv, 801) and into the future, still goes by the old familiar name of 'Little Dorrit' that looks back to former times. 'Amy Clennam', by stressing a relationship different from the one we had been used to, would have sounded more promising, but this new name is never mentioned and the omission is certainly no accident: Little Dorrit she has always been and Little Dorrit she remains, faithful to a dream, faithful to two men whose images have long since been blurred into one.

The disparity in years between Arthur and Amy has bred from the start transfers of feelings and ambiguities that will never be erased. We remember how, when he gave her the name of 'Little Dorrit', she looked up to this 'grave brown gentleman' as to the father she had never had, thoughtful, selfless, truly paternal – 'She thought what a good father he would be. How, with some such look, he would counsel and cherish his daughter' (I, xiv, 161) – while he at once had called her 'my child' (I, xiv, 160) and was henceforth to harbour fatherly feelings for 'his poor child' (I, xxii, 257), 'his delicate child' (II, viii, 504), even 'his adopted daughter' (I, xvi, 184).

This is the relationship that links them to each other for most of the novel. Even after her own feelings have taken a new turn, and distressed though she is that her love is not reciprocated, Amy takes a perverse pleasure in playing the role of child-woman in which she has been cast by her creator. Her letters from Italy, signed 'Your poor child' (II, iv, 457; II, xi, 538), are little masterpieces in masochistic negation; she even prides herself on not being lovable, or sexually attractive: 'I have no lover, of course' (II, xi, 537), she writes, and if the reader of the book can perceive a veiled love declaration in this pathetic 'of course', the reader of the letter, who is still hopelessly infatuated with another woman, cannot be expected to read between the lines. Amy's awareness of this infatuation delightfully increases the exquisite agony of her love's labours. Identifying herself with her 'rival' whose own unhappy marriage mirrors her frustration and secret heartaches, she writes from Venice where she has befriended Pet: 'I could not keep it out of my mind that if I was Mrs Gowan (what a change that would be, and how I must alter to become like her!) I should feel that I was rather lonely and lost, for the want of some one who was steadfast and firm in purpose' (II, iv, 455).

But the discreet Phaedra is unlikely to get her message over to a slightly hard-of-hearing Hippolytus[17] and the generous intervention of her own rejected lover will be necessary to put an end to this misunderstanding and open Arthur's eyes. It is John Chivery who acts as go-between and, 'for the sake of the loved one' (II, xxvii, 714), offers to his rival the present of 'Miss Dorrit's love' that has been denied him. Arthur receives the news like a man suddenly 'awakened from sleep, and stupefied by intelligence beyond his full comprehension' (II, xxvii, 710), but his amazement is short-lived and the interior monologue that follows, a well-argued demonstration that he was in love from the first, cleverly reverses the situation and the responsibilities:

Consider the improbability. He had been accustomed to call her his child, and his dear child, and to invite her confidence by dwelling upon the difference in their respective ages, and to speak of himself as one who was turning old ...

He had her two letters among other papers in his box, and he took them out and read them. There seemed to be a sound in them like the sound of her sweet voice. It fell upon his ear with many tones of tenderness, that were not insusceptible of the new meaning ...

Consider the improbability.

But, it had a preponderating tendency, when considered, to become fainter. There was another and a curious enquiry of his own heart's that concurrently became stronger. In the reluctance he had felt to believe that she loved any one; in his desire to set that question at rest; in a half-formed consciousness he had had, that there would be a kind of nobleness in his helping her love for any one; was there no suppressed something on his own side that he had hushed as it arose? ...

He had kissed her when he raised her from the ground, on the day when she had been so consistently and expressively forgotten. Quite as he might have kissed her, if she had been conscious? No difference? (II, xxvii, 711–12)

But rethinking the past does not obliterate it and the old relationship survives the new, giving a faintly incestuous nature to the final union of this strangely assorted couple. How else could it be when their vows are exchanged within the walls of the prison where Arthur in his turn has been incarcerated and conspicuously placed in the room which had been Amy's father's for so long? The memory of old Dorrit haunts the place, compelling Arthur to the most disturbing identification:

Imprisonment began to tell upon him. He knew that he idled and moped. After what he had known of the influences of imprisonment within the four small walls of the very room he occupied, this consciousness made him afraid of himself. Shrinking from the observation of other men, and shrinking from his own, he began to change very sensibly. Anybody might see that the shadow of the wall was dark upon him. (II, xxviii, 715)

Gradually, his behaviour models itself on that of his predecessor, he grows physically and morally weaker and weaker, thus allowing Amy to play at nurse as in the past:

and drawing an arm softly round his neck, [she] laid his head upon her bosom, put a hand upon his head, and resting her cheek upon that hand, nursed him as lovingly,

and GOD knows as innocently, as she had nursed her father in that room when she had
been but a baby, needing all the care from others that she took of them. (II, xxix, 736)

The author, who means no harm, takes God to witness as to the complete
innocence of all this. In all innocence, Arthur can embrace his beloved as a
father would embrace his child: 'He took her in his arms, as if she had been
his daughter' (II, xxix, 739). In all innocence Amy finds a father again in
finding a husband.

Arthur's imprisonment is the most worrying episode in the whole novel.
The lover of justice is now in the dock. He who wanted to take away the sins
of the world has committed the sin of the age. He who did not want a soiled
inheritance has speculated his fortune and that of his best friend away. He
who was 'Nobody' has become 'Everybody'. And it is this very man, 'weak
and erring', that Little Dorrit chooses for a husband. We feel all the more
inclined to worry on seeing the heroine, who embodies all the values of the
novel (including clear-sightedness), make such a blind choice. Is there no
way out of the infernal circle? Will history repeat itself? Will the curse that
weighed down the fathers hang over their children for ever and ever?
   The omnipotent novelist fortunately breaks the spell. The new 'Pupil of
the Marshalsea' (II, xxvii), although more guilty than his predecessor, is
better able to learn his lesson and will be a better man when he gets out.
   Provided he does get out, which is not so easy since he has no money to
pay off his debts and Amy, now ruined, cannot help in any way. But we may
trust Dickens to find a solution, even if it means fetching, as he does, a
providential man from abroad. Daniel Doyce reappears in the nick of time
with his money, his expertise, his optimism, his energy and his moral
philosophy: 'Every failure teaches a man something, if he will learn; and you
are too sensible a man not to learn from this failure', he tells Arthur whom
he also assures that the business stands 'in greater want of [him] than ever it
did' and that 'a new and prosperous career' is opened before them 'as
partners' (II, xxxiv, 797).
   Besides clearing Arthur from his difficulties, Doyce's return in the last
chapter would seem to strike a real note of hope for the whole of society.
Dan, the engineer, belongs to that race of enterprising men that people the
books of Smiles and Carlyle, and whose talent and efficiency should free
'Britannia' from the 'Do-Nothingism'[18] of Barnacles and such like. But the
hopes are no sooner raised than Meagles damps them down. Dan, he says, is
recognized abroad as the aristocrat of talent he is: 'He's medalled and
ribboned, and starred and crossed, and I don't-know-what all'd, like a born
nobleman', but these things 'won't do, over here. In that particular, Britannia is a Britannia in the Manger – won't give her children such distinctions

herself, and won't allow them to be seen, when they're given by other countries' (II, xxxiv, 796).

Dan's new partnership with Arthur would also seem of good omen with its emphasis on work as opposed to reliance on speculation or inheritance. But the demonstration would be more convincing if the novelist himself did not rely on luck and fathers to engineer this happy ending. For had not Doyce happened to turn up, poor Arthur might well have remained in gaol for life, like a new William Dorrit. And it is in the guise of a father, 'a jolly father' (II, xxxiv, 796) that the liberator makes his appearance.

The spiritual fatherhood of Doyce is pointed out no fewer than three times within a single chapter. Hardly has he arrived than the 'jolly father' asks Amy if she will do him the honour of regarding him 'in the light of a father' (II, xxxiv, 798) and, on her wedding-day, he waits for her inside the church 'in this paternal character' (II, xxxiv, 801) as she and her betrothed walk up to the altar. This role is all the more remarkable as the man, as far as we know, is not a family man. We therefore cannot miss the hint: the country, Dickens tells us, must get rid of its Patriarchs and Fatherly impostors, but it cannot do without paternal guides.

Paradoxical as it may seem, *Little Dorrit*, which is Dickens's most virulent satire of the patriarchal system, is also the novel that ends with the most explicit celebration of paternity. But the Dickens novel needs fathers because Dickens is so deeply attached to the paternal image and Doyce embodies the new ideal. It does not follow that the happy ending marks the beginning of perfect utopia. Thanks to Doyce's intervention, Arthur can at last become 'Somebody' and receive at the end the blessing of his creator. But eternal damnation continues to weigh on the rest of humanity and the last sentence regrettably confirms Meagles's sceptical remarks:

They went quietly down into the roaring streets, inseparable and blessed; and as they passed along in sunshine and in shade, the noisy and the eager, and the arrogant and the froward and the vain, fretted, and chafed, and made their usual uproar. (II, xxxiv, 802)

The redemptive mission that the hero had undertaken by making 'Everybody's Fault' his personal business ends in shade and sunshine, in semi-failure and semi-victory. The communion of sinners cannot be turned overnight into a communion of saints for, even in the Dickens world, there is no salvation for all, there is only individual grace.

7 Dickens's disinherited boy and his great expectations

> He must dream—
> Of what? Of Paradise! – Ay! dream of it,
> My disinherited boy! – 'Tis but a dream;
> For never more thyself, thy sons, nor
> fathers, shall walk in that forbidden
> place of joy!
> > Byron, *Cain*

Bastard or foundling?

My father's family name being Pirrip, and my christian name Philip, my infant tongue could make of both names nothing longer or more explicit than Pip. So I called myself Pip, and came to be called Pip. (i, 1)

The inaugural paragraph of *Great Expectations* does more than acquaint the reader with the name of its hero. For all the light-hearted, matter-of-fact and somewhat childish simplicity of its style, it establishes at the onset a complex relationship between a son and his father; it encapsulates within two short sentences the ontological drama of one whose identity should not be mistaken for identification and it alerts, in so doing, our critical attention.

Pip's self-christening, in the surname of the father and in the first name of the son, is at once an act of bondage and a gesture of autonomy. Without denying the contingencies of his birth – his ritual visits to his parents' burial ground even show a keen sense of rootedness and allegiance – the child, thanks to his lingual, therefore linguistic, awkwardness, early frees himself from the dictates of family onomastics: 'it's a kind of a family name what he gave himself when a infant, and is called by' (x, 71), Joe will say later, echoing Pip's first statement, 'I called myself Pip, and came to be called Pip.'

Severance, to be sure, does not preclude reverence. But in calling himself 'Pip', therefore adopting for a name the smallest common denominator between his genitor's patronymic and his own Christian name (acknowledged as personal, though also inherited at first hand from Philip Pirrip the Elder), the young orphan is paying, in a literal sense, lip-service to the narcissism of his dead and buried father. 'Dead and buried' indeed is the

'Philip Pirrip, late of this parish' whose name is no more than a few signs inscribed on a tombstone, a name never to be passed on to the son, as it should legitimately be: Pip is Pip from the start and will remain so right up to the end.

The circuitous phrase, 'my father's family name', shows lasting impertinence on the part of the narrator – no longer the blundering, inarticulate infant whose tongue slipped inadvertently, but an elderly, polite gentleman – and expresses an ambivalent claim to kinship and alienation. No legitimate son in his right mind would ever choose, unless in jest, to introduce himself so deviously when a plain statement, 'my family name', would do just as nicely. The incongruous interpolation of the genitive creates a grammatical and sentimental disruption in the sentence and distorts the relationship between possessor and possessed: the name belongs to the father, the father belongs to the son, and the son belongs nowhere. And if, undeniably, the formulation gives pride of place to the child's sire as life-giver, it also most cheekily dismisses him as name-transmitter.

Before we proceed beyond the first page, our attention is drawn again to the importance of naming. Self-awareness, Pip tells us, is simultaneous and, it would seen, synonymous with linguistic awareness:

My first most vivid and broad impression of the identity of things, seems to me to have been gained on a memorable raw afternoon towards evening. At such a time I found out for certain, that this bleak place overgrown with nettles was the church-yard; and that Philip Pirrip, late of this parish, and also Georgiana wife of the above, were dead and buried; and that Alexander, Bartholomew, Abraham, Tobias, and Roger, infant children of the aforesaid, were also dead and buried; and that the dark flat wilderness beyond the churchyard, intersected with dykes and mounds and gates, with scattered cattle feeding on it, was the marshes; and that the low leaden line beyond was the river; and that the distant savage lair from which the wind was rushing, was the sea; and that the small bundle of shivers growing afraid of it all and beginning to cry, was Pip. (i, 1)

In thus rehearsing the 'identity of things', Pip puts himself *in medias res* and begins his life-story like a Book of Genesis, where creation and naming are not to be dissociated. Then, the master of words, he signs his name at the bottom of his list as any artist would do at the bottom of a picture or any poet at the bottom of a sonnet. As we read these lines, we soon realize that we are attending nothing less than the birth of a writer: self-authored in the midst of the world that he has just conjured up and himself the word made flesh, Pip is not brought to life in a traditional manner like any of his famous predecessors. No Mrs Thingummy, no Dr Chillip, no Doctor Parker Peps is called to the rescue as they were to help forth Oliver, David or Paul. His is an oral delivery, a kind of posthumous birth among the graves of distant, almost imaginary parents:

As I never saw my father or my mother, and never saw any likeness of either of them (for their days were long before the days of photographs), my first fancies regarding what they were like, were unreasonably derived from their tombstones. The shape of the letters on my father's, gave me an odd idea that he was a square, stout, dark man, with curly black hair. From the character and turn of the inscription, '*Also Georgiana Wife of the Above*,' I drew a childish conclusion that my mother was freckled and sickly. (i, 1)

A beautiful tribute is paid here to the poetic powers of the written word. Like all writers, it is as a reader that Pip begins his career. Like all budding autobiographers, it is the book of his origins that he is first given to read. And, of course, he rewrites it. There is little else he could do. Those parents are so far away that he has in fact no choice but to recreate them before he recreates himself.

But, behind the fiction of the freckled mother and of the dark, curly-haired father, the reality of the 'real' Georgiana and of the 'real' Philip is clearly perceptible and the information scattered over the page about this couple whose only daughter 'married the blacksmith' and whose five eldest boys 'gave up trying to get a living exceedingly early in that universal struggle' tells us a great deal about the predicament of their youngest surviving son. Within a single page, we have learnt enough about the young tomb-reader to know 'for certain' that he is more to be pitied for his wretched condition than envied for his talent. So does indeed the 'small bundle of shivers growing afraid of it all and beginning to cry', an exhausted and pathetic demiurge abandoned to himself in the wilderness, a king without a kingdom, as helpless as Lear on the heath, as vulnerable as little Oedipus exposed on the mountain.

For, in proclaiming his singularity, Pip in fact proclaims his utter solitude. Undeniably the most proletarian and the most desperately orphaned of all Dickens's heroes, he embarks upon life without any of the romantic assets that in many novels can ensure success to even the most destitute. He has not the advantage of illegitimacy or of mysterious origins, which were so promising in 'the Parish Boy's Progress'; nor can there be in his case any whisperings of some secret legacy: the Pirrips do not belong to the class of testators in which as a rule Dickens places his heroes. Philip Pirrip the Elder was even so ignorant of conventions and proprieties that he has mistakenly christened his last-born child after himself, when any bourgeois would have known that this is the prerogative of the eldest son and rightful heir to the property.[1] But what does it matter to one born so low whether he be called Philip, Alexander or Bartholomew? 'Pip' in fact expresses this helplessness with a vengeance and brings the orphan child down to the level of the poorest, the Dicks, the Johnnies and the Joes, who cannot afford a family name and do not even know that most people can – 'never heerd of sich a think'. Unlike Jo, the *Bleak House* crossing sweeper, the son of Philip Pirrip knows very well, of course, that 'everybody has two names' and that Pip 'is short for a longer name', but he none the less thinks it 'long enough for *him*' (*BH*, xi, 134), long enough for a boy who has no one but himself to rely on, no birthright, no prospects of inheritance, no expectations whatever, and whose only chance, with such a nickname of a name, would be to belong to a fairy tale.

Should we therefore already begin to doubt the promises of the title? We should and we do. But only up to a point. For what novel-reader worthy of the name would be prepared to renounce the pleasure of subscribing to the illusion of the text and of letting himself be mystified by a story whose main attraction, as may be perceived on reading the first lines, is its equivocation?

Great Expectations is indeed a fundamentally ambiguous novel: it has, as we shall see, the narrative ambiguity of a story which hesitates between verisimilitude and implausibility, the ideological ambiguity of a message which hesitates between utopia and resignation, the psychological ambiguity of a hero who hesitates between two heroic callings, the formal ambiguity of a text which hesitates between several literary genres, the functional ambiguity of a method which hesitates between irony and detachment.

The reader's participation in this enterprise is amply solicited: he is invited to play the double game of credulity (through his identification with Pip as a hero) and of alienation (through his identification with Pip as a narrator), to suspend at will 'his disbelief and (what is harder) his belief'.[2] Gullible and cautious, the dupe of the narrator and his confidant, he has to cope with two simultaneous, contradictory readings, so that at the end his romantic self will be somewhat disappointed, whereas his critical (and Pumblechookian) self will exclaim triumphantly: 'But what else could be expected! what else could be expected!' (lviii, 450).

One of the main difficulties is to decide whether Pip's story, 'the classic legend of the nineteenth century', as Robert Stange calls it,[3] is, in any final analysis, a Victorian success story after the *David Copperfield* pattern or Dickens's tale of lost illusions. Another is to appreciate the hero's modernity. If we consider with Marthe Robert that 'modernity' in fiction-writing must be understood as 'the self-searching, self-questioning literary movement which uses as subject matter its own doubt and belief in the value of its message',[4] we can with no further hesitation call *Great Expectations* a modern novel, but it does not follow that the hero of this modern novel is himself a modern hero; and, paradoxically, the question that remains to be solved is precisely whether Pip is not an old-fashioned hero in a very modern novel. Or, to use Robert's terminology, is he still at the end the modern oedipal 'bastard' that we first discovered on his father's grave or has he not regressed into the more archaic type of the romantic 'foundling', reading backward, in this event, his *Entfremdungsroman* or 'Family Romance'?

The 'Family Romance' in the Freudian theory is a story which the child makes up for himself 'as a correction of actual life',[5] a day-dream which serves 'as the fulfilment of wishes' during the early years of his life, when he has to free himself from parental authority, and which might be compared to a serial story in two main episodes.

The first episode begins with the child's disappointment with his parents after an early period of idolatry. As he grows up and comes to realize that he is not, or no longer, the sole object of parental care and affection, has to face the necessity of sharing his parents' dispensation of love, food and security with unwanted siblings, and as he furthermore 'gets to know other parents and compares them with his own, and so acquires the right to doubt the incomparable and unique quality which he had attributed to them',[6] he feels betrayed and humiliated and embarks upon a compensatory dream in which he rewrites his life-story, imagining himself to be a lost child adopted by strangers. He is the noble 'foundling' whose true parentage will of necessity be discovered some day, and things will be set to rights at last.

The second episode takes place when the child grows aware of a sexual difference between his genitors and realizes that only his father's parental authenticity can be a matter of doubt. He then focuses on his father his genealogical uncertainty and takes on a new part as 'bastard' child of a familiar mother and of some distant, preferably aristocratic, father, thus ridding himself in his imagination of the father who does not come up to his expectations.

If, as Freud invites us to do, we consider that fiction, especially popular romance, is primarily based on wish fulfilment, we may assume with Marthe Robert that the two heroic types of the Family Romance have quite naturally found their way into literary works of fiction: the foundling, a romantic dreamer, has developed into the fairy-tale hero, relying on benefactors, benevolent uncles and fairy godmothers; the bastard, a realist, is the hero of modern fiction, pugnacious, self-reliant and solitary. Among Robert's long list of 'bastards' we find colonists like Robinson Crusoe and ambitious young men like Rastignac or Julien Sorel.

If we now try to sort out Dickens's heroes according to these criteria, Oliver Twist, although a bastard in the ordinary sense of the term, will appear at once as the ideal, almost paradigmatic 'foundling', whereas Charles Darnay, born d'Evrémonde and legitimate heir to a title and to a fortune, will qualify immediately as the ideal 'bastard'. But these two pure types are remarkable exceptions, and there is, on the whole, much overlapping between the two categories. David Copperfield, the runaway child who fights his way up into fame and affluence after the fashion of his creator, is very much on the bastard side, though, in seeking the help of his aunt Betsey, who acts as surrogate parent, the young Oedipus shows that he cannot entirely resist the old attraction of Telemachus for some protective parental figure. The double temptation is in fact shared by all the other Dickens heroes, none so well as John Harmon, as we shall see in the next chapter. The Dickens novel might in fact be described as an oedipal novel with Telemachus in the leading role: the movement is always away from the father and back again, back to origins.

Structurally, *Great Expectations* follows this pattern. When, after long years of absence in Cairo, Pip comes back to his native place and visits his friends at the forge, he finds himself in the presence of another little Pip, the son of Joe and Biddy, his namesake and *alter ego*: '. . . and there, fenced into the corner with Joe's leg, and sitting on my own little stool looking at the fire, was – I again!', he writes (lix, 457). The next morning, Pip takes the child out for a walk to, of all places, the old churchyard where it all began:

I took him out for a walk next morning, and we talked immensely, understanding one another to perfection. And I took him down to the churchyard, and set him on a certain tombstone there, and he showed me from that elevation which stone was sacred to the memory of Philip Pirrip, late of this Parish, and Also Georgiana, Wife of the Above. (lix, 457)

We have now come full circle and reached the end of the novel. There do follow two or three pages on the Estella–Pip relationship, but this love-story is of such limited significance to the novel as a whole that Dickens could rewrite its conclusion at will and reorientate it without damaging or improving the book. Altering or suppressing the return of the son to the graves of his parents would, on the contrary, have greatly impaired the meaning of the novel; and when Dickens reworked his ending, he knew better than to rework this scene and reconsidered only what came next.

This act of filial piety is really essential: it confirms to the reader that *Great Expectations* is first and foremost the novel of a son and, more important still, it reminds him that it is the novel of the son of Philip Pirrip. This is all the more necessary as, in between, the relationship between this son and this father is not openly made the subject of the plot: it even seems erased, ruled out of the book. Pip, unlike Oliver, has no reason to seek his father when he knows so well where to find him. He has no reason either to hate, suspect or despise him as Arthur Clennam and John Harmon do, and between the first and the last chapters he never mentions him, never gives him a thought. He has, we remember, never set eyes on him, and no one, as far as we know, ever told him what he looked like or what sort of man he was. The return of the prodigal son is not a return to someone he ever knew, but

to someone he imagined in the days when he was a young epigraphist. His
filial pilgrimage is a journey back towards some idea, or some ideal maybe,
early derived from a few words inscribed on a tombstone.

We might well also make the journey back to this first chapter, as the
conspicuously self-referential narrator invites us to do, if we are to appreciate what exactly he is returning to. He is returning, of course, to his first
'fancies' which, on reflection, prove to have been rather stereotyped images
of a fragile mother and of a strong, dark, impressive father, the sort of man
that any boy would like to take after or to imitate to strengthen his own
image of himself. He is also returning to the poetic appeal of their epitaph
and to his misreading of its convoluted phrasing: 'At the time when I stood
in the churchyard, reading the family tombstones,' he explains, 'I had just
enough learning to be able to spell them out. My construction even of their
simple meaning was not very correct, for I read "wife of the Above" as a
complimentary reference to my father's exaltation to a better world' (vii,
39). A father in Heaven, a mother magnified by the magic formula which
commemorates her – 'Also Georgiana. That's my mother' (i, 2) – two people
whom the popular, conventional poetry of an inscription have immortalized
into almost mythical figures, such are the parents he is returning to.

These wishful representations do not, unfortunately, provide the whole
picture. The child sobbing among the graves is also, as we have seen, a child
who has been cruelly slighted by the very people whom he is so willing to
idealize; he has been slighted by their death, their inability to provide for
him, and even their lack of concern in not taking him with them like the
other five little boys. The scene in the churchyard precisely takes place at a
crucial moment of awareness when Pip is beginning to estrange himself
from his genitors and to 'bastardize' himself, when, in other words, he has
just set about adding a new episode to his family romance 'as a correction of
actual life' or in retaliation for being mishandled.

But something strange occurs then. For the narrative agencies, who are
dreaming on his behalf, begin at this very moment to write his romance for
him in order to turn him eventually into an adopted son. Instead of
remaining a bastard for life, he will be given a chance of becoming a
foundling and being provided for. But, left in the dark about the identity of
his adoptive parent, he will also be given the liberty of projecting his
parental ideals on whomsoever he wishes. As blind as Oedipus, he blindly
goes on living his oedipal drama through vicarious relationships, imaginary
experiences, adapting his dreams to these mysterious circumstances, mis-
placing his affections and expectations, faithless to his origins, faithful to his
ideals.

The romance begins as early as chapter 1, when Pip is still weeping on his
father's grave and, as in David Copperfield's fantasy, Lazarus is raised from

the dead: '"Hold your noise!" cried a terrible voice, as a man started up from among the graves at the side of the church porch' (i, 1–2). Even before being identified as a convict 'in coarse grey, with a great iron on his leg', the newcomer is unmistakably recognized as 'the ghost of a man's', or for that matter of a boy's, 'own father' (xxvii, 208) and the recognition is greatly helped by associations with the earlier novel: are we not, after all, reading a new episode of Dickens's own 'Family Romance'?

Only years later, when the convict returns and proclaims himself to be Pip's 'second father' (xxxix, 304), will the reader grasp the full meaning of this ghostly apparition. But, meanwhile, the mystery attached to the event will not impair his innermost conviction that the man who sprang up as a father-figure might reappear some day as something like a father, a conviction often strengthened in the course of the novel by incidental, premonitory coincidences and narratorial side-lighting. Pip, for his part, will not see beyond the event itself until, some sixteen years later, 'the truth of [his] position' comes 'flashing' on him (xxxix, 303). And it is certainly the greatest dramatic irony of this first-person narrative that the hints dropped throughout for our benefit and information should come from the very man who, as a character, was primarily concerned, yet remained so long in the dark.

Another, concomitant irony concerns the child's identity in its long unsuspected relation with the newcomer:

'Tell us your name!' said the man. 'Quick!'
  'Pip, sir.'
'Once more,' said the man, staring at me. 'Give it mouth!'
  'Pip, Pip, sir.' (i, 2)

That an escaped convict should prove so eager to know the name of a child whom he has just met by chance and whom in all likelihood he will never meet again (there is at this stage no reason why he should) seems quite inexplicable, even goes against common sense. This behaviour cannot be ascribed to vain curiosity or be taken for convict 'manners'. Yet the question is asked twice, as if the man wanted to make sure that he gets the answer right. The obvious explanation that comes to mind is that this verbal exchange meets dramatic requirements: Dickens wants to secure the future of his story and how could a sheep-farmer from the depths of Australia ever find the track of the boy unless he knew him by name? Something very similar occurs in Hugo's *Les Misérables* when Jean Valjean, the escaped convict, meets Petit-Gervais on the road and robs him of a silver coin:

'What is your name?' Jean Valjean said.
  'Little Gervais, sir.'
'Be off,' said Jean Valjean.[7]

Throughout the novel, Jean Valjean will be pursued in the literal and in the figurative sense by his misdeed. A warrant is issued for the arrest of the (long unidentified) thief, and the name of the child will be to the last the name of his guilt.

Magwitch feels no guilt for emptying the pockets of the boy whom he turned upside down on first meeting him; but Pip's name, as we are going to see, will have its own symbolic value.

When Jaggers comes to the forge eleven years later to inform Pip of his good fortune, he does not merely satisfy himself that Joe Gargery's apprentice answers to the name of 'Pip', but he imparts to him the peremptory and sole condition to his inheritance demanded by his mysterious benefactor, namely that he should always go by that name:

'Now, Mr Pip,' pursued the lawyer, 'I address the rest of what I have to say, to you. You are to understand, first, that it is the request of the person from whom I take my instructions, that you always bear the name of Pip. You will have no objection, I dare say, to your great expectations being encumbered with that easy condition. But if you have any objection, this is the time to mention it.'

My heart was beating so fast, and there was such a singing in my ears, that I could scarcely stammer I had no objection.

'I should think not!' (xviii, 130–31)

In a novel so meticulously sifted by the critics, little attention has been paid to this strange demand. No explanation, of course, is offered by Jaggers. None will ever be offered by Magwitch either. But this is not a sufficient reason for not giving it proper consideration.

Magwitch's likely motivations seem easy enough to detect. The former runaway convict wants to express his gratitude to the boy who once brought him food, a file and a glimpse of humanity, and whose name in his memory stands (rightly or wrongly) for human fellowship. In asking him to stick to this name, he is trying, not unlike Miss Havisham, to stop the clocks and arrest time. His money will go to the little child as he knew him and as he wishes to imagine him always, unchanged, unspoilt by time, child-like, generous, loyal and weak enough, moreover, still to require his protection.

Other, less noble motives may be hazarded. The social outcast who intends to have his revenge on the oppressive and unfair society that has victimized him ever since he was born may wish to confer respectability on a name that connotes destitution and misery, as he turns this little speck, self-dubbed 'Pip', into a moneyed gentleman. And this vicarious ambition seems gratified when they meet again: 'I tell it, fur you to know as that there hunted dunghill dog wot you kep life in, got his head so high that he could make a gentleman – and, Pip, you're him!' (xxxix, 304).

But, more important still, Magwitch has decided to make Pip his son and heir: 'You're my son,' he says, 'more to me nor any son. I've put

away money, only for you to spend' (xxxix, 304). Under normal circumstances (especially in a Dickens novel), the new father would naturally wish
to bestow his name as well as his fortune on his adopted child,[8] but if a
convict's money can be bequeathed easily enough (for *pecunia non olet*), how
could a man who lives in banishment bestow a tainted name on someone he
loves dearly and wishes to protect from such misfortunes and humiliations
as he himself has had to endure? Not to mention the fact that he must long
remain anonymous to ensure the suspense of his own plotting and that on
his return he has to go by a false name. Besides, the name of 'Provis' that this
*provi*dential father assumes for a pseudonym, if it corresponds well to the
role of donor that he has assigned himself, would ill suit the one placed at
the receiving end.

If the adoptive father's liberality is unfettered, his power on onomastics
is, as we see, very limited, and his choice to have Pip stick to the name of
'Pip' may appear as a poor makeshift. It is, none the less, a means of
strengthening the father–son relationship between him and his protégé: in
compelling his adoptive son to renounce his rightful identity, Magwitch
gets the upper hand of an old rival, Philip Pirrip the Elder, the dead and
buried father. Should Pip, in growing up, decide to revert to the name of
Philip Pirrip (a not unlikely hypothesis), the ghost of the real father would
forever be in the way, a constant reminder of the laws of genetics, disturbingly suggestive of usurpation, whereas, thanks to a little clause in a legal
document, he is ousted for good.

Or so it seems. For, given the rather paradoxical character of his demand,
does not the new father run the risk, in time, of being double-crossed by his
own stratagem? And is it not, ironically, on the understanding that he will
keep his bastard's name that Pip is allowed to become a foundling? As the
narrative proceeds, this request will prove indeed to have harboured one of
the major ambiguities of the book, the enduring enigma being whether the
foundling will turn out to be 'somebody's child', 'anybody's' or 'nobody's'
[*LD*, II, ix, 524).

Jaggers, the man who takes 'nothing on its looks ... everything on evidence' (xl, 317), is unduly hasty in his judgement when he calls the
demand of Pip's protector an 'easy condition'. On second reading, it even
sounds rather ironic, though whether the irony be the speaker's or the
writer's is a conjectural matter. To be Pip by order is just as absurd as to
play to order, and the hero finds himself once again in the impossible
situation of one whose wish has become another's command; direly put to
the test, he must from now on be at once free and obedient, true to himself
and true to his word. Self-naming had made the child father to the man,
but now that a man is father to the self-named child, the meaning of Pip's

name is as double-edged as its graphic appearance, a mirror-image of itself.

Pip's name is officially made the touchstone of his moral strength and of his loyalty to himself and to the past. Unfortunately, the child has early learnt to distrust and disown himself. Hectored by grown-ups, rebuked and ordered about by his sister, always under the threat of Tickler, and the subject of the most contemptuous conversations, only solaced by Joe's spoonfuls of gravy and inefficient outpourings of love, how could he be expected to be strong and self-reliant? On the occasion of his first visit to Satis House, his weakness and diffidence already induced him to betray himself, even before crossing the threshold of Miss Havisham's dressing-room:

'Who is it?' said the lady at the table.
'Pip, ma'am'.
'Pip?' (viii, 53)

His name is returned to him like a slap on the face or a misdirected note: 'Not known at the address', says the question-mark. So deep is the humiliation, so strong the desire to be recognized and acknowledged that, with no hesitation, Pip disowns his name at once and places himself in the most disgraceful bondage: 'Mr Pumblechook's boy, ma'am. Come – to play', he explains. Not Joe's boy, or even Mrs Joe's, but Pumblechook's, of all men. Commonsense readers will argue that this is the best means for Pip of making himself known to the mistress of the place, since Pumblechook is the very man who recommended him to her and who has just left him outside the gate. But was it necessary to put it that way, to create this grammatical dependence as if in testimony of some filial or menial connection with a most hated, self-imposed benefactor? And when, a moment later, Pip is asked to play, why should he hit upon the 'desperate idea of starting round the room in the assumed character of Mr Pumblechook's chaise-cart' (viii, 54)? The answer rests in one word, the word coined by Carlyle, 'gigmanity'. For Pip, who has seen so little of the world, but heard so often his sister's praises of the man, the local corn-chandler is a paragon of gentility and his chaise-cart, by any conceivable stretch of imagination, the most enviable symbol of prestige. The chaise-cart is part and parcel of Pumblechook, as suggested by the way this character is introduced: 'Uncle Pumblechook ... was a well-to-do corn-chandler in the nearest town, and drove his own chaise-cart' (iv, 21). Pumblechook's *own* chaise-cart clinches any argument: 'as Mr Pumblechook was very positive and drove his own chaise-cart – over everybody – it was agreed that it must be so' (vi, 38), we read, for instance. Pumblechook's *own* chaise-cart is the proper vehicle to carry young boys with great expectations up to town: 'you do not know', Mrs Gargery says to Joe, 'that Uncle Pumblechook, being sensible that for anything we can tell, this boy's fortune may be made by his going to Miss Havisham's, has offered to take him into town to-night in his own chaise-cart' (vii, 47). Pumblechook's *own* chaise-cart is such an object of veneration that Pip feels 'unequal to the performance' of impersonating it on that memorable occasion (viii, 54), though he will succeed better on his next visit: 'I started at once, . . . and we went away at a pace that might have been an imitation (founded on my first impulse under that roof) of Mr Pumblechook's chaise-cart' (xi, 79). (We note that the 'own' is dropped as soon as the imitation succeeds.)

This instance of self-betrayal is a minor offence compared to the next, which takes place after Pip has pledged himself to Jaggers always to bear the name of Pip. Only too pleased to be removed into the upper spheres of gentility, the young Rastignac has just arrived in London, where he will share house with Herbert Pocket, whom he has identified as 'the pale young gentleman' of Satis House. Pip's new friend asks: 'Will you do me the favour to begin at once to call me by my christian name, Herbert?' Pip assents quite willingly and in his turn introduces himself, though under a name more genteel-sounding than Pip: 'I informed him in exchange that my christian name was Philip', he says. But, genteel as it may sound and authentic as it may be, Philip will not do: 'I don't take to Philip', Herbert replies, 'I tell you what I should like. We are so harmonious, and you have been a blacksmith – would you mind it?' 'I shouldn't mind anything that you propose', Pip answers, 'but I don't understand you.' Herbert then explains himself: 'Would you mind Handel for a familiar name? There's a charming piece of music, by Handel, called the Harmonious Blacksmith.' 'I should like it very much', acquiesces Pip, who has already forgotten the 'easy' condition to his great expectations (xxii, 168).

As on the previous occasion, Pip acts on the initiative of a social better: the 'bastard' will go by any name to rise in society. But, in so doing, he is also the victim of irony, lets himself be 'handled' by others and aligned with the comic or hateful characters to whom, as Sylvère Monod remarks, Dickens mischievously allots preposterous names ending in 'le',[9] Drummle, Wopsle, Hubble, and even the venerable and respectable Pumble(chook). The musical reference, besides, is as jarring as it is harmonious; in rechristening Pip, Herbert unwittingly performs variations on the theme of social determinism, 'once a blacksmith's boy, always a blacksmith's boy', which is repeatedly underlined in the book.

Pip, of course, is deaf to these prophetic undertones. He even takes his new identity as a token of enfranchisement and is soon helped in this delusion by curious circumstances. When he next goes down to the village by stagecoach, convicts are among his fellow-travellers and one of them he recognizes as the man who had once brought him the two greasy one-pound notes on behalf of his old fugitive friend of the marshes. The newly made gentleman dreads mutual recognition and is happily relieved on realizing that his new name may prevent it: '"Good-bye, Handel!" Herbert called out as we started. I thought what a blessed fortune it was, that he had found another name for me than Pip' (xxviii, 215).

The coach journey is nevertheless a journey back into the past, a nightmarish revival of Act I, scene i, as the convict's conversation precisely runs on his own adventures in the marsh country and his connection with the man who since then 'got made a Lifer' (xxviii, 216). Throughout the journey, Pip is obsessed with the fear of being identified, as if the mask of pseudonymity was thinning down to transparency:

> After overhearing this dialogue, I should assuredly have got down and been left in the solitude and darkness of the highway, but for feeling certain that the man had no suspicion of my identity ... Still, the coincidence of our being together on the coach, was sufficiently strange to fill me with a dread that some other coincidence might at any moment connect me, in his hearing, with my name. (xxviii, 217)

Reading this, we think we can hear Miss Havisham's voice still ringing from the distance: 'Good-bye, Pip! – you will always keep the name of Pip, you know' (xix, 149), she had said to him when he had come to take his leave before starting for London. We know she had said it to exasperate the Pockets and lead them on to believe that she was Pip's benefactress, but the reach of the sentence goes much beyond the narrow bounds of petty family conflicts; in the broader context of the novel, the remark, after a time, acquires some autonomy and may read as a key sentence, possibly *the* key sentence of the novel, an ironic and prophetic summary of the plot, a cruel epitome of the social fable. What Miss Havisham knows and cynically expresses here is that Pip is no foundling of hers and has no future except in his past that dooms him to being a bastard for ever.

But the crowning irony of Pip's fantastic journey down to the end of the night is that it ultimately takes him to the discovery, on reading the local paper, that he is a most ludicrous father-seeker:

> 'Our readers will learn, not altogether without interest, in reference to the recent romantic rise in fortune of a young artificer in iron of this neighbourhood ... that the youth's earliest patron, companion, and friend, was a highly-respected individual not entirely unconnected with the corn and seed trade ... It is not wholly irrespective of our personal feelings that we record HIM as the Mentor of our young Telemachus, for it is good to know that our town produced the founder of the latter's fortunes. Does the thought-contracted brow of the local Sage or the lustrous eye of local Beauty inquire whose fortunes? We believe that Quintin Matsys was the BLACKSMITH of Antwerp. VERB. SAP.' (xxviii, 218)

For all its preposterous, convoluted style, the paragraph that Pip lights upon as he rests at the local inn, holds much truth about his character and destiny. It cruelly reminds him that if Miss Havisham is to be his Ulysses, he must needs accept his old Mentor into the bargain and remain to the last 'Mr Pumblechook's boy'. It says in funny terms what the novel reveals in more heartfelt accents, namely that the incompetent Oedipus is also doomed to be a pathetic Telemachus.

When 'our young Telemachus' discovers his 'real' father, he is quite dumbfounded, and Oedipus wakes up again. Reluctant at first to recognize him, he is bound, after a time, to identify the man with a 'strange' face (xxxix, 299) as *his* convict: 'but I knew him! ... I could not have known my convict more distinctly than I knew him now ... I knew him ... though, a moment before, I had not been conscious of remotely suspecting his identity' (xxxix, 301). But he immediately estranges him again as '*the* Convict' (303, my emphasis), 'some terrible beast' (304). Words of hatred and rejection crop up, 'repugnance', 'abhorrence', 'dread': 'I recoiled from his touch as if he had been a snake', he writes (305). He is on the verge of fainting – 'the room began to surge and turn' (304) – on the verge, as any psychoanalyst would tell us, of performing a suicide in effigy, behaving as if, short of destroying the unwanted father, he wished to destroy the father's unwilling son. Even his sense of identity is shaken for a while: 'I hardly knew ... even who I was' (xl, 311).

This aggressive stage is short-lived, however, and, after a few days, Pip, quite reasonably, opts for a compromise: he decides simultaneously to renounce his benefactor's patronage and to stand by the man who, at the peril of his life, has crossed the seas just to see him. But both his decision and the words he chooses to account for it betray fundamentally oedipal motivations. Fearing that, 'under the disappointment', Magwitch might put himself 'in the way of being taken', which, since he is a 'lifer', would mean death by hanging, he thinks it wise not to impart to him his intentions concerning the inheritance which, he explains, 'would make me regard myself, in some sort, as his murderer' (xli, 324–5). If Dickens had read Freud, he would never have dared to write this sentence! But what post-Freudian reader can fail to react at the word 'murderer' in such a context? And, in expressing his fear of being the 'murderer' of the man who calls him 'my son', how could Pip fail to draw our attention to the parricidal drive of his nature and to remind us of Pumblechook's oracular words, 'take warning, boy, take warning!', which had been uttered, as Pip had remarked at the time, 'as if it were a well-known fact that I contemplated murdering a near relation, provided I could only induce one to have the weakness to become my benefactor' (xv, 110).

Pip, like Oedipus, is afraid of the oracle and his fears are even better justified because, unlike Oedipus, he has from childhood, and long before hearing the Pumblechookian warnings, been obsessed with fears or visions of murder of a parricidal type. The avuncular Pumblechook himself had been his first imaginary victim when, at the end of the Christmas meal, he had choked on his drink and Pip, who had poured the tar into the brandy bottle, believed, as he recalls, that he 'had murdered him somehow' (iv, 25). Then, there had been the hallucination on the occasion of his first visit to Satis House when he had fancied that his 'patroness'[10] was hanging by the neck from a beam of the brewery. But listening to Wopsle's theatrical reading of Lillo's tragedy, and being forced by Pumblechook into the most disquieting identification with George Barnwell, the uncle-murderer,[11] had been the most trying experience, breeding unjustified guilt that circumstances had soon dramatically helped to justify; returning home to discover that Mrs Joe had been beaten almost to death, poor Pip had inevitably connected the real-life and the fictitious dramas: 'With my head full of George Barnwell', he writes, 'I was at first disposed to believe that *I* must have had some hand in the attack upon my sister' (xvi, 133). By the time of the convict's return, the intertext, especially *The London Merchant* and the Hamlet theme that has started running and will run on through the novel, has much contributed to building up a disquieting atmosphere of guilt and nightmarish visions of uncle-murder. Magwitch himself, the 'second father', is soon turned into an 'uncle' (xl, 309) and later referred to as 'Uncle Provis'.[12]

Magwitch, the gentleman-maker, is also perceived as a repulsive creaturely creator, a sort of monstrous Frankenstein that Pip would like to run away from : 'The imaginary student pursued by the misshapen creature he had impiously made, was not more wretched than I, pursued by the creature who had made me, and recoiling from him with a stronger repulsion, the more he admired me and the fonder he was of me' (xl, 320), he writes, establishing a strange confusion between creator and creature. In Mary Shelley's myth, it was the maker who was repelled by his creature; here, on the contrary, it is the creature who wishes to run away from his misshapen creator and, it would seem, from his own misshapen self.

Running away from the father could also mean running away from murderous temptations. 'I did not wish to be a parricide',[13] Oedipus explains to the Corinthian messenger who wants to know why he left the town where his parents live; but Pip, as we have seen, cannot let the man down, which precisely might cause his death. So all he can do to sever any filial bond that might link him with his provider is to give up his expectations. He will certainly help the man, he will protect him, he will be true to him, he will even indulge his illusions, let him be a father, or rather let him take himself for one, he will act *as* a son, but knowing all the time that he is playing a part, with this secret like a barrier between them. Even towards the end, when his 'repugnance' has 'melted away', Pip writes: 'in the hunted wounded shackled creature who held my hand in his, I only saw a man who had meant to be my benefactor' (liv, 423). But 'had meant to be' is a far cry from 'had been'!

It must be conceded that there is ironic bitterness in this 'had meant to be' and that the convict's money would now be less unacceptable than it had been a few weeks earlier, as we may gather from a conversation Pip has with Jaggers about the 'fate' of Magwitch's wealth. 'Mr Jaggers was querulous and angry with me for having "let it slip through my fingers"', he says, but it 'would be idle' now to try 'for some of it' and he will not 'be sickened with the hopeless task' of establishing a claim which he knows is unjustified: 'I was not related to the outlaw, or connected with him by any recognizable tie' (lv, 425).

Inheriting Magwitch's wealth would anyway spoil the moral of Dickens's social fable. During the third stage of his adventures, Pip's progress has been towards solitude and renunciation. After renouncing the convict's money, the hero ostensibly declines any form of patronage, even from the person whom he had so long imagined to be his benefactress: 'Miss Havisham was good enough to ask me ... whether she could do nothing for me,' he tells Wemmick, 'and I told her No' (li, 388). By thus refusing help from anyone, Pip gives up all thoughts of being a 'foundling' and goes back to square one, when he was the son of a poor man.

The real father's poverty is actually sublimated by the death of the adoptive one. With his fortune now forfeited to the Crown and no legacy to hand down to his so-called 'son', Magwitch in the prison dies like a pauper. In fact, he dies two deaths: his own, which rehabilitates him as a man, even as a gentle man, and the death of the father long buried in the churchyard, whose ghost he had been when he had first 'started up from among the graves' (i, 1–2) and whom he impersonates to the very last.

Now that the ghost has gone to rest for good, Oedipus is cured of his parricidal leanings and Telemachus can give up his quest. A timely fever will help the hero exorcize old dreams and borrowed identities, and become himself again. Recovering from his cathartic malady, he becomes again, if not the Pip of older times, at least one very like him: 'I fancied I was little Pip again' (lvii, 442), he says. With Joe looking after him 'in his old unassertive protecting way', 'like a child in his hands' (lvii, 442), Pip is born again to himself.

But it would certainly be a gross misreading of the book to say that in this scene Pip finds a new father or that a son is born to Joe. The relationship between these two characters had never had that kind of ambiguity. Joe is assuredly a 'fatherly', even a 'motherly' man: he feeds, protects, nurses; but he is, and always was, too honest, too 'unassertive' and too much like 'a larger species of child' (ii, 7) ever to play father to his 'best of friends'.

Significantly, when the stranger at the Three Jolly Bargemen enquired about their relationship, he felt unable to define it:

'Son of yours?'
    'Well,' said Joe, meditatively ... 'well – no. No, he ain't.'
    'Nevvy?' said the strange man.
    'Well,' said Joe, with the same appearance of profound cogitation, 'he is not – no, not to deceive you, he is *not* – my nevvy.'
    'What the Blue Blazes is he?' asked the stranger. (x, 71)

It is precisely because he is no prevaricator that Joe can be a mediator between the true and the false Pips. The moral touchstone of the book, he alone can help the hero find his true metal and his true identity. Joe is the father who might have been, not the father who was or ever pretended to be. And this is the reason why, at the end of the novel, he can still father a Pip of his own, a little Pip Gargery whose happy story will never be worth the telling.

For repetition implies difference. 'There ... was – I again!' exclaims Pip on seeing Joe's little boy, but Joe is more matter-of-fact: 'We giv' him the name of Pip for your sake, dear old chap', he says, 'and we hoped he might grow a little bit like you, and we think he do' (lix, 457). Not Pip's double, but his mirror, Pip Gargery will merely help the son of Philip Pirrip to recognize and accept himself, draw the line between what is, what was, and what might have been, and return to his origins.

Thus, Dickens's odyssey brings him back to familiar shores, where Pip is waiting for him. He will now learn 'for certain' that his 'true legitimacy' rests on his semi-bastardy, half Philip, half Pirrip, 'as if in the Family Romance there were some sort of secret pact between aesthetics and logic, stipulating that the Bastard can never betray the Foundling who survives within him without running the risk of a *literary* impoverishment – a loss of depth, ambiguity and poetry – and of losing at least some of the social advantages due to him'.[14] Oedipus will survive and learn self-reliance only in harbouring Telemachus somewhere in his heart of hearts, but their different roles will no longer be confused. For was it not Oedipus who had embarked on a foolish voyage, looking for imaginary fathers and accepting self-imposed ones? Was it not Telemachus who had lost his bearings, blindly murdering parental figures in his dreams and *actes manqués*? But this strange comedy of errors ends with the hero's wanderings, when the Tale of Lost Illusions becomes the Novel of Regained Identity.

From tale to fable

Even making allowances for the moral and philosophical advantages of deprivation, the outcome of Pip's adventures is not entirely satisfactory.

The 'sacrifice of so much portable property' (lv, 428), the unhonoured pledges of the title, the enigmatic, and anyway unverifiable, promises of the last sentence will leave any reader with a sense of frustration, and any Dickens reader with the puzzling realization that the story does not end like an old play.

G. K. Chesterton long ago summed up the situation: 'All his books', he says of Dickens, 'might be called *Great Expectations*. But the only book to which he gave the name of *Great Expectations* was the only book in which the expectation was never realised.'[15] A justifiably provocative remark on a provocative novel, though, like all sweeping statements, it cannot receive unqualified approval: if we took it literally, what should we make of the *Dombey* plot or of Rick Carstone's tragic fate?

Recent criticism has improved on Chesterton. *Great Expectations* emerges no longer as the 'only' but as the most outstanding illustration of Dickens's self-contradictions. The view almost unanimously held is that the providential myth – the 'Dickens myth' as Geoffrey Thurley calls it[16] – remained from first to last Dickens's narrative *pattern*, whereas the Great Expectations *theme*, 'so complacently approved in *Oliver Twist*',[17] soon became an object of suspicion and criticism.

The undermining process begins as early as *The Old Curiosity Shop* according to Gabriel Pearson, who reads Grandfather Trent's 'illegitimate dreams of wealth' as Dickens's 'first criticism' of the theme.[18] But real demolishing is more patently observable from *Martin Chuzzlewit* onwards as, in book after book, and with growing acuteness, the structural principle of the Dickens novel becomes its own subject-matter. 'Expectations', a word conspicuously absent from *Oliver Twist*, in which desires were fulfilled without even having to be expressed, occurs ever increasingly in the later novels, where it is loaded with derogatory, ironic connotations. Often synonymous with 'greed', 'ambition', 'illegitimate claims', it is, among other examples, the word Old Martin Chuzzlewit chooses to inveigle Pecksniff: 'I confide in you to be my ally; to attach yourself to me by ties of Interest and Expectation' (*MC*, x, 157). It is also a favourite term with mealy-mouthed Uriah Heep: 'You have heard something, I des-say, of a change in my expectations, Master Copperfield, – I should say, Mister Copperfield?' (*DC*, xxv, 323). A word of ill omen, it often triggers off catastrophes and ironic reversals of plot: 'I have been bred up from child-hood with great expectations', declares Martin Chuzzlewit, 'and have always been taught to believe that I should be, one day, very rich. So I should have been, but for certain brief reasons which I am going to tell you, and which have led to my being disinherited' (*MC*, vi, 94). 'It began when I taught him to be too covetous of what I have to leave, and made the expectation of it his great business' (*MC*, li, 780), complains Anthony

Chuzzlewit who finds himself hoist with his own petard on realizing that his son Jonas, whose cupidity outdoes his own, has it in his mind to poison him. Serves him right, thinks the reader, always ready to applaud comic retribution. But, with *Dombey and Son*, things take a more serious and ironic turn as the thwarting of the father's misdirected expectations costs the life of his young son. And with *Bleak House*, the great expectations theme acquires a really tragic dimension: 'Rick, Rick!' cries Jarndyce to his ward (Pip's forerunner in many ways) in a vain effort to exhort him against building castles in the air, 'for the love of God, don't found a hope or expectation on the family curse! Whatever you do on this side the grave, never give one lingering glance towards the horrible phantom that has haunted us so many years. Better to borrow, better to beg, better to die!' (*BH*, xxiv, 302). But Rick will learn his lesson too late, on his death-bed, drawn as he is by the magnet of expectations like his ambiguously comic counterpart, mad little Miss Flite:

'My father expected a Judgement,' said Miss Flite. 'My brother. My sister. They all expected a Judgement. The same that I expect.'
'They are all—'
'Ye'es. Dead, of course, my dear,' said she.
. . .
'Would it not be wiser,' said I, 'to expect this Judgement no more?'
'Why, my dear,' she answered promptly, 'of course it would!'
'And to attend the Court no more?'
'Equally of course,' said she. 'Very wearing to be always in expectation of what never comes, my dear Fitz-Jarndyce! Wearing, I assure you, to the bone!'
. . .
'But, my dear,' she went on, in her mysterious way, 'there's a dreadful attraction in the place . . . There's a cruel attraction in the place. You *can't* leave it. And you *must* expect.' (*BH*, xxxv, 439–40)

The message is always the same: expectations pervert and destroy and are an obstacle to prosperity. In *A Tale of Two Cities*, Charles Darnay's self-reliance is even expressed in terms of non-expectations: 'he had expected neither to walk on pavements of gold, nor to lie on beds of roses: if he had had any such exalted expectation, he would not have prospered. He had expected labour, and he found it, and did it, and made the best of it. In this, his prosperity consisted' (*TTC*, II, x, 123). When, a year later, the familiar motif of 'Great Expectations' is appointed, so to speak, eponymous hero of Dickens's new novel, no reader can fail to perceive the ironies and threats which are at work in the title. Nor does the subversion of the plot come to us as a surprise, but it comes none the less as a disappointment and we cannot help feeling 'vaguely convinced' that the hero, as he himself puts it, has been 'very much ill-used by somebody' (xvii, 122).

Our uneasiness is not easy to account for. Perhaps it finds its origin in that of the author himself, in the slightly apologetic tone of his conclusion, in his ambiguous treatment throughout of his subject and of his hero. For *Great Expectations* is a complex and ambiguous book, not just a great expectations novel, but a novel about great expectations novels, not just a novel with a hero, but a novel about the notion of hero, not just Pip's autobiography, but the confessions of his biographer, a novel in which, Geoffrey Thurley notes, 'the Dickens myth' is 'raised to the surface, laid upon the table, dissected, criticized'.[19] This cannot be done without entailing much suffering on the part of both surgeon and patient. A most crucially self-critical and self-questioning enterprise, the book, which has no less than the Dickens novel for its subject-matter, must have been a most uncomfortable experience for the writer, who felt furthermore compelled to create most uncomfortable situations for his new protagonist.

In order to serve the pedagogical purpose of the fable, Pip is trapped from the very start into assuming his own creator's self-inconsistencies and impersonating several incompatible heroic parts at the same time, while romance and reality are played against each other. As early as chapter 8, the story takes indeed a rather disconcerting turn when the young child is suddenly taken from the brutally realistic environment in which he was born into the fantastic world of Satis House. The reader himself, on being introduced to the place with no rhetorical warnings to suspend his belief, feels as if he had just entered real Wonderland. Within the conventions of literary fiction at least, Miss Havisham's house is a real house with real dark, mysterious passages, where the clocks have really stopped and from which the light of day has really been shut out; and the mistress of the place really is a withered bride, really wearing a yellowed bridal dress and yellowed bridal flowers. Metaphorical language will, admittedly, enhance the 'Astonishing' (xiii, 96) character of the place and of its inhabitants: beautiful, scornful Estella behaves 'as if' she were 'a queen' (viii, 52) and looks 'like a star' (viii, 54), and 'corpse-like' Miss Havisham (viii, 55), with her 'crutch-headed stick', will later be said to look 'like the Witch of the place' (xi, 78–9); but, even divested of such ornaments, the world Pip enters at this stage is more romantic by far than any of the places where Dickens's fairy-tale heroes end up and find shelter: Oliver's resting-place after the workhouse and the thieves' kitchen is no better than a cottage and Bob Cratchit's castle remains to the end a poor Englishman's house. But such is the paradoxical nature of *Great Expectations* that it has all the outward signs of romance and yet is not a romance. All the fairy-tale motifs are there – the enchanted house, death-in-life, the captive Princess, the weird witch-like lady – but the hero himself is not a fairy-tale hero. He has in truth no right to be one: literary convention forbids it as he is also the narrator of his own story.

A fairy-tale hero, always a third person, has no say in what happens, plays no part in either forwarding the plot or relating his life-story, has no awareness even that it is being recorded. Oliver Twist, therefore, might be described as a fairy-tale hero, even though he is placed in a realistic setting.[20] Pip, on the contrary, is an ordinary hero placed, at least for a time, in a fairy-tale scenery. But, being the story-teller, he is held responsible for all that happens to him and for the way it is told, a twofold responsibility whose two aspects are closely linked since his chief difficulty as a character is to appreciate people and events at their fair value, whereas his main endeavour as a narrator is to show that he was in his youth a most incompetent reader of the book of his life.

'Reader' is not a far-fetched simile: from the moment he enters Satis House, Pip acts like someone who has inadvertently found his way into a work of fiction which he improves, as he reads on, with his own marginal notes. As long as he remains an outsider, the 'common labouring boy' (viii, 55) who comes to play at Satis House for the day and goes back at night to the forge, which he knows is where he belongs, his metaphorical embellishments are rather harmless and do not alter the meaning of the book. Real misconstructions begin when he finds himself changed overnight into a young man with great, yet greatly unexpected, expectations and, urged by circumstances to take himself for a fairy-tale hero, forces his way into the wrong book and the wrong literary genre.

He has the 'givens' of the plot: his great expectations, a mysterious benefactor. His imagination provides at once the missing information, finds the setting, names the other actor: Satis House, Miss Havisham. Hasty as it may be, and mistaken as it will prove, his choice is admirably true to the workings of desire and its inner contradictions. 'What I wanted, who can say? How can *I* say, when I never knew?' (xiv, 101) he had admitted not so long ago, describing the discontent of his 'restlessly aspiring self'; and what place could best satisfy his frustration and insatiable desire than Satis House itself, the official abode of wish fulfilment where wishes are never fulfilled? Satis House is a wicked place, as Pip has learnt from the start, a place where he has been humiliated, made to play, made to cry, made to love, and beggared always, but there is 'a cruel attraction in the place' just as there was in Chancery and this is where, 'against reason, against promise, against peace, against hope, against happiness, against all discouragement that could be' (xxix, 219), he chooses to belong and play the leading part.

This cannot be done unless he revises his text and suits his similes to the occasion, which he does without the slightest hesitation: the 'Witch of the place' is with no further delay promoted 'fairy godmother' to justify his own magic transformation: '"This is a gay figure, Pip," said she, making her crutch stick play round me, as if she, the fairy godmother who had changed me, were bestowing the finishing gift' (xix, 149). When he leaves her, the 'as if' has been dropped and she has become '*my* fairy godmother' (xix, 149, my italics), though she still has 'weird eyes' and her magic wand still is a 'crutch stick'.

Such tricks, if they provide an interesting insight into the nature of the human heart and into the art of self-delusion, are totally out of place in a would-be fairy tale. A fairy-tale hero has no business and no power to delude himself in that way. He lives surrounded with characters endowed with well-defined functions, 'helpers', 'donors', 'opponents',[21] and he is never mistaken for long as to which is which. Neither is the reader, who tells good from evil with unerring intuition, no matter how hard villains try to deceive him, for the narrator himself has a firm hold on the text and leaves no room for incertitude. But a first-person narrative permits the double mystification and the shared uneasiness as to which 'as if' is the right one.

Through the agency of his narrator, Dickens actually compels us to read *Great Expectations* as we do mystery tales or uncanny stories which, contrary to fairy tales, are usually written in the first person in order precisely to create mixed feelings in the reader, uneasily torn between suspicion about the tale and regard for the teller: the reported events seem unbelievable but the reporting 'I' ought to be reliable as first-hand witness of the facts. He will indeed be all the more so if he records his own past incredulity, insists on the uncanny character of his adventures and adds as a saving clause, 'Was there ever such a fate!' (xli, 324).[22]

Reliable in this narrow sense, but never authoritative, Pip's narrative gives us imperfect and contradictory information: facts, hints, mere surmises from which we cannot fairly sort out the truth. We are *told* by Pip that Miss Havisham must be his benefactress but given no proof of it; we are *shown*[23] disturbing coincidences and made to suspect some connection between the hero's progress and his shameful past; and we have, of course, strong premonitions that the convict will reappear, for what would become of literature if characters were lost on the way? But it is not until we discover with the hero himself that Provis is the 'donor' (xxxvi, 274) that we know the real story. Reading an ordinary ironic novel, we would have been taken long ago into the narrator's confidence. Reading a fairy tale, we would merely ascertain that our guesses were right. As things are, we are never better informed than the protagonist but what information we get is better sign-posted and, not being personally involved, we are freer to draw our conclusions. In fact, although we read the same story as the hero, we read quite a different book, and the two books even belong to two different fictional modes: ours could be affiliated to 'realistic fiction' with a hero belonging to the 'low mimetic mode', his would come under the heading 'naive romance', 'being closer to the wish-fulfilment dream'.[24] The latter affiliation is explicitly propounded by the narrator himself who, after being long behind-hand in grasping the meaning of his life-story, proves a sharper critic than might have been expected and audaciously steals a march on the structuralists:

Betimes in the morning I was up and out. It was too early yet to go to Miss Havisham's, so I loitered into the country on Miss Havisham's side of town – which was not Joe's side; I could go there to-morrow – thinking about my patroness, and painting brilliant pictures of her plans for me.

She had adopted Estella, she had as good as adopted me, and it could not fail to be her intention to bring us together. She reserved it for me to restore the desolate house, admit the sunshine into the dark rooms, set the clocks a going and the cold hearths a blazing, tear down the cobwebs, destroy the vermin – in short, do all the shining deeds of the young Knight of romance, and marry the Princess. I had stopped to look at the house as I passed; and its seared red brick walls, blocked windows, and strong green ivy clasping even the stacks of chimneys with its twigs and tendons, as if with sinewy old arms, had made up a rich attractive mystery, of which I was the hero. (xxix, 219)

The last and catastrophic stage of Pip's expectations is heralded by a new reference to literary fiction:

In the Eastern story, the heavy slab that was to fall on the bed of state in the flush of conquest was slowly wrought out of the quarry, the tunnel for the rope to hold it in its place was slowly carried through the leagues of rock, the slab was slowly raised and fitted in the roof, the rope was rove to it and slowly taken through the miles of hollow to the great iron ring. All being made ready with much labour, and the hour come, the sultan was aroused in the dead of the night, and the sharpened axe that was to sever the rope from the great iron ring was put into his hand, and he struck with it, and the rope parted and rushed away, and the ceiling fell. So, in my case; all the work, near and afar, that tended to the end, had been accomplished; and in an instant the blow was struck, and the roof of my stronghold dropped upon me. (xxxviii, 297)

The allusion is to 'Misnar, the Sultan of the East',[25] a moral tale by James Ridley. Misnar has been defeated by his brother Abubal who has invaded his country, dispossessed him of all he had, and driven him out of his pavilion where he now celebrates his victory. But during the night a heavy stone, artfully concealed in the roof, is suddenly released when the rope that fastened it is severed by the Sultan, and the invaders are crushed to atoms.

The analogy Pip establishes here between himself and Abubal does more than express the crumbling of his hopes and castles in the air; it implies no less than the well-deserved destruction of an impostor. The once 'Knight of romance' now identifies himself with the villain of the tale and, by so doing, invites us to reconsider his heroic status. Even if the comparison with the wicked usurper of the tale is blatantly undeserved (for he never tried to take another's place), it is undeniable that Pip is no longer 'superior in *degree*',[26] and we are now faced with the difficulty, pointed out by Frye, 'in retaining the word "hero"'[27] to describe his new fictional position. Once more, Chesterton helps us out of our dilemma: '*Great Expectations*', he writes, 'may be called ... a novel without a hero ... I mean that it is a novel which aims chiefly at showing that the hero is unheroic.'[28]

More precisely, Pip suddenly discovers that he is the hero of a totally different plot from the one he had imagined, and that the cards must be reshuffled. In Magwitch's plot – for *he* was the novelist who engineered it all from New South Wales – Pip retains his position as subject of the quest and as receiver,[29] but he is now a modern type of receiver who gets rewarded for a good action, not the hero by divine right he had thought he was.

The other major novelty is the almost entirely new cast of actants. As Magwitch comes in as 'donor' or 'sender', Miss Havisham has to go. And not only is she dislodged from the sender's square, but she disappears from the plot altogether, having no part to play either as helper or as opponent. It is quite clear now that, had she never existed, or had he never met her, Pip's great expectations would have been just the same. Only his bitterness would have been less acute.

The first consequence of Miss Havisham's departure, as Pip immediately perceives, is that Estella has no reason to stay as the object of his quest: 'Miss Havisham's intentions towards me, all a mere dream; Estella not designed for me' (xxxix, 307). And with Estella no longer starring, *exit* Drummle whose part as opponent belongs to the discarded plot. *Exeunt* in their turn the greedy Pockets, who have nothing to fear any longer from Pip's expectations. And thus, the whole world of Satis House recedes into the background. The real actants in the new drama, Magwitch, Jaggers, Wemmick, Compeyson, Orlick, belong either to the world of crime or to the world of the law, so that, from a narrowly structural point of view, Pip is the hero of a novel that turns out to be much more of the Newgate than of the silver-fork type, however earnestly he had wished it to be so.

Had it not been for Pip's fictions and misconstructions, *Great Expectations*, we now come to realize, would have been a much more straightforward novel. 'The Return of the Convict', as it might have been called, would not have been lacking in romantic appeal, thanks to the mythical figure of the outcast in the part of provider; but, with no other plot in which to mirror itself, it would have been deprived of its ironic and nostalgic dimension and the novel as a whole would have lost much aesthetically. As things are, the 'real' plot, Dickens's, can never be read as a self-contained story, and Pip's dream pattern remains to the end superimposed on Magwitch's, blurring the picture. Miss Havisham's shadow, in particular, hovers formidably over the sender's square, making her absence so conspicuous that she gains in charisma what she loses in power and becomes active as a 'non-actant': 'You made your own snares,' she tells Pip, '*I* never made them' (xliv, 341), but we know that she long humoured his misconstructions and was the ironist of the book, who never spoke 'straight'[30] the better to deceive him. What she has done and will later feel so guilty about (xlix, 378) cannot and will never be entirely undone.

Irony is a cruel game and, even granting that Pip deserves moral castigation, we cannot help feeling that he has been, by and large, more sinned against than sinning, that his conversion from Romanticism to Victorianism corresponds to Dickens's own attempt at ridding himself of his own romantic dreams, that he has been 'ill-used' because he was 'used' as his creator's whipping-boy and that he is severely punished for sticking to literary and moral standards which are in the process of being discarded. Had Pip been born twenty years earlier, he would have been less unlucky. But in 1860, he is chastised for the unpardonable anachronism of taking himself for Oliver Twist!

This seems all the more unfair as Dickens's enterprise never really carries conviction. It is even quite remarkable that, under the pretext of destroying romance, the novelist should have allowed himself in this book, as in no other before, the right to build a most romantic story, which his very *coup de théâtre* destroys most romantically. When romance is over and realism has taken over, irony indeed loses its edge and takes on a new quality: mellowed and melancholy, it becomes almost elegiac.

Should he still be looking for literary analogies when he reaches the final stage of his expectations, Pip would have hardly any choice left but to identify himself with the hero of a *Bildungsroman* of the low mimetic mode. This he does implicitly as he gives up his false pretences and takes himself for what he is, an ordinary young man, 'the *eiron* ... who deprecates himself, as opposed to the *alazon*',[31] now placed in the school of experience and adversity and making good progress towards self-knowledge, self-denial and self-reliance. To all appearances, he is now cured of romance.

But Dickens is not. And when it comes to concluding, he is obviously at a loss what to do with his hero who, 'bred to no calling, and ... fit for nothing' (xli, 324), is now moneyless, fatherless and patronless. The result is a series of dead-ends, false starts, false endings. Pip first goes back to the village with a view to working with Joe and getting married to Biddy, which would be the normal conclusion of the social fable, but Dickens cannot face the idea that his hero should 'build up his fortunes again from scratch in the old village' and marries Biddy to Joe to make it impossible. He then 'whisks him off to the East', where, in Humphry House's words, 'gentlemen grow like mushrooms',[32] a decision which testifies less to his 'colonial optimism'[33] than to his incurable romanticism, for, as much as to 'the East', Pip is whisked off 'to the land of the Arabian Nights', a place of which Herbert, less foolishly than one might have thought, had for years on end sketched 'airy pictures' (lii, 395) and where it is a tradition with writers to play fairy godmothers to their blue-eyed boys.

The two paragraphs describing Pip's Egyptian years are assuredly most unromantic. Pip's promotion is presented as the result of his self-helping exertions and the stress is on work, frugality, 'industry and readiness' (lviii, 456). In becoming Herbert's partner he is also clearly rewarded for helping his friend in the past with his expectations money. But he is fortunate enough not to be paid in his own coin: in Clarriker's crucible, Magwitch's money and Miss Havisham's have been melted into one metal so that, at a symbolic level, he now comes into a double inheritance. So, as a matter of fact, had Herbert done before him, which paved the way for a more complex symbolic ending: the gentleman by birth and the former blacksmith's boy, two modern aristocrats of virtue-turned-into talent, are now placed on an equal footing, co-partners in the firm, co-heirs to the money of a convict and of a lady. Such is Dickens's modern version of the old wish-fulfilment dream, a subtle compromise between a tale and a fable.

Inheritance or death

They calls me Adam Bell, 'tis true,
'Cause Adam was the fust man,
I'm sure it's very plain to you,
I'm a *litterary dustman.*
Street Ballad (1830s)

'You are an alchemist; make gold of that!'
Shakespeare, *Timon of Athens*

Money and origins

A writer's last book inevitably reads as a literary testament. *Our Mutual Friend*, Dickens's last completed novel, strikingly fulfils that function in a way *Edwin Drood*, his last but unfinished one, does not. Never before had Dickens been so concerned with the problems of fiction-making, reading, listening, believing. 'What to believe', Boffin's 'chief literary difficulty' (III, vi, 476), is also that of Podsnap's or Veneering's guests during those 'wondering dinner[s]' (III, xvii, 618) where the plot is mirrored, distorted and discussed, offering an unprecedented instance of grotesque 'mise-en-abyme'. Nor will the instance ever be repeated: a sort of postscript to the *œuvre*, *Drood* will not dramatize further the author's concern with the relationship between teller and listener.

There also emerges, as in Montaigne's famous essay 'On Vanity', an impression of disenchantment. Silas Wegg, public reader, rhymer, plotter, 'a literary man – *with* a wooden leg –' (I, v, 49), already has one foot in the grave as had indeed his creator who at the time badly suffered from gout and walked with a limp. This ludicrous representative of the art of story-telling is also associated throughout with the pervading notion of decay which is so characteristic of the novel as a whole: Gibbon's *Decline and Fall* is, aptly, the book Boffin asks him to read, and, after much declining and falling, he ends up in a scavenger's cart among the rubbish, an anticipation of his oncoming return to the dust which was from the first his favourite element. We saw him in turn selling street-ballads in the most 'dusty corner' (I, v, 44) of the town, 'stumping . . . through the mud' (I, vii, 85), prodding the dust-heaps with his peg, trying to unearth the last will of old Harmon, befriending a taxidermist, dreaming of turning dust into gold by despoiling his listener and patron, the Golden Dustman, of his property, performing in short endless variations on the theme of Ecclesiastes, 'all are from dust and all turn to dust again', that pervades the whole novel. Are not these testamentary and testamental variations, like Montaigne's idle musing over the vanity of writing, the 'excrements of an old mind'[1] obsessed with death, dismemberment, disintegration?

With no fewer than three wills on which to make the plot hinge, the novel might also be described as the novelist's testament on testaments, a final assessment of the question of parentage and inheritance that from *Oliver Twist* onward was so central to his preoccupations. What we read here on the subject sounds all the more conclusive as, for the first time in years, the time of writing and that of the events related in the novel are made to coincide almost exactly. The choice of the preterite admittedly suggests an interval of a sort, but this is corrected both by the narrator's opening statement which sets the action 'In these times of ours' (I, i, 1), and by the use of the present tense in the final scene (as, indeed, in the closing chapters of each book), which thus offers an immediate commentary on what has just taken place. There is no harking back any longer as in the two preceding inheritance novels, *Great Expectations* and *Little Dorrit*, to the Regency or pre-Victorian days of the novelist's childhood, no Marshalsea prison,[2] no child-hero, no dominant father-figure. The *hic et nunc* of this new book precludes the return to fictional autobiography and would seem to ensure more detachment, more objectivity and more serenity.

The society depicted in these pages is, as a consequence, very different from that in which Arthur or Pip were placed. We are in 1864 and a gap of forty years separates the events of the new and the old fictions. As far as *Little Dorrit* is concerned, this certainly ought to be qualified, for the novel in fact covers two different periods. Officially, the story is set 'Thirty years ago' (*LD*, I, i, 1), roughly 1825, the time when, Dorrit-like, John Dickens underwent the humiliating experience of being imprisoned for debt in the Marshalsea, but we know from the novelist himself that the Circumlocution Office is none other than a thinly disguised caricature of the British Civil Service at the time of the Crimean War and that Merdle's bankruptcy was directly inspired by the recent Sadleir affair,[3] which brings the story back to the year of grace 1855. But, even if we consider the period of ten years or so which took England from the defeat at Balaklava to the first steps towards administrative and electoral reform, and Dickens from one set of social chronicles to another, we can note a significant evolution in British society. The aristocracy, which had already for a long time been threatened by the onset of industrial capitalism, is now rapidly losing its prestige along with its sinecures. No one would now share Meagles's unquestioning veneration of blue blood or Mrs Pocket's passion for red books.

Representatives of the nobility are anyway very few and harmless at that. Lady Tippins, 'old Lady Tippins (relict of the late Sir Thomas Tippins, knighted in mistake for somebody else by His Majesty King George the Third, who, while performing the ceremony, was graciously pleased to observe, "What, what, what? Who, who, who? Why, why, why?")' (I, x, 118), is not even genuine and only ironists can pretend to take her for 'high society' (IV, xvi, 813). Twemlow is a colourless and effeminate character whom nobody takes seriously and whom Podsnap 'tolerates' as 'a well-connected old female who will do no harm' (II, iii, 248). More remote even than Lord Decimus, 'the sublime Snigsworth' never steps on the stage where, all too clearly, he has no part to play. Invisible in the flesh, the man is merely represented by a portrait, 'a full-length engraving', in which he appears 'snorting at a Corinthian column, with an enormous roll of paper at his feet, and a heavy curtain going to tumble down on his head; those accessories being understood to represent the noble lord as somehow in the act of saving his country' (III, xvii, 620); but the antiquated setting, the imminent curtain-fall, the permanent threat weighing over his head, are signs that he is one of the last remaining specimens of an endangered species.

Large, parasitic families are therefore no longer prominent on the scene. The only epigones of the Barnacle clan are a certain Tapkins family which the narrator names but never presents. Their social role merely consists in leaving cards that read 'rather like a Miscellaneous Lot at an Auction; comprising Mrs Tapkins, Miss Tapkins, Miss Frederica Tapkins, Miss Antonina Tapkins, Miss Malvina Tapkins, ... Miss Euphemia Tapkins ... [and] Mrs Henry George Alfred Swoshle, *née* Tapkins' (I, xvii, 209); but, for all we know, these cards receive no response, or if they are acknowledged nobody cares to inform us. A group of harmless, powerless, faceless females, the Tapkins ladies and their daughters are no more than a name whose phonetic resemblance with that of Tippins casts by analogy some doubt on their authenticity. Even the rhetoric of the (only) two paragraphs devoted to them, repetitive and mechanical as it is, conveys the sclerosis and narcissism of a social class which remains blind to its impending end and still allows itself airs.

The aristocracy has become indeed so inoffensive that Dickens does not hesitate, at the end of the novel, to entrust its most benign and uninspired representative with a message which he knows very well to be at once utopian and outdated. Twemlow's splendid redefinition of the 'gentleman' – 'I beg to say that when I use the word gentleman, I use it in the sense in which the degree may be attained by any man' (IV, xvii, 819–20) – certainly corresponds to the author's own democratic and meritocratic inclinations, but, revolutionary though it is, this statement marks a return to the old aristocratic ideal of chivalry when a 'gentleman' could be defined as 'a man of chivalrous instincts and fine feelings': Twemlow restores to the term the greatness it has lost in a century in which a 'gentleman' is nothing more than 'a man of money and leisure',[4] and, quite typically, Dickens suddenly becomes nostalgic and dreams of lost values when it is too late to recapture them.

This may well be a sign of his own disillusionment. The decadent aristocracy has not been dethroned (and is not likely to be for some time) by a new class of true 'gentlemen'. One evil has simply been replaced by another. As in real life, the bourgeoisie in this new novel is well and truly present as a class, but Daniel Doyce has not founded the dynasty he had dreamt of. The Barnacles have disappeared from the Dickensian scene but 'Barnacleism' has been succeeded by 'Podsnappery', which can hardly be seen as an improvement, and, on a lower level, by 'Weggery', which is even worse. In fashionable circles, the important dignitaries in the Church and the State, 'Bishop' and 'Bar', have been replaced by businessmen, 'Boots' and 'Brewer'. Bourgeois mercantilism has triumphed over the old order and no attempt is made any longer at pretending to feel any reverence for the old spiritual values: the world of *Our Mutual Friend* is that of modern capitalism where materialism prevails.

Origins no longer matter. The questions which worried Grimwig or Brownlow, 'Where does he come from? Who is he? What is he?',[5] can now be answered in a single word, 'Shares':

As is well known to the wise in their generation, traffic in Shares is the one thing to have to do with in this world. Have no antecedents, no established character, no cultivation, no ideas, no manners; have Shares. Have Shares enough to be on Boards of Direction in capital letters, oscillate on mysterious business between London and Paris, and be great. Where does he come from? Shares. Where is he going to? Shares. What are his tastes? Shares. Has he any principles? Shares. What squeezes him into Parliament? Shares. Perhaps he never of himself achieved success in anything, never originated anything, never produced anything! Sufficient answer to all; Shares. O mighty Shares! (I, x, 114)

Polite society, in which the patriarchal pattern is no longer the structuring element, is now very much like a huge club of share-holders, a society of best friends after the model set at Westminster: 'before Veneering retired from Parliament, the House of Commons was composed of himself and the six hundred and fifty-seven dearest and oldest friends he had in the world' (IV, xvii, 815). At Veneering's first dinner-party, Twemlow had been quite puzzled by 'the insoluble question whether he was Veneering's oldest friend, or newest friend' (I, i, 7), but as the novel proceeds, he gets used to the system and can candidly encourage his oldest or newest friend to join 'the best club in London' (II, iii, 246) and come in for Pocket-Breaches.

Needless to say, the bond of friendship which links all these men is none other than the 'cash-nexus' referred to so often by Carlyle, a bond which, from a practical angle, is an improvement on the blood ties that it has replaced since it can be broken and taken up again just as often as one wants, depending simply on the ups and downs of the money market. No sooner do the Lammles have their possessions seized than they lose not only their friends but their very identity and become nonentities, 'these deceiving what's-their-names' (III, xvii, 624), to quote 'skittish' Lady Tippins. Had the good lady been alerted to Dickens's art of coining surnames, she might have guessed earlier that the former Miss Akershem was no better than a shammer (Acre-sham),[6] a fake 'lady of property' (I, x, 114). Sham is over, anyway, and for Society these have-nots are now be-nots. Poor Veneering, the 'mushroom man' (I, xi, 131) who sports a brand new coat of arms 'in gold and eke in silver' (I, ii, 10) and is in fact a belated snob, will meet a similar fate to those two fortune-hunters. As long as the cheat has a bank account, his naïve attempt at misleading the world about his origins does not disturb anyone and his friends are quite willing to put up with the pretence. But as soon as it becomes clear that the man has lied about his property and that, just like his name, his fortune is a 'veneer', 'Society' discovers 'that it always did despise Veneering, and distrust Veneering, and that when it went to Veneering's to dinner it always had misgivings' (IV, xvii, 815). Only the gold and silver of the crest had made him acceptable.

Podsnap, with more worldly wisdom, seeks no such subterfuge as birth to assert himself in society. Everything about him is a clear sign that he is worth his weight in solid silver: 'A corpulent straggling epergne', 'a big silver ring', 'silver salt-cellars', 'silver spoons' (I, xi, 131), and when he plays host, the narrator is there to testify to the 'substance' of his guests: 'The majority of the guests were like the plate, and included several heavy articles weighing ever so much' (I, xi, 131).

Even Boffin, old Harmon's former servant, who for his part is worth his weight in true gold, is shamelessly courted by this *beau monde* who are 'attracted by the gold dust of the Golden Dustman' (I, xvii, 209) and not really put off by his origins. Money has no smell for the new capitalists who are not over-fastidious.

G. K. Chesterton, with his usual perspicacity, points to what, by Victorian standards, is another lack of fastidiousness: '*Our Mutual Friend*', he writes, 'is literally full of Jews.'[7] No doubt he has in mind Alfred Lammle and his friends, he 'with too much nose in his face, too much ginger in his whiskers, too much torso in his waistcoat, too much sparkle in his studs, his eyes, his buttons, his talk, and his teeth' (I, ii, 10), they, 'mostly asthmatic and thick-lipped', and 'for ever demonstrating to the rest, with gold pencil-cases which they [can] hardly hold because of the big rings on their forefingers, how money [is] to be made' (II, iv, 261). Despite his flattering portrait of Riah, the good Jew who falls victim to a Christian money-lender, Dickens, it is true, does not succeed in concealing his antisemitic feelings or in convincingly making up for Fagin: 'It seems', Chesterton writes, 'as if he had avenged himself for the doubt about Fagin by introducing five or six Fagins – triumphant Fagins, fashionable Fagins, Fagins who had changed their names. The impeccable old Aaron stands up in the middle of this ironic carnival with a peculiar solemnity and silliness. He looks like one particularly stupid Englishman pretending to be a Jew, amidst all that crowd of clever Jews who are pretending to be Englishmen.'[8] As with Trollope in *The Way We Live Now*,[9] Dickens has admittedly one excuse: his antisemitism is actually, deep down, a form of anti-materialism. The novelist indeed suggests, and rightly so, that, far from revealing true generosity, the tolerance of his moneyed contemporaries is motivated basically by calculating and opportunist instincts. A single principle, that of self-interest, dictates the conduct of this new class of big businessmen and allows them to come to terms with both their xenophobia (there is, on one occasion, a 'foreign gentleman' among Podsnap's guests) and their social prejudice: the Stock-Exchange Jews, in other words, are tolerated for the same reasons as Boffin. Similarly, polite society does not disapprove of Lizzie because she is proletarian but only because she brings no dowry. A money magnate when asked to comment on Eugene's misalliance puts it quite bluntly: 'A man may do anything lawful for money. But for no money!—Bosh!' (IV, xvii, 819).

This London society could be described in exactly the terms used some thirty-five years earlier by Balzac, speaking of Paris:

There, even bloodstained or filthy money betrays nothing and stands for everything. So long as high society knows the amount of your fortune, you are classed among those having an equal amount, and no one asks to see your family tree, because everyone knows how much it costs. In a city where social problems are solved like algebraic equations, adventurers have every opportunity in their favor. Even supposing this family were of gypsy origin, it was so wealthy, so attractive, that society had no trouble in forgiving its little secrets.[10]

But Dickens does not share the indifference displayed by his contemporaries as regards origins and their ready acceptance of these spontaneous moneyed generations. Even at the risk of appearing old-fashioned and provocative, he does not hesitate, in this social context, to introduce a plot about going back to roots. *Our Mutual Friend*, like *Oliver Twist*, will have only one objective – that of giving back to the hero both his patronymic and his patrimony and of establishing a direct link between what he has, who he is, and where he comes from.

But since 1837, the novelist has lost his superb optimism, and his legitimism is not as serene or unquestioning as it had once been. John Harmon, the new Oedipus, has sadly no illusions for he knows the face of Laius and, like Arthur Clennam, although for different reasons, he is dogged by scruples. The obstacles he meets no longer come from without, as they did in Dickens's first novel of origins, but from within, as they did in *Little Dorrit*.

The inheritance itself, if not 'bloodstained', is very 'filthy', and it at once 'betrays' much and 'stands for' a great deal. The heir's deceased father, we are told, was 'a tremendous old rascal who made his money by Dust' (I, ii, 13) and his fortune is enormous. Dickens is, of course, as vague as ever concerning figures but leaves no doubt as to the man's affluence: 'I don't know how much Dust, but something immense' (I, ii, 13), says Mortimer Lightwood about the marriage portion once settled on John's sister, and the property now left to the son is said to be 'very considerable' (I, ii, 15). The sale of a dust-mound at mid-century could be very lucrative indeed: according to William Miller, Henry Dodd, a dust-contractor well known to Dickens, 'gave his daughter as a wedding-present a dust-heap that realized 10 thousand pounds'[11] and if we believe R. H. Horne it might have netted four times as much money.[12]

Critics and historians have not been sparing in details about the substance those dust-heaps were made of. Henry Mayhew draws the following list:

A dust-heap, therefore, may be briefly said to be composed of the following things, which are severally applied to the following uses:–
1. 'Soil', or fine dust, sold to brickmakers for making bricks, and to farmers for manure, especially for clover.
2. 'Brieze,' or cinders, sold to brickmakers, for burning bricks.
3. Rags, bones, and old metal, sold to marine-store dealers.
4. Old tin or iron vessels, sold for 'clamps' to trunks, &c., and for making copperas.
5. Old bricks and oyster shells, sold to builders, for sinking foundations, and forming roads.
6. Old boots and shoes, sold to Prussian-blue manufacturers.
7. Money and jewellery, kept, or sold to Jews.[13]

Added to this was 'the garbage and offal collected from the houses and markets'[14] and the contents of cesspools. Humphry House writes:

One of the main jobs of a dust-contractor in Early Victorian London was to collect the contents of the privies and the piles of mixed dung and ashes which were made in the poorer streets; and the term 'dust' was often used as a euphemism for decaying human excrement, which was exceedingly valuable as a fertilizer.[15]

Harvey Peter Sucksmith also speaks of 'that Victorian bowdlerized version of a dung hill, the "dust heap"'.[16] But there is no bowdlerization in Dickens's novel: dung and human faeces are part of the picture even though the information is conveyed indirectly. It occurs during a reading session held at Boffin's place, when Wegg opens 'Merryweather's Lives and Anecdotes of Misers' and selects the life of Daniel Dancer:

'Page a hundred and nine, Mr Boffin. Chapter eight. Contents of chapter, "His birth and estate. His garments and outward appearance. Miss Dancer and her feminine graces. The Miser's Mansion. The finding of a treasure. The Story of the Mutton Pies. A Miser's Idea of Death. Bob, the Miser's cur. Griffiths and his Master. How to turn a penny. A substitute for a Fire. The Advantages of keeping a Snuff-box. The Miser dies without a Shirt. The Treasures of a Dunghill—"'

'Eh? What's that?' demanded Mr Boffin.

'"The Treasures," sir,' repeated Silas, reading very distinctly, '"of a Dunghill." Mr Venus, sir, would you obleege with the snuffers?' This to secure attention to his adding with his lips only, 'Mounds!'

Mr Boffin drew an arm-chair into the space where he stood, and said, seating himself and slyly rubbing his hands:

'Give us Dancer.' (III, vi, 481)

The image of wealth as dust, bad enough as it is, is rather traditional: ever since the seventeenth century 'dust' has been a slang word for 'money' and 'cash'[17] and Dickens himself has used it more than once before. In *Bleak House*, Krook's rag and bottle shop gave us a foretaste of Harmon's dustyard and the Smallweeds, all 'blackened with dust and dirt' (*BH*, xxxix, 492), 'rummaging and searching, digging, delving, and diving among the treasures of the late lamented', were the worthy predecessors of Wegg and Venus. Watching their proceedings, Guppy and Weevle were set wondering like Boffin's guests:

What those treasures are, they keep so secret, that the court is maddened. In its delirium it imagines guineas pouring out of teapots, crownpieces overflowing punchbowls, old chairs and mattresses stuffed with Bank of England notes. It possesses itself of the six-penny history . . . of Mr Daniel Dancer . . . and transfers all the facts from those authentic narratives to Mr Krook. Twice when the dustman is called in to carry off a cartload of old paper, ashes, and broken bottles, the whole court assembles and pries into the baskets as they come forth. (*BH*, xxxix, 491)

In *Little Dorrit*, it is the bank itself that the narrator describes as a dumping-ground: on the death of her husband, Mrs General, he tells us, 'began to inquire what quantity of dust and ashes was deposited at the bankers' (*LD*, II, ii, 435).

The association with animal or human excrement, hardly more subversive, is more derogatory, though not new either: many examples of literary references to scatological gold will come to mind, such as the golden coins dropped by Peau d'Ane's donkey[18] or the gold chamber-pots in Thomas More's *Utopia*. Dickens had also made the connection before: the name of Merdle, 'the name of the age' (*LD*, II, v, 469), inspired by the French 'merde',[19] was clearly meant to suggest that the financier with the Midas touch, 'a Midas without the ears who turned all he touched to gold' (*LD*, I, xxi, 241), would eventually turn all he touched into something less valuable, reminding us in fact of a remark in one of Freud's letters to Fliess: 'I can scarcely enumerate for you all the things that I (a modern Midas) turn into – excrement. This fits in perfectly with the theory of internal stinking. Above all, money itself. I think the association is through the word "dirty" as a synonym for "miserly".'[20] But what makes the association so disturbing now is that it concerns the hero's inheritance. And more disturbing even is the fact that the heir is by no means put off at the thought of inheriting this filth. If he feels reluctant to get into his money, it is for other reasons. He has always known what his father's fortune was made of and never refers to it as dirty. It is as if his homecoming was an unquestioning return to the primeval ooze, the excremental clay[21] or dust of origins. Adam, after all, was the 'fust dustman'.

The hero's misgivings, unlike the reader's, concern the giver rather than the gift and a study of the plot focusing on the father–son relationship is therefore necessary to understand what is going on.

Death in effigy

Everything begins with the arbitrary decision of a father who, in order to demonstrate his authority, even beyond the grave, imposes on his son, as a condition of inheritance, a wife of his own choice. This is not the first example of such uncompromising behaviour on the part of old Harmon: fourteen years earlier, he had already disinherited his daughter when she had refused to marry the husband he had selected for her, and then turned his son out for taking sides with his sister. But, on the verge of death, he has finally decided to favour legitimacy and to leave his fortune to the outcast, his rightful son and heir who is now his sole descendant since, in the meantime, the daughter has died. It proves, however, to be a poisoned gift because of the stinging clause requiring the son to marry a woman whose only claim to fame so far is her crabby disposition.

Strangely enough, this son who, as a boy, had been bold enough to stand up to his father while he was alive, is ready now to give in meekly to the whims of the dead man. He has been living as an exile in the Cape of Good Hope during all the years of their estrangement but, on his father's death, he decides to return home to take over the succession and sells his house before leaving, a detail which leaves no doubt about his intention to accept without demur the most arbitrary stipulations in the will. Of course it is well worth his while: a fortune of 'upwards of one hundred thousand pounds' (I, viii, 88) is waiting for him, a fair sum indeed in comparison with the mere seven hundred pounds 'realized by the forced sale[22] of his little landed property' (I, iii, 31).

John does indeed suggest later that his unconditional obedience was motivated by the lure of gain: 'I was already growing avaricious' (II, xiii, 366) he admits to himself. But this argument is in complete contradiction with the psychological coherence of the character whose actions, throughout the story, are always totally disinterested. Its validity is, moreover, disproved in the confession itself, when John analyses his hesitations and uneasiness at the time of his return: 'When I came back to England, attracted to the country with which I had none but most miserable associations, by the accounts of my fine inheritance that found me abroad, I came back, shrinking from my father's money, shrinking from my father's memory, mistrustful of being forced on a mercenary wife, mistrustful of my father's intention in thrusting that marriage on me' (II, xiii, 366).

But if we are to believe him when he claims that neither his father's memory nor his father's money held any attraction for him, we surely have good cause to wonder why he bothered to come back at all when he was so happy abroad! The incoherence of such an attitude is quite as disconcerting as the unconditional acceptance of the father's will and neither can convincingly be held to be in character. It seems hardly reasonable to take these contradictions to be indicative of a changeable or indecisive nature when in general the reader cannot fail to admire John for his moral rigour and his determination.

So we have here a story which, as far as the psychology of the character is concerned, is simply not convincing. The only explanation seems to be that the novelist has deliberately subordinated psychological plausibility to what are clearly urgent necessities. With the return of the prodigal son, Dickens pays homage once more – and for the last time, as it turns out – to the omnipotence of the father-figure. Through the procrastinating and prevaricating of his fictitious character, he, once more, gives expression here to his own oedipal torments (which have remained unsolved long after his father's death) and to his own fatherly dreams. John comes back, not because *he* wants to but because *Dickens* wants him to, because it is necessary that the ambiguous drama of revolt against the father and of filial submission should once again be acted out so that, in the long term, the father's will might be done.

A most fortunate coincidence allows the hero to play this double game, to stop being his father's son so that he can become it again. On reaching his native shores, John is set upon and left for dead in the river, but this immersion in the Thames does not prove fatal and becomes a welcome opportunity for him to die socially and spiritually: he learns of his death through the newspapers and can henceforth break with the past, be freed, for ever if he so wishes, of his father's name and of his father's money, become a new person and start a new life. Breaking with the past, however, is not so easy; a morbidly narcissistic instinct prompts him to go and have a look at the body of the drowned man which he identifies as his own; a rash move indeed, since, at the sight of the remains of his double, he becomes inordinately troubled, arouses the suspicions of the police and has to invent a name for himself in order to satisfy the superintendent's legitimate curiosity, thus jeopardizing his efforts to conceal his true identity. The anonymous stranger who had gone into the police station comes out as Julius Handford but he will have to think about changing his name as quickly as possible if he wants to avoid further trouble with the police: 'So John Harmon died, and Julius Handford disappeared, and John Rokesmith was born' (II, xiii, 372).

John Rokesmith is an assumed name which will turn out to have a longer life than Julius Handford. It is the name by which the hero will be known to the majority of the characters throughout most of the novel and it is the name he will still be bearing on the day of his marriage to his allotted partner who will choose him for his face and not for his fortune of which she has as yet no knowledge. But being dressed in borrowed robes does not make for a very comfortable existence. There are moments of doubt, self-alienation, self-destruction even. John frequently becomes an anonymous character again, being referred to simply as 'a man', 'a certain man', 'a stranger', 'a secretary', 'an unknown friend' or even just a 'nobody' (*passim*). Fortunately, however, he is finally unmasked: John Rokesmith is recognized as the ex-Julius Handford and accused, not without reason, of being mixed up in the murder of John Harmon. It is high time for all the misunderstandings to be cleared up and for him, as his own murderer, to bring himself back to life by retrieving his old identity, reassuming 'his true other name' (IV, xiii, 770). Thus the person he is and the person he pretends to be at last become one and the same, putting an end to a deep sense of disquiet, and the narrator himself makes no attempt to hide his satisfaction at seeing his hero recover his integrity in agreeing to become 'John Harmon now for good, and John Rokesmith for nevermore' (IV, xiii, 777).

The chronic metempsychosis of the hero helps us to understand why *Our Mutual Friend*, of all of Dickens's novels, is the only one whose title, while clearly intended as a reference to one particular character, conspicuously avoids naming him. The title, however, evasive though it may be, does not hide any mystery. It has never been Dickens's intention to conceal the true identity of this latter-day Proteus, from the reader at any rate. As early as the end of chapter 4 (the end of the first instalment in the serialized version), the narrator makes his meaning quite clear, just in case the reader has not yet understood: 'if Mr Julius Handford had a twin brother upon earth,' he writes, 'Mr John Rokesmith was the man' (I, iv, 43). And from now on, whenever the hero takes on a disguise, the narrator is there to guard against any misunderstanding:

Here he ceased to be the oakum-headed, oakum-whiskered man on whom Miss Pleasant Riderhood had looked, and, allowing for his being still wrapped in a nautical overcoat, became as like that same lost wanted Mr Julius Handford as never man was like another in this world. In the breast of the coat he stowed the bristling hair and whisker, in a moment, as the favouring wind went with him down a solitary place that it had swept clear of passengers. Yet in that same moment he was the Secretary also, Mr Boffin's Secretary. For John Rokesmith, too, was as like that same lost wanted Mr Julius Handford as never man was like another in this world. (II, xiii, 365–6)

In his postscript, Dickens confirms that his intention was not to mystify but, on the contrary, to inform his reader: 'When I devised this story, I foresaw the likelihood that a class of readers and commentators would suppose that I was at great pains to conceal exactly what I was at great pains to suggest: namely, that Mr John Harmon was not slain, and that Mr John Rokesmith was he' (p. 821). The whole point of the intrigue surrounding 'Our Mutual Friend' is precisely to take the hero, with the help of a succession of assumed names which the reader is never taken in by, from his incognito state – a form of protest, amounting to death – to the serene acceptance of his identity in accordance with the laws of inheritance and of what might be termed 'natural society'.

It would seem therefore that, rather than call his novel 'John Harmon', Dickens chose an enigmatic circumlocution in order to emphasize from the outset the complicity that he intended to create between himself and his readers at the expense of his characters. Even the author of the expression will long be unaware of its significance. When he first refers to John as 'Our Mutual Friend', Boffin has no reason to suspect that there might be something mysterious about the stranger. He simply comes as a prospective employer to ask Mrs Wilfer some questions about a young man whom he has only seen briefly and whom he is still wondering whether or not to take into his service:

'By-the-by, ma'am,' said Mr Boffin, turning back as he was going, 'you have a lodger?'

'A gentleman,' Mrs Wilfer answered, qualifying the low expression, 'undoubtedly occupies our first floor.'

'I may call him Our Mutual Friend,' said Mr Boffin. 'What sort of a fellow *is* Our Mutual Friend, now? Do you like him?'

'Mr Rokesmith is very punctual, very quiet, a very eligible inmate.'

'Because,' Mr Boffin explained, 'you must know that I am not particularly well acquainted with Our Mutual Friend, for I have only seen him once. You give a good account of him. Is he at home?'

'Mr Rokesmith is at home,' said Mrs Wilfer. (I, ix, 111)

There is really no justification on psychological grounds for Boffin resorting at this stage to such a periphrasis, which at most can be seen as a way of expressing his distrust of the newcomer. But his insistence is all too obvious for the reader not to detect, behind his clumsy volubility, the skill of the narrator in putting across his personal message and in using his character as an innocent go-between. Through this amusing subterfuge, we discover that John is the hero mysteriously referred to in the title and from now on we know for certain who is to be identified behind this puzzling circumlocution. John becomes not only 'Our and the Wilfers' Mutual Friend' for Boffin (I, xv, 178), but 'Our and the narrator's Mutual Friend' for the reader.

When, later on, Bella talks with John Rokesmith about Lizzie's 'unknown friend' and wonders who this mysterious person might be, the expression rings a bell in the mind of the reader and gives him the secret pleasure of recognizing his superiority since he knows the answer to the girl's question. This pleasure is increased by a subtle shift from direct to free indirect speech in which we can hear the narrator's intonation ironically superimposed on the voice of the speaker:

'You look rather serious, Miss Wilfer,' was the Secretary's first remark.

'I feel rather serious,' returned Miss Wilfer.

She had nothing else to tell him but that Lizzie Hexam's secret had no reference whatever to the cruel charge, or its withdrawal. Oh yes though! said Bella: she might as well mention one other thing; Lizzie was very desirous to thank her unknown friend who had sent her the written retractation. Was she indeed? observed the Secretary. Ah! Bella asked him, had he any notion who that unknown friend might be? He had no notion whatever. (III, ix, 529–30)

Scenes of this kind make us appreciate our privileged position as omniscient readers: we hold the solutions to the problems set by the characters and behind their dissimulation we can easily discern the truth which the narrator has made known to us from the start.

But for a Dickens reader the title holds another secret. Even if Boffin delights in repeating the expression 'Our Mutual Friend', which he believes to be the fruit of his invention, the formula is not his own. Uneducated though he is, the man is quoting a famous author, and that famous author is no other than Charles Dickens who, in *Little Dorrit*, had already put the words into Flora Finching's mouth: '... it's better that we should begin by being confidential about our mutual friend ... very proper expression mutual friend' (*LD*, I, xxiv, 276), Flora had said to Amy Dorrit, meaning, of course, Arthur Clennam and rightly underscoring the aptness of the expression, given the genuine friendship that existed between the three of them. In its new context, the expression, on the contrary, can only have an ironic and premonitory value. But, as a quotation, it highlights, ten years on, a striking resemblance between the two heroes who are thus referred to in the very same terms. Our new mutual friend, like his predecessor, is a man who has been cut off from his roots, a 'man from Somewhere ... Man from Nowhere, perhaps!' (I, ii, 12), a homeless, stateless wanderer who comes 'from many countries' (I, viii, 96), a 'living-dead man' (II, xiii, 373), a ghostly figure, 'a haunting Secretary, stump – stump – stumping overhead in the dark, like a Ghost' (I, xvi, 208), a 'nobody' (I, viii, 95), a man in short whose way of formulating references to himself very often suggests unreality, as his choice of modals shows: 'There was no such thing as I within my knowledge', he says (II, xiii, 369) in the scene in which he most dramatically buries himself mentally and begins to imagine what 'the late John Harmon' 'would probably' have done or what he 'might have thought' (II, xiii, 374–5). This, therefore, is not a new theme, but it is now made even more complex, as we are about to see, due to the triple effect of anonymity, homonyms and assumed names.

The intuition which leads Boffin, in his conversation with Mrs Wilfer, to avoid naming 'Our Mutual Friend' by the only name he as yet knows him by shows considerable insight. John's assumed names are no more permanent indeed than 'Chokesmith' or 'Artichoke', the nicknames which Mortimer Lightwood invents for this 'individual of the hermit-crab or oyster species' (II, xvi, 413). Julius Handford is simply the assumed name, rarely used in fact, of the self-murderer whose own initials it faithfully reproduces. John Rokesmith is a provisional name, a prolepsis of himself ('Mr Rokesmith followed close upon his name', II, viii, 313), a precautionary mask and, more than anything else, the expression of a rejection.

In his study of Stendhal, Jean Starobinski offers a shrewd analysis of pesudonymity:

A pseudonym is adopted, first of all, out of shame or resentment, as a way of repudiating the name that has been passed on by the father ... If a name is really to be taken as an identity and if, through the name, the essence of a human being can be reached and violated, then refusing the patronymic amounts to murdering the father. This is the least cruel form of murder in effigy.[23]

What is true of an author adopting a pen-name is bound to be true of whoever refuses to assume his father's identity. Dickens, the novelist who had called himself Boz during the early stages of his career, must have known what it meant very intimately and what symbolic use of the phenomenon could be made in his fiction. But he has so far used it sparingly, as if he were afraid of its implications: the only memorable instance of such dramatic form of rejection of the father is that of Charles d'Evrémonde in *A Tale of Two Cities* where, being justified on historical grounds, the adoption of an assumed name did not sound so subversive as in the later novel. John's repudiation of his father's name is a much more daring and unambiguous gesture.

Nor is it exceptional. The example provided by the main character finds a counterpoint in that of a minor one, as if the disease was spreading. Fanny Cleaver also rejects her father's name, evoking as it does severance or dependence, and prefers to enter another naming system: 'Something sparkled down among the fair hair ..., it was Jenny Wren's eye, bright and watchful as the bird's whose name she had taken' (II, xi, 347), we read. The girl's rebellion is even more violent than John's since she has gone so far as to reject her Christian name. Only by bringing about this transfer is she able to accept her disability, her own 'inheritance of shame': Jenny will take on what Fanny has rejected.

As has already been the case in *Little Dorrit*, the roles of father and daughter are dramatically reversed here, but the relationship is conducted in quite a different way. The inversion is now proclaimed loud and clear by the daughter herself, both in public and in private: 'my bad child', 'bad old boy', 'you naughty, wicked creature' (II, ii, 241 and *passim*), such are the expressions she normally uses to address her drunken father or refer to him in conversation. This is a far cry from the respectful 'Father' which Little Dorrit would never have dreamt of questioning. The situation is, besides, openly deplored by the narrator himself when he speaks of 'this dire reversal of the places of parent and child' (II, ii, 241). What was once simply observed and suggested is now spelt out and commented upon.

The situation is so completely irreversible that not only does the daughter assume a new name, but the father himself meekly accepts this false identity as his child's genuine name: '"How's my Jenny?" said the man, timidly. "How's my Jenny Wren, best of children, object dearest affections broken-hearted invalid"' (II, ii, 240). This is an act of unnaming and of self-repudiation, an abdication of authority as yet unheard of in Dickens. The father figure has never before suffered such degradation. And Jenny's father completes his self-abasement by losing his own name. What reader could indeed say, without stopping to think, who Mr Cleaver is? The moment Fanny broke with her origins, 'Mr Cleaver' ceased to exist. A name will eventually be found for this helpless wretch thanks to his daughter's work as a dolls' dressmaker, a name put forward by Eugene Wrayburn when introducing him to his friend Mortimer: '"My dear Mortimer – Mr Dolls." Eugene had no idea what his name was, knowing the little dressmaker's to be assumed, but presented him with easy confidence under the first appellation that his associations suggested' (III, x, 537). Interestingly, in Arthur Hayward's *The Dickens Encyclopaedia*, the character is only to be found under the name of Mr Dolls![24]

But Fanny Cleaver's adoption of an assumed name is of a different order from that of John Harmon. Her action is both aggressive and playful; it is conspicuously and even flagrantly flaunted: 'Try Jenny', she insolently replies, for instance, to the no less insolent 'Miss What-is-it?' (II, v, 280) proffered by Fledgeby when he first meets her in Riah's company. Her trick, in other words, is an open secret and, being intended for public consumption, it brings the expected result, a release from suffering. John's choice, on the contrary, to keep the secret for himself alone is both a social imposture and an act of misanthropy. 'To abstract a name and place one's self under it', Victor Hugo writes, '[is] to be a false signature in flesh and blood, to be a living false key, to enter among honest folk by picking their lock.'[25] The victim of his own pretence, the impostor finds himself leading a double life and this schizophrenic state, artificial though it may be, is none the less devastating in its effects, producing alienation not only from the father, but from mankind in general and threatening, in the long term, to divorce the 'false' from the 'real self' irretrievably.[26] Parricide is no doubt the intention, as Starobinski demonstrates, but on closer inspection this use of a false name is a form of suicide. It is even a rather special kind of suicide which could perhaps be more aptly described as 'infanticide' since, in destroying himself, the son kills his father's child.

Reverting to the family name is therefore the only way for the son to be reconciled not only with his father, but with his fellow-creatures and most of all with himself. When, in true detective story style, the narrator of the novel finds a convenient pretext for unmasking 'Our Mutual Friend', he does much more than gratify the reader's love of sensation, he brings John Harmon back to life. Beginning as a very unchristian parody of baptism, the book ends as a very Dickensian fable of resurrection.[27]

The holy sacrifice

The opening of the grand finale strikes a triumphant note:

Mr and Mrs John Harmon had so timed their taking possession of their rightful name and their London house, that the event befell on the very day when the last waggon-load of the last Mound was driven out of the gates of Boffin's Bower. (IV, xiv, 779).

The 'Dickens myth' has once more come true: one after another, the mounds of dust have been conjured away; Harmony Jail has been turned into a golden Bower;[28] and John has recovered both his patrimony and his patronymic, two notions yoked together by a superb zeugma which perfectly encapsulates the Dickensian ideal.

Zeugmas in Dickens are, as a rule, patently highlighted stylistic devices used mostly for comic ends: to emphasize, for example, Mr Gamfield's loss of control when he is said to be 'alternately cudgelling his brains and his donkey' (*OT*, iii, 13), or Lady Tippins's vanity in 'showing her entertaining powers and green fan' (*OMF*, II, iii, 249), or again Guppy's bumptiousness in offering Esther 'the ouse in Walcot Square, the business, and myself' (*BH*, lxiv, 756). But here the combination is self-evident, reminding us rather of Mr Brownlow who made no distinction between 'parentage' and 'inheritance' or of old Martin Chuzzlewit who, after unmasking Pecksniff, proclaimed in the same breath the hypocrite's double failure: 'And hear me, you, who ... are Bankrupt in pocket no less than in good name!' (*MC*, lii, 803). Name and fortune are really one and the same in the narrator's mind and he says so quite naturally.

It will be noticed, however, that combinations of this type are only taken seriously with reference to characters belonging to the middle class. As soon as he touches either extreme of the social hierarchy, Dickens turns such confusions into a subject for comedy or satire. Poor Sloppy, for instance, is almost held responsible for not having 'had the good sense and good taste to *inherit* some other name' (II, ix, 323, my italics). Rogue Riderhood's pride in his first name sounds absurd only because of his low social origins which prevent him from tracing it back beyond the third generation: '... being by the Chris'en name of Roger, which took it arter my own father, which took it from his own father, though which of our fam'ly fust took it nat'ral I will not in any ways mislead you by undertakin' to say' (III, xi, 549). But those at the top of the tree are held up to ridicule for diametrically opposite reasons: Sir Leicester Dedlock, for instance, smugly satisfied as he is with inheriting the 'family gout', which 'has come down, through the illustrious line, like the plate, or the pictures, or the place in Lincolnshire' (*BH*, xvi, 196). Tulkinghorn will later point out to Lady Dedlock the need for an aristocrat to make no distinction between property, appearances and ancestry, which sounds very close indeed to Dickensian orthodoxy, but the speaker is too fearsome and the tone of his speech too dogmatic and arbitrary for us not to detect narratorial disapproval:

'When I speak of Sir Leicester being the sole consideration, he and the family credit are one. Sir Leicester and the baronetcy, Sir Leicester and Chesney Wold, Sir Leicester and his ancestors and his patrimony'; Mr Tulkinghorn very dry here; 'are, I need not say to you, Lady Dedlock, inseparable.' (*BH*, xli, 511).

All too clearly, the holy alliance between parentage and inheritance becomes unholy, ludicrous and contemptible as soon as plebeians or aristocrats are concerned. But, restrictive though it is, Dickens's 'legitimism' is quite essential to the outcome of his 'restoration' plots and, from *Oliver Twist* onwards, his bourgeois heroes have all ended up where they truly belonged.

Reinstating John, however, involves a more complex ritual than reinstating Oliver since both the name and the fortune have to be made acceptable and go through a process of regeneration. The role of the Boffins in the restitution of the 'rightful name', closely connected with their rejection of the 'wrongful inheritance' (IV, xiii, 772), ought to be emphasized here. In turn usurpers, go-betweens and donors, Nicodemus and Henrietta are in fact the true celebrants of this ceremony which for simplification's sake we normally choose to call 'plot', and this is where the episode of the hunt for an orphan takes on all its significance.

On hearing the news of John's death, these good people, who have no offspring, conceive the idea of adopting a boy and making him their son and heir. Surely, there would be nothing strange about this decision if the child in question was intended to take the place of the children they have not had, but what they have in mind is altogether different:

Mrs Boffin ... then said, gradually toning down to a motherly strain: 'Last, and not least, I have taken a fancy. You remember dear little John Harmon, before he went to school? Over yonder across the yard, at our fire? Now that he is past all benefit of the money, and it's come to us, I should like to find some orphan child, and take the boy and adopt him and give him John's name, and provide for him. Somehow, it would make me easier, I fancy. Say it's only a whim—'
    'But I don't say so,' interposed her husband. (I, ix, 100–101)

It is, indeed, quite natural that they should wish to call the boy John in memory of the dead man or, rather, of the young child they had once cherished so very dearly; but one might expect them, as adoptive parents, to give their own surname to their successor rather than that of their former master who, moreover, had never been a very loving father: 'John Boffin' would be perfectly appropriate. Surprisingly, however, they behave as if their sole intention in putting a male heir in the dead man's place was to ensure the survival of a patronymic which otherwise would be fated to disappear: the child will be called 'John Harmon', not even 'John Harmon Boffin', which would have been a rather suitable compromise.[29]

The whole operation is carried out with much difficulty. By a stroke of luck, Mrs Milvey, who is given the task of finding the ideal orphan, comes up with a child already called Johnny:

'Is that the dear child in your lap?' said Mrs Boffin.
    'Yes, ma'am, this is Johnny.'
    'Johnny, too!' cried Mrs Boffin, turning to the Secretary; 'already Johnny! Only one of the two names left to give him!' (I, xvi, 198)

Dickens thus avoids any of the problems, moral, religious or psychological, that a change of Christian name could have provoked or implied. The other name will prove easy enough to change since everything takes place as if the child did not have one. All we know about Johnny is that he is Betty Higden's great-grandchild on the maternal side, 'the child of my own last left daughter's daughter' (I, xvi, 198), she says. It is therefore as if he were anonymous, and there is really nothing to stop him from becoming 'John Harmon', if not before God, at least before men.

But the Boffins' gesture, however noble, brings the plot to an impasse. There is henceforth one John Harmon too many and the resurrection of the true heir to the name suddenly becomes seriously jeopardized. Particularly unsettling is the scene during which the false John Rokesmith learns of the existence of the false John Harmon, thus dramatizing the double imposture:

'Good-bye for the present, Miss Bella,' said Mrs Boffin, calling out a hearty parting. 'We shall meet again soon! And then I hope I shall have my little John Harmon to show you.'

Mr Rokesmith, who was at the wheel adjusting the skirts of her dress, suddenly looked behind him, and around him, and then looked up at her, with a face so pale that Mrs Boffin cried:

'Gracious!' And after a moment, 'What's the matter, sir?'

'How can you show her the Dead?' returned Mr Rokesmith.

'It's only an adopted child. One I have told her of. One I'm going to give the name to!'

'You took me by surprise,' said Mr Rokesmith. (I, ix, 111)

Caught out at his own game, 'Our Mutual Friend' seems more than ever condemned to lie about his identity and to renounce his fortune, now that a poor child is about to enjoy it. No doubt he would do so if fate (another word for the narrative agencies) did not intervene again to unravel the plot by bringing about the death of the innocent usurper.

This is, admittedly, a very cruel and most uncalled-for episode. Yet, at a symbolic level, it is quite essential, a sort of play within the play in the course of which the love relationship between a father and his son is acted out for the benefit of the spectator. Johnny's short-lived existence exorcizes John's past, cancels out the fourteen years of rupture and exile, and brings the hero directly from his cosseted childhood with the Boffins to the present time when he is about to succeed his double.

Johnny has therefore come into the world to serve the cause of the hero, 'born to die,' like Paul Dombey, so that another should live. John is, of course, the sole and privileged witness of the sacrificial rite, a ceremony during which, the legatee of his 'namesake' (II, ix, 330), he inherits the right to become himself again and even receives a message of love for Bella into the bargain:

With a weary and yet a pleased smile, and with an action as if he stretched his little figure out to rest, the child heaved his body on the sustaining arm, and seeking Rokesmith's face with his lips, said:

'A kiss for the boofer lady.'

Having now bequeathed all he had to dispose of, and arranged his affairs in the world, Johnny, thus speaking, left it. (II, ix, 330)

The sacrifice being accomplished, its effects are immediate. No sooner has Johnny died than John's very looks are restored to him: a few days after the event, Mrs Boffin, who so far had been blind to the familiar features, suddenly recognizes the John Harmon of former days under the guise of the Secretary, as she will later explain to Bella: 'Too many a time had I seen him sitting lonely, when he was a poor child, to be pitied, heart and hand! Too many a time had I seen him in need of being brightened up with a comforting word! Too many and too many a time to be mistaken, when that glimpse of him come at last' (IV, xiii, 770). The 'glimpse', interestingly, comes only after a mother–child relationship is established, following the death of Johnny:

John Rokesmith's manner towards Mrs Boffin at this time was more the manner of a young man towards a mother, than that of a Secretary towards his employer's wife. ... The completeness of his sympathy with her fancy for having a little John Harmon to protect and rear, he had shown in every act and word, and now that the kind fancy was disappointed, he treated it with a manly tenderness and respect for which she could hardly thank him enough. (II, x, 331–2)

Having gone through the process of identification with the other John Harmon, the hero can from now on accept himself for what he is and begins to consider taking back his real identity: '. . . John Harmon is dead. Should John Harmon come to life?' Were it not for others, the answer would of course be 'yes', but John is too scrupulous and too unselfish to jump to easy conclusions:

Now, take no. The reasons why John Harmon should not come to life. Because he has passively allowed these dear old faithful friends to pass into possession of the property. Because he sees them happy with it, making a good use of it, effacing the old rust and tarnish on the money. Because they have virtually adopted Bella, and will provide for her. Because there is affection enough in her nature, and warmth enough in her heart, to develop into something enduringly good under favourable conditions. Because her faults have been intensified by her place in my father's will, and she is already growing better. Because her marriage with John Harmon, after what I have heard from her own lips, would be a shocking mockery, of which both she and I must always be conscious, and which would degrade her in her mind, and me in mine, and each of us in the other's. Because if John Harmon comes to life and does not marry her, the property falls into the very hands that hold it now. (II, xiii, 372)

After long debating with himself in true Hamlet style – 'If yes, why? If no, why? ... Take yes, first ... Now, take no ... What would I have? ... What course for me then? ...' – John, who throughout the scene has been in fact speaking for the novelist, comes to the decision that 'John Harmon shall come back no more' (II, xii, 373). But his wish to come to life again betrays itself immediately: 'That I may never, in the days to come afar off, have any weak misgiving that Bella might, in any contingency, have taken me for my own sake if I had plainly asked her, I *will* plainly ask her', he says to himself (II, xiii, 373). He does declare his love to the 'boofer lady' who rejects him outright, thus condemning him to remain among the dead, though much against his will now, and it is with no light heart that the Sexton Rokesmith buries John Harmon 'many additional fathoms deep' (II, xiii, 378) at the end of the chapter.

Everything from now on is subordinated to Bella's progress, and her moral education will take up almost the whole of the second part of the book. The novelist will take advantage of this extra time to solve the disputes between Boffin and Silas Wegg and, as a result of their nego-tiations, transform and expurgate his hero's patrimony. But John, now recognized by those who love him as a son, has already become a living person for his protectors. In connivance with them, he is already managing his fortune, taking part in their masquerade and waiting for the moment when he can proclaim his name to the face of the world. Johnny has brought him back to life.

The alchemist

Admittedly, John's return to square one is somewhat disappointing. The 'happy ending', all things considered, amounts to no less than the fulfilment of all the father's wishes, including the most absurdly tyrannical. For it is only after marrying the wife bequeathed him 'like a dozen of spoons' (I, iv, 37) that John takes back his patronymic and gets into his inheritance. At the end of the book, old Harmon has carried the day, and it will have taken no fewer than eight hundred pages to come to this, eight hundred pages to come round full circle!

Does this mean that these are eight hundred pages too many and that Dickens could have done without his plot? Must we conclude that his story is futile, being built up only to be knocked down again?

The answer must be yes if we consider only the strict facts: all John needed to do on his return, some might say, was to submit to the demands of his testator and the triple legacy – a wife, a name and a fortune – would have fallen to him quite naturally. But our appreciation will be altogether differ-ent if we realize that at the end of the story nothing is quite the same as before, neither the legacy in its revived triple form, nor the hero risen again from the dead. A closer look at the novel will show that what John went through were true ordeals and not peripeteias designed simply to spin out the tale, that through the crucible of suffering, a hermetic transformation has slowly taken place, regenerating individuals and reasserting values, and that, ironically, although the father's wishes have been accomplished, they are not his last wishes.

In fact, we come to learn that this father was not only the tyrannical miser described to us in the first chapters but a most 'unhappy self-tormenting' man (IV, xiv, 787), not knowing whom he could entrust either with his confidence or his property and spending the end of his life making one will after another. This changeable and capricious testator thus turns out to be the author of a trilogy, three wills on which the plot hinges.

Let us look again at the basic elements. First of all there is the original will, which triggers off the narrative process by bringing the hero back from exile. This will leaves all the property to John (on condition that he marries Bella), with the exception of a mound of refuse reserved for Boffin in recognition of his loyal and faithful services. If John refuses to obey his father's commands, or if he dies, everything goes to Boffin. Then, the second will bequeaths everything to the Crown, except for the famous heap of rubbish, still reserved for the old servant, whereas the third will, which we hear of much later, makes Boffin sole legatee. Will number three is therefore, because of its date, the only valid document and Boffin knows this all along. But a sense of propriety leads him to conceal the truth even though it favours him: out of respect for the dead man to begin with, then because of his desire not to wrong the son when he has recognized him. He is reluctant, however, to destroy the deed and so hides it among the pile of scrap which is the constant part of his inheritance. Wegg's machinations finally force him to reveal the existence of this piece of paper which alone can render the second will invalid and, in doing this, he becomes, albeit unwillingly, the sole heir of Harmon senior.

In other words, had Boffin asserted his rights on the death of his master, there would have been no homecoming, no return of the prodigal. As things are, the novelist, whose wishes coincide with those of the author of the first will and of the scrupulous servant, will devote himself to restoring the natural order of succession, telling us a story less about inheritance than about reinstatement. In order to do so, he will engineer a series of complications, not the least of which will be the son's refusal of the succession which his father has in fact already deprived him of. This double profanation of the sacred institution of inheritance by the reciprocal repudiation of the testator and the legatee will require the corrective and purging work of the plot, justifying incorrect or delayed revelations.

For, besides giving fresh impetus to the action, the existence of the three wills enables Dickens to establish three levels of information: John has no knowledge of the last two wills for a long while, and Bella for even longer; Wegg and Venus are aware of will number two, but not of the one that came next; Boffin and his wife alone share the secrets of the novelist. This creates interesting and ironic situations, allowing different characters to be sounded out and desires to be assessed. John's inheritance itself, at first debased by the predatory appetites of Bella, Wegg, Venus and Alfred Lammle, will eventually be reinstated thanks to the intervention of Nicodemus and Henrietta Boffin whose devotion to the just cause of the Harmon Dynasty will play a vital role in the outcome of the story. During the interregnum, they alone will impersonate the legitimate desire of the son and heir, and they alone will in due time bring to light the facts concerning the successive provisions of old Harmon's wills.

Thus, truth will finally out, but not before Boffin has seized the opportunity of pulling the strings of the plot. Like Magwitch in Dickens's previous novel, this very ordinary man is given indeed a strategic role. He boldly takes over from the storyteller and, although illiterate, reveals unsuspected literary talents. He invents, plots, improvises and puts off disclosing the secrets for as long as he wishes.[30] He conducts the intrigue as if it were a game and, since it is an instructive game, adopts a maieutic approach when, with the help of his wife, he delivers people's minds of the dramatic and moral enigmas through rhetorical questioning:

'Old lady, old lady,' said Mr Boffin, at length; 'if you don't begin somebody else must.'
'I'm a-going to begin, Noddy, my dear,' returned Mrs Boffin . . .
'Bella, my dear. Tell me, who's this?'
'Who is this?' repeated Bella. 'My husband.'
'Ah! But tell me his name, deary!' cried Mrs Boffin.
'Rokesmith.'
'No, it ain't!' cried Mrs Boffin . . . 'Not a bit of it.'
'Handford then,' suggested Bella.
'No, it ain't!' cried Mrs Boffin . . . 'Not a bit of it.'
'At least, his name is John, I suppose?' said Bella.
'Ah! I should think so, deary!' cried Mrs Boffin. 'I should hope so! Many and many is the time I have called him by his name of John. But what's his other name, his true other name? Give a guess, my pretty.'
'I can't guess,' said Bella, turning her pale face from one to another.
'*I* could,' cried Mrs Boffin, 'and what's more, I did! I found him out all in a flash, as I may say, one night. Didn't I, Noddy?'
. . .
'. . . So what . . . might you think by this time that your husband's name was, dear?'
'Not,' returned Bella, with quivering lips; 'not Harmon? That's not possible?' (IV, xiii, 769–70)[31]

Bella, gradually discerning the truth, can continue the story alone:

'Oh, I understand you now, sir!' cried Bella. 'I want neither you nor any one else to tell me the rest of the story. I can tell it to *you*, now, if you would like to hear it.'
   'Can you, my dear?' said Mr Boffin. 'Tell it then.'
   'What?' cried Bella, holding him prisoner by the coat with both hands. 'When you saw what a greedy little wretch you were the patron of, you determined to show her how much misused and misprized riches could do, and often had done, to spoil people; did you? Not caring what she thought of you (and Goodness knows *that* was of no consequence!) you showed her, in yourself, the most detestable sides of wealth, saying in your own mind, "This shallow creature would never work the truth out of her own weak soul, if she had a hundred years to do it in; but a glaring instance kept before her may open even her eyes and set her thinking." That was what you said to yourself; was it, sir?' (IV, xiii, 775)

Thus, the young woman discovers at last what we had long since suspected, namely that part of the intrigue was simply a show put on by actors for her own benefit.

   In the following chapter, the tale will be taken up by John who, informed by his benefactors of his father's different wills, passes the information on to Wegg and discourses at length on the moral of this story which is beginning now to sound more like a fable. But, like Bella, John is telling Boffin's fable.

   For Boffin is not only a medium for the narrator, a storyteller, a stage director and a *deus ex machina*: he is above all an instructor and a moralist. He not only instigates the dramatic action but also and firstly upholds the moral code. In this novel dedicated to the reassertion of values, he is the philosopher's stone, responsible for all the different transfers and transformations: Bella will stop being mercenary to become 'true golden gold' (IV, xiii, 772), the inheritance will be purified, and the defiled name of the father will be hallowed once more.

   There is, to be sure, a striking discrepancy between the complexity of the role and the simplicity of the character. But Boffin has no need of the subtleties of the inner life since he lives only for others. What happens to him is of no importance and nobody (whether character or reader) shows any concern about what will become of him after the apotheosis of John and Bella. Boffin has no life of his own, he is simply an instrument. Even his moment of glory on the death of his master brings him no respite from servitude: he becomes at once the novelist's servant. He only exists to serve: to serve the aims of the author, to serve the cause of the heir, to serve as a mediator between the son and his father.

   In order to carry out his mediation, he will identify himself with those he wants to reconcile even if, from time to time, this leads us to believe that he is supplanting them. We see him in turn taking the place of the father and that of the son, and even, occasionally, monopolizing both roles at the same time.

Interestingly, the first word that occurs to him when speaking of his former master, who is also his testator, is the ambivalent term 'governor' (I, v, 50) which, in the nineteenth century, in familiar language, can mean either 'master' or 'father'. The first meaning goes back to the beginning of the century (1802), whereas the second only made its official appearance in 1827. Obviously, this new meaning was a misuse of language, a form of impertinence which, by analogy, emphasized what could at times be an unbearable relationship inside the family. (Incidentally, it is significant to note that it was the sons and not the daughters who opted for this new term – 'Applied *by sons* to their fathers', says the *Oxford English Dictionary*[32] – sons being no doubt more aware than their sisters of the authority and authoritarianism impersonated by the father whom they would have to dislodge in order to assert themselves.) The evolution of the word in Dickens's fiction follows fairly closely the change recorded in the dictionary. 'Governor', or 'gov'ner', is the word Sam Weller uses to refer to Pickwick, his fatherly master, keeping the name 'father' for his true sire, Tony.[33] Twenty years later, 'governor' will be used by Tip and Sparkler, in *Little Dorrit*, when speaking of their father and step-father respectively.[34] It is also the term often used jokingly by Dickens himself when referring to his own father.[35] Thus when Boffin restores to this word its original meaning, it is inevitably contaminated by the new connotations. The choice of vocabulary clearly confirms that, albeit unintentionally, the man is the author of a double imposture: in taking the place of the 'governor', he is also taking the place of the governor's son.

But Dickens is an upholder of tradition and he has no wish for his fiction to serve as a model for the sanctioning of a usurpation simply on the ground of the beneficiary's virtue. What is essential is that the bourgeois, like Caesar, should be rendered what is his. The last two wills, therefore, will have to be erased so that neither the Crown nor the old servant, however honest he may be, can take possession of what rightfully belongs to another. Boffin and his wife sense themselves that there is something fraudulent about the legacy, 'our wrongful inheritance' (IV, xiii, 772) as Mrs Boffin calls it. As much as their generosity, it is indeed the faith they share with Dickens in the natural order that will bring about the final rehabilitation of the fallen son. After a while, the unwilling impostor is duly promoted, self-promoted in fact, to the rank of donor: 'I owe everything I possess solely to the disinterested, uprightness, tenderness, goodness (there are no words to satisfy me) of Mr and Mrs Boffin' (IV, xiv, 788) are the terms John will use to express his gratitude and sum up the whole story. After being a surrogate son, Boffin thus becomes a surrogate father. He is the unexpected link that fits into the genealogical chain as if to strengthen and consolidate it. He gives with love and affection what the father, in his bitterness and vain

resentment, had refused. Thanks to his mediation, a posthumous reconciliation is brought about and the illusion of appeasement created at long
last: 'It looks as if the old man's spirit had found rest at last; don't it?' (IV,
xiii, 778) says Mrs Boffin when things are set to rights again.

Another 'as if' follows close upon the first: 'And as if his money had
turned bright again, after a long, long rust in the dark, and was at last
beginning to sparkle in the sunlight' (IV, xiii, 778), adds the good lady.
With remarkable insight, Mrs Boffin hits here on a metaphor which has
been running throughout the novel, the metaphor of hermetics. The alchemist, Bachelard explains in his studies of scientific imagination, performs a
drama which consists in debasing what will be reinstated, defiling what will
be cleansed: 'Il faut salir pour nettoyer',[36] he writes. If silver is eventually to
be converted into gold, it must in the first place be converted into a 'silvery
mud' by the *aqua fortis*. The risk must be taken of spoiling the baser metal to
transform it into the more noble: 'il faut risquer l'argent pour gagner l'or, il
faut perdre pour gagner'.[37] This is exactly what Dickens has been doing in
this novel, and what Mrs Boffin suddenly realizes: John's inheritance is at
last washed clean of its grimy connotations, the golden dust has, like Bella,
been turned into 'golden gold'.

Boffin himself, while performing the part of a miser, had to undergo the
hermetic experience: 'was the Golden Dustman passing through the furnace
of proof and coming out dross?' (III, v, 461) the narrator had wondered at
one point, using the very image of Bella's educator: 'She'll come through it,
the true golden gold' (IV, xiii, 773). But when all is said and done, the values
are reasserted and 'Golden Dustman' becomes a false antithesis just as
'golden gold' becomes a false pleonasm. Dickens the alchemist has worked
the miracle.

Dickens, like most writers, could be said to have been the author of one book
and if *Oliver Twist* is that one novel which he wrote over and over again, it is
in *Our Mutual Friend* that the original pattern is most visible, when the
wheel has come full circle. Yet, in spite of appearances, John Harmon's filial
pilgrimage is a far cry from Oliver's. The usual peregrinations do bring him
back to his father's place, but they do so with a difference. Someone has
stepped in now between the father and the son: *Our Mutual Friend* is a novel
in which Dickens reaps harvests that he has sown in the course of his own
literary journeys and more particularly in *Great Expectations*. It is a novel in
which Magwitch has made Boffin necessary and Brownlow outdated.

John Harmon is assuredly reinstated at the end of the book, recovering his
father's money and his father's name, but he gets nothing in direct succession from his old sire: everything comes to him from the hands of Boffin,
Boffin the servant, the ungenteel, illiterate man who, by divesting himself of

his inheritance, ensures the 'genuine' succession. Boffin's role even makes John's story much closer to Pip's than might at first meet the eye: formidable as it had seemed, the ghost of old Harmon, which presided over the novel and haunted John's memory, turns out to have been no more than his son's Miss Havisham, a tyrant whose power to pass on his money and the girl that went with it proves after all to have been quite deceptive. Boffin's mediation is, after Magwitch's, the greatest ideological revolution in the Dickens plot.

Conclusion: Oedipus or Telemachus?

> This is my son, mine own Telemachus,
> To whom I leave the sceptre and the isle.
> Tennyson

Testaments are holy writs. For those who inherit 'the sceptre and the isle', abiding by their laws is a sacred obligation. Sons in Dickens all have an innate sense of the sacredness of the bond that links them to their testators and they behave accordingly. Even Oliver, bastard though he is and totally unacquainted with the existence of the deed that concerns him, spontaneously conforms to the wishes expressed in his father's will and never stains 'his name with any public act of dishonour, meanness, cowardice, or wrong' (*OT*, li, 351), while rebellious John Harmon eventually obeys each and every one of his father's instructions. Such filial piety, which nothing justifies, is a sort of driving force over which they have no control: it is in the nature of the Dickens plot to feature Telemachus and to dramatize his quest.

But when sons begin to question their fathers and yet continue to honour paternity, when they spurn their fathers' money and yet retain their respect for the notion of inheritance, the rite of succession becomes a deeply tragic act. In *Our Mutual Friend*, global identification of the son and heir with the person of the father and with the father's property is both a necessity and a curse, so that neither the initial pretence of parricide nor the final utopian reconciliation are truly satisfying: they both show evidence of a wounded form of idealism which, of course, is that of the novelist.

Dickens reveals himself to be torn, like so many of the century's moralists, between his beliefs and his observations, his dreams and his condemnations. A hardened parricide, he is constantly finding for his orphans, whether they be heroes or minor characters, substitutes for the fathers whom he has deprived them of. There are in his novels paternal figures of all kinds: adoptive fathers, step-fathers, grandfathers, godfathers, foster fathers, spiritual fathers, from Brownlow to Boffin, not forgetting Fagin, Micawber, Jarndyce, Daniel Doyce, Meagles and Magwitch, and they are all there to fill the space left empty, if only temporarily, until values can be miraculously reasserted and testators and their wills serenely accepted.

For, despite his criticisms and his obvious inclination to break away, Dickens remains deeply attached to the old ideals of belonging and tradition. His use of the parricide theme does not amount to a call for violence and revolution, unless, taking the term 'revolution' in its etymological sense, one is to understand it as a return to a former situation which would inevitably be placed outside the limits of history, in some mythical golden age. The only exception is the murder of Monseigneur in *A Tale of Two Cities* which is the anticipation of the regicide that will mark the end of the French monarchy. It is said of the murderer that 'because Monseigneur was the father of his tenants – serfs – what you will – he will be executed as a parricide' (*TTC*, II, xv, 162); and by analogy, Charles d'Evrémonde's break from family and fatherland appears dangerously subversive. But the inexorable movement away from patriarchy which characterizes the nineteenth century favours a less political treatment of the theme of parricide in the other novels in which destruction is a form of nostalgia. 'The Oedipus complex appears most plausible in a society in which the father's authority has been greatly weakened but not completely destroyed; that is, in Western society during the course of recent centuries', writes René Girard.[1] 'The Oedipus complex', he goes on, 'waxes as the father wanes. It has become routine to ascribe all sorts of psychic disorders to an Oedipus whose Laius remains obstinately out of sight.'[2] This is illustrated perfectly by Dickens's novels in which fathers, as a rule, are either shown in a very unfavourable light or not shown at all. But, although their abdication and incompetence account for much unease and latent rebelliousness, they remain the keystone of the family unit and of society at large, and their essential prestige remains unquestioned to the last. The result is that, paradoxically, Dickens actually kills fathers in order to present a more glorified image of paternity; he only disinherits sons for a trial period, in order to turn what is a due into a reward; his acts of despair, deep down, are acts of faith, and his Oedipus is invariably upstaged by Telemachus.

But can we really separate these two mythical figures? Are they not rather two sides of the same person? Here again, Girard provides an answer to what are apparently conflicting temptations, the wish to follow and the wish to kill the father: 'we can say that those desires that the world at large, and the father in particular, regard as emanating from the son's own patricide-incest drive actually derive from the father himself in his role as model',[3] he maintains, basing his argument on the notion of mimetic desire and of the father as the son's desire-model: 'It is the father who directs the son's attention to desirable objects by desiring them himself.'[4] It is, moreover, the father himself who first suggests the parricide wish: 'The incest wish, the patricide wish, do not belong to the child but spring from the mind of the adult, the model. In the Oedipus myth it is the oracle that puts such ideas into Laius's head, long before Oedipus himself was capable of entertaining any ideas at all ... The son is always the last to learn that what he desires is incest and patricide.'[5] In *The Women of Trachis*, Sophocles provides an even more remarkable instance than in *Oedipus the King* of the father's death-wish as a model for the son's parricide wish. At the end of the play, Heracles, the protagonist, who lies writhing in agony in his poisoned tunic, asks his son Hyllos to kindle a fire and place him on the pyre so as to free him from his pain: 'Do as I say, for this must be done. Or else, cease to call yourself my son', he orders. 'Oh, father,' Hyllos exclaims, 'what are you asking of me? To be your murderer, to assume the guilt of your death!'[6] What appears to be 'impious rebellion', Girard comments, 'is in fact an absolute sub-mission to the paternal command'.[7] This, in fact, is the reason why 'in Greek tragedy, as in the Old Testament, the "good" son cannot generally be distinguished from the "bad" son'.[8]

The prodigal son too is indeed fated to return to his father's home, just as Oedipus is fated to succeed Laius on the throne of Thebes. The father himself, who knows that he is mortal, has no choice but to 'will' his death in order, somehow, to succeed himself. Writing a testament amounts to writing the next chapter of a long story which, like Scheherazade's tales, is a means of preventing irretrievable extinction. The son may well untell the father's story, but his version of the tale will none the less be the story of a succession, intended to go on for ever and ever.

Such untelling or retelling is what Dickens's inheritance plots are all about. To be or not to be their fathers' sons, that is the question that his latter-day Hamlets ask themselves, the internal conflict they have to cope with, and the novels in which they star are all tales of two heroes, the piously filial and the parricidal. Writing in pre-Freudian days, Dickens had never heard of the now so familiar Oedipus complex, and it seems that he never even came across Sophocles; if he had, he would not have failed to refer to a myth that is so central to his own preoccupations. But he might be said to have been the inventor of the 'Hamlet complex', and to have understood long before Ernest Jones that Shakespeare's 'undecided Prince' (*GE*, xxxi, 240) was the very embodiment of the filial condition. The Dickensian Hamlet, part Oedipus, part Telemachus, is a guilt-ridden character because of his double nature, his loyalty and his defiance being always at cross purposes.

It is the 'everlasting yes' that always carries the day at the end of the novels, but not without the help of the narrative agencies that are needed to engineer a symbolic and often complex process of reconciliation. Accept-ance, as we have seen, may entail renouncement: Pip must give up his wrong expectations to accept himself as the son of a poor man, and Boffin must give up his wrongful inheritance so that John Harmon should be his father's genuine successor. Besides 'the sacrifice of so much ... property' (*GE*, lv, 428), these rituals require human immolations: Fagin, Magwitch, little Johnny and many others are sacrificed to the same cause, the survival of a dynasty and the reinstatement of legitimacy. But Dickens feels no qualms about all this, 'so careful of the type [he] seems, so careless of the single life'.

Careless of both, he would actually seem to be at times, as when the murdered innocent is also the rightful heir. Thus, the death of Paul Dombey, which contradicts the standard pattern, seems to be a spectacular instance of the inconsistency of the great expectations myth, and it certainly would be so if the novel ended with the sacrificial rites. But, as it turns out, the child who was 'born to die' simply dies to be reborn and the cruelty of the episode proves in the long term to be far from gratuitous when, having killed his father's dreams, the unwilling little Oedipus returns from a long journey around the world and re-enters his father's home as Telemachus in disguise. Such is the complexity of ceremonies round which there are ironies at work and in which violence is a form of the sacred.

Notes

INTRODUCTION: TO HAVE OR NOT TO BE

1 Monroe Engel, *The Maturity of Dickens* (Cambridge, Mass.: Harvard University Press, 1959), p. 103.
2 J. Hillis Miller, '*Our Mutual Friend*', in Ian Watt (ed.), *The Victorian Novel* (London: Oxford University Press, 1971), p. 123.
3 Humphry House *The Dickens World* (1941; London: Oxford University Press, 1965), p. 58.

1 PARENTAGE AND INHERITANCE

1 Humphry House, *The Dickens World* (1941; London: Oxford University Press, 1965), pp. 55–105.
2 Arnold Kettle, 'Dickens: *Oliver Twist*' (1951), in G. H. Ford and Lauriat Lane Jr (eds.), *The Dickens Critics* (1961; Ithaca, New York: Cornell University Press, 1966), pp. 252–70; and '*Our Mutual Friend*', in J. Gross and G. Pearson (eds.), *Dickens and the Twentieth Century* (1962; London: Routledge & Kegan Paul, 1966), pp. 213–25.
3 Monroe Engel, *The Maturity of Dickens* (Cambridge, Mass.: Harvard University Press, 1959), pp. 59–67 and 96–7.
4 Ross H. Dabney, *Love and Property in the Novels of Dickens* (London: Chatto & Windus, 1967), *passim.*
5 Grahame Smith, *Dickens, Money, and Society* (Berkeley and Los Angeles: University of California Press, 1968), *passim.*
6 Ibid., p. 136.
7 Earle R. Davis, *The Flint and the Flame: The Artistry of Charles Dickens* (Columbia: University of Missouri Press, 1963), pp. 134–5.
8 Edgar Johnson, *Charles Dickens: His Tragedy and Triumph*, 2 vols. (Toronto: Little, Brown & Co, 1952), Vol. 1, p. 280.
9 Kettle in Ford and Lane (eds.), *The Dickens Critics*, p. 260.
10 Davis, *The Flint and the Flame*, p. 144.
11 Smith, *Dickens, Money, and Society*, p. 126.
12 Sigmund Freud, 'Moses and Monotheism', translated by Katherine Jones, in *The Standard Edition of the Complete Psychological Works of Sigmund Freud*, 24 vols. (London: The Hogarth Press, 1975), Vol. 23, p. 114.
13 Ibid., pp. 117–18.
14 Arthur L. Hayward, *The Dickens Encyclopaedia* (1924; London: Routledge & Kegan Paul, 1969), p. 158.

15 George H. Ford, '*David Copperfield*' (1958), in Ford and Lane (eds.), *The Dickens Critics*, p. 353.
16 John Kucich, 'Action in the Dickens Ending: *Bleak House* and *Great Expectations*', *Nineteenth-Century Fiction* 23 (June 1978), 104.
17 Letter to T. J. Thompson, 29 March 1844, *The Letters of Charles Dickens* (Oxford: The Clarendon Press, 1977), Vol. IV, p. 89.

2 DOMESTIC AND NATIONAL

1 John Forster, *The Life of Charles Dickens*, new edition with notes and index by A. J. Hoppé, 2 vols. (1872–4; London: Dent & Sons, 1966), Vol. 1, p. 22.
2 Edgar Johnson, *Charles Dickens: His Tragedy and Triumph*, 2 vols. (Toronto: Little, Brown & Co, 1952), Vol. 1, pp. 307–8.
3 Cf. Dickens, preface to *Oliver Twist* (1841), Clarendon edition, p. lxii.
4 Forster, *Life*, Vol. 1, p. 35.
5 Dickens, letter to Washington Irving, 21 April 1841, *The Letters of Charles Dickens* (Oxford: The Clarendon Press, 1969), Vol. II, p. 268.
6 I am using the word in the sense Greimas gives to it. See A. J. Greimas, *Sémantique structurale* (Paris: Larousse, 1966). For a summary of the 'actantial model', see Terence Hawkes, *Structuralism and Semiotics* (1977; London: Methuen, 1985), pp. 87–95.
7 Sigmund Freud, 'Creative Writers and Day-Dreaming', translated by I. F. Grant Duff, in *The Standard Edition of the Complete Psychological Works of Sigmund Freud*, 24 vols. (London: The Hogarth Press, 1975), Vol. 9, pp. 146–7.
8 Ibid., p. 148.
9 See Johnson, *Charles Dickens*, Vol. 1, p. 42: the mother of John Dickens died on 28 April 1824 and he was released from prison at the end of May. 'The £450 willed to John', Johnson specifies, 'was more than enough to relieve his difficulties'.
10 Northrop Frye, *Anatomy of Criticism* (1957; Princeton, New Jersey: Princeton University Press, 1971), p. 97.
11 Freud, 'Creative Writers', *Works*, Vol. 9, p. 150.
12 Barbara Hardy, *Tellers and Listeners* (London: The Athlone Press, 1975), p. vii.
13 Robert Newsom, *Dickens on the Romantic Side of Familiar Things: Bleak House and the Novel Tradition* (New York: Columbia University Press, 1977), p. 108.
14 Ibid., p. 106.
15 Dickens, letter to Kolle (Autumn 1834), quoted by Johnson, *Charles Dickens*, Vol. 1, p. 98.
16 Johnson, *Charles Dickens*, Vol. 1, p. 258.
17 Dickens, letter to Dolby, 25 September 1868, quoted by Johnson, *Charles Dickens*, Vol. 2, p. 1100. On the subject, see Philip Collins, *Dickens and Education* (London: Macmillan, 1965), pp. 34–7.
18 This is the title of ch. 4 in Newsom's study.
19 Marxist criticism of Dickens's novels left R. J. Cruikshank with the 'bemused feeling that *Das Kapital* was written by an economist called Karl Dickens and *Great Expectations* by a German émigré named Charles Marx who is buried at Highgate', foreword to *The Humour of Dickens* (London: News Chronicle, 1952), quoted by Ada Nisbet, 'Charles Dickens' in Lionel Stevenson (ed.), *Victorian Fiction. A Guide to Research* (Cambridge, Mass.: Harvard University Press, 1964), p. 80.

20 André Gide's famous 'Familles, je vous hais!' appeared in 1897, *Les Nourritures terrestres* (Book IV).
21 Samuel Beckett, *Endgame* (1957).
22 Albert Camus's novel *L'Etranger* (1942) has been translated as *The Outsider* and as *The Stranger*.
23 The hero of Kafka's *The Castle* (1926).
24 Adam Polo, the hero of J. M. G. Le Clézio's *La Fièvre* (Paris: Gallimard, 1965).
25 Harold Pinter, *The Birthday Party* (1960; London: Methuen, 1971), Act II, p. 47 and p. 50.
26 John Fowles, *The French Lieutenant's Woman* (1969; London: Panther, 1971), p. 85 and p. 319.
27 Peter Laslett, *The World We Have Lost* (London: Methuen, 1965), p. 5.
28 Published in 1859, *Self-Help* was one of the most popular books of the time. In his preface to the Centenary Edition (London: John Murray, 1958), Asa Briggs writes: 'There are few books in history which have reflected the spirit of their age more faithfully and successfully than Smiles's *Self-Help*', p. 7.
29 Arthur O. Lovejoy, *The Great Chain of Being* (1936; Cambridge, Mass.: Harvard University Press, 1953), p. 59.
30 Voltaire, 'Chaîne des êtres créés: Great Chain of Being', *Philosophical Dictionary*, translated by Theodore Besterman (Harmondsworth: Penguin, 1971), pp. 107–8.
31 Lovejoy, *The Great Chain of Being*, p. 183.
32 Pascal, *Pensées*, L. Brunschvicg (ed.), (Paris: Hachette, 1907) 'Disproportion de l'homme', p. 347.
33 See Richard H. Tawney, *Religion and the Rise of Capitalism* (1926; New York: Mentor Books, 1955) and Max Weber, *The Protestant Ethic and the Spirit of Capitalism* (1904; New York: Scribner, 1958).
34 Asa Briggs, *Victorian People* (1954; Harmondsworth: Pelican, 1965), p. 142.
35 Dostoevsky's expression, quoted by George Ford, *Dickens and His Readers* (1955; New York: Norton, 1965), p. 193.
36 See Garrett Stewart, *Dickens and the Trials of Imagination* (Cambridge, Mass.: Harvard University Press, 1974).
37 Maurice Blanchot, *La Part du feu* (Paris: Gallimard, 1949), p. 27.

3 THE PARISH BOY'S PROGRESS: A PILGRIMAGE TO ORIGINS

1 Steven Marcus, *Dickens from Pickwick to Dombey* (London: Chatto & Windus, 1965), p. 63.
2 Sylvère Monod, *Dickens the Novelist* (Norman, Okla.: University of Oklahoma Press, 1968), p. 129.
3 Michael Slater, 'On Reading *Oliver Twist*', *The Dickensian* 70 (May 1974), 77.
4 Percy Fitzgerald asserts that the headlines were supplied by W. H. Wills, but the editors of the Clarendon edition insist that 'Dickens clearly claimed responsibility' and that 'the style of the headlines often suggests his hand' (p. xxx).
5 See Clarendon, p. lxii.
6 Marcus, *From Pickwick to Dombey*, pp. 67–8.
7 Clarendon, p. lxii.
8 Marcus, *From Pickwick to Dombey*, p. 79.

9 Bunyan, *The Pilgrim's Progress* (London: Oxford University Press, 1945), p. 12.
10 According to André Jolles, fairy-tale heroes and the heroes of realistic short stories can be defined by these questions (*Einfache Formen*, 1930) quoted by Tzvetan Todorov, 'Poétique', in *Qu'est-ce que le structuralisme?* (Paris: Le Seuil, 1968), p. 142.
11 J. H. Miller, *Charles Dickens, The World of his Novels* (Cambridge, Mass.: Harvard University Press, 1958), p. 43.
12 G. K. Chesterton, *Appreciations and Criticisms of the Works of Charles Dickens* (London: Dent & Sons, 1911), p. 48.
13 This was to be the title of a chapter of *Bleak House* (ch. 9) also devoted to the question of mysterious origins.
14 See Henry Fielding, *Tom Jones*, eds., Martin C. Battestin and Fredson Bowers, 2 vols. (Oxford: The Clarendon Press, 1974), Vol. 2, Bk XVIII, ch. ix, p. 954: 'I was as ignorant of his Merit as of his Birth', declares the shame-faced Squire Allworthy.
15 Q. D. Leavis, in F. R. and Q. D. Leavis, *Dickens the Novelist* (1970; Harmondsworth: Pelican, 1972), pp. 134–5.
16 A. Kettle, 'Dickens: *Oliver Twist*' (1951), in G. Ford and L. Lane Jr (eds.), *The Dickens Critics* (1961; New York: Cornell University Press, 1966), p. 255.
17 Ibid., p. 263.
18 On 'bastards' and 'foundlings' in 'The Family Romance', see below, chapter 7, pp. 98–9.

4 THE SONS OF DOMBEY

1 This passage was cancelled at the proof stage of the book: Dickens had overwritten himself and had to make cuts because of the space restrictions imposed on him by serial publication; see Clarendon edition p. 2, note 2. But the whole chapter, which relates the birth of Son, conveys the feeling of a long expected event.
2 Robert Stange, 'Expectations Well Lost: Dickens' Fable for his Time', *College English*, 16 (October 1954). Reproduced in G. Ford and L. Lane Jr (eds.), *The Dickens Critics* (1961; Ithaca, New York: Cornell University Press, 1966), p. 296.
3 John Forster, *The Life of Charles Dickens*, 2 vols. (1872–4; London: Dent & Sons, 1966), Vol. 2, p. 20.
4 Reproduced in Paul D. Herring, 'The Number Plans for *Dombey and Son*: Some Further Observations', *Modern Philology* 68 (Nov. 1970), 151–87.
5 Forster, *Life*, Vol. 2, p. 30.
6 Ibid., p. 20.
7 Ibid., pp. 20–1.
8 J. Butt and K. Tillotson, *Dickens at Work* (1957; London: Methuen, 1968), p. 103.
9 Herring, 'The Number Plans', 186–7.
10 Kathleen Tillotson, *Novels of the Eighteen-Forties* (Oxford: The Clarendon Press, 1954), p. 170. 'Inevitably', also writes Geoffrey Thurley, 'one thinks of Lear', *The Dickens Myth* (London: Routledge & Kegan Paul, 1976), p. 123.
11 Butt and Tillotson, *Dickens at Work*, p. 106.
12 *Cymbeline*, I, i, 7.
13 *Cymbeline*, I, iv, 36–7.

14 This imagery has often been commented upon by critics. See in particular Julian Moynahan, 'Dealings with the Firm of Dombey and Son: Firmness *versus* Wetness', in J. Gross and G. Pearson (eds.), *Dickens and the Twentieth Century* (1962; London: Routledge & Kegan Paul, 1966), pp. 121–31.

15 See Ernest Schanzer, introduction to *The Winter's Tale* (Harmondsworth: Penguin, 1975), p. 10.

16 Forster, *Life*, Vol. 2, p. 21.

17 22 November 1846, *The Letters of Charles Dickens* (Oxford: The Clarendon Press, 1977), Vol. IV, p. 658.

18 The word 'governor' is used on several occasions by Captain Cuttle in reference to Walter's master (ix, 124 and xvii, 231). Dickens was no doubt playing on the double meaning of the term, indifferently used in the nineteenth century for 'father' or 'employer'. See below, chapter 8, p. 145.

19 The child referred to might arguably be identified as Florence, Dombey's only living child, who has now found her way into his heart: the narrator tells us that 'he knew her, generally'. But we are also told that he 'would go on with a musing repetition of the title of his old firm twenty thousand times' and that he 'would count his children – one – two – stop, and go back, and begin again in the same way' (lxi, 817–18), so that it is difficult to decide which child he has in mind. The expression 'his child' remains vague enough anyway for the reader to choose his interpretation and I presume the author's vagueness was intentional.

20 Genesis, 30, 1–8.

21 On Dickens and Charity Schools, see Philip Collins, *Dickens and Education* (London: Macmillan, 1963) and Norris Pope, *Dickens and Charity* (London: Macmillan, 1978), chapter 4, 'The ragged school movement'.

22 Cancelled at proof stage, see Clarendon, p. 21, note 1.

23 Forster, *Life*, Vol. 1, pp. 23–4.

24 Ibid., p. 25.

25 'The Trusty Agent', referring to him, is also the title of chapter 45.

26 Dombey is forty-eight (i, 1), Carker thirty-eight or forty (xiii, 172).

27 Butt and Tillotson, *Dickens at Work*, p. 99. The passage referred to in their quotation was cancelled at proof stage 'after Dickens had decided to reserve Walter for a happier future' (see Clarendon, pp. 79–80, note 2).

5 NEMO'S DAUGHTER AND HER INHERITANCE OF SHAME

1 Esther means 'star'.

2 Victor Hugo, *Les Misérables*, translated by Lascelles Wraxall (1862; New York: Limited Editions Club, 1938), Vol. V, Bk VII, p. 224.

3 This is very unlikely, judging by the conversation Esther and her mother later have on the subject: 'Does *he* suspect?' Lady Dedlock asks. 'No', Esther replies, 'No, indeed! Be assured that he does not!' (xxxvi, 451). However, the hypothesis of a white lie cannot be excluded.

4 The title of chapter 9, which rightly underscores the importance of indirectness in this novel.

5 Ernest Rhys (ed.), *Pascal's Pensées* (Everyman's Library, 1931), pp. 676–7. 'Type', the word chosen by the translator for Pascal's 'figure', is used, of course, in its obsolete meaning, 'A figure or picture of something; a representation; an

image or imitation (*rare*)-1774' (*Oxford English Dictionary*). 'Cipher', for 'chiffre', should also be understood here as 'A symbolic character -1614' (ibid.).

6 Charles Hartshorne and Paul Weiss (eds.), *Collected Papers of Charles Sanders Peirce*, 8 vols. (Cambridge, Mass.: The Belknap Press of Harvard University Press, 1965), *Principles of Philosophy*, Vol. I, chapter 6, 'On a new list of categories', p. 295. In other writings, Peirce changed the term 'likeness' into 'icon'.

7 From the Greek 'symballein', to put together, to reunite.

8 From the Greek 'diaballein', to disperse, to throw apart.

9 For a further analysis of Esther's emancipation, see Anny Sadrin, 'Charlotte Dickens: The Female Narrator of *Bleak House*', *Dickens Quarterly*, Vol. IX, No. 2, June 1992.

6 'NOBODY'S FAULT' OR THE INHERITANCE OF GUILT

1 Letter to Mrs Watson, 10 November 1855, quoted by J. Butt and K. Tillotson, *Dickens at Work* (1957; London: Methuen, 1968), p. 230.

2 The badly organized dispatch of supplies and munitions to Balaklava, the appalling sanitary services, the inefficiency in transmitting orders and information that caused many deaths were widely condemned in the British press at the time. On 29 January 1855 Roebuck proposed a motion in Parliament asking for the opening of an enquiry. To advocate the reorganization of the Civil Service, the Administrative Reform Association was founded a few months later and Dickens soon joined it, 'considering that what is everybody's business is nobody's business ... before any serviceable body with recognised functions can come into existence', as he explained in the speech he made at the third meeting of the association (27 June). See K. J. Fielding (ed.), *The Speeches of Charles Dickens* (Oxford: The Clarendon Press, 1969), pp. 198–208.

3 In fact, as the previous note indicates, the two questions were closely linked. For a discussion, see C. P. Snow, 'Dickens and the Public Service', in M. Slater (ed.), *Dickens 1970* (London: Chapman & Hall, 1970), pp. 125–49.

4 *Household Words* 336 (30 August 1856), pp. 145–7 (italics mine). 'Nobody' survived Dickens. He reappears in 1875, trimmed with Dickensian rhetoric, under the pen of Samuel Smiles: 'That terrible Nobody! How much he has to answer for. More mischief is done by Nobody than by all the world besides. Nobody adulterates our food. Nobody poisons us with bad drink ... Nobody has a theory too – a dreadful theory. It is embodied in two words – *Laissez faire* – Let alone', *Thrift* (1875; London: John Murray, 1905), pp. 376–7.

5 10 November 1855, quoted by Butt and Tillotson, *Dickens at Work*, p. 230.

6 Ibid., p. 230.

7 J. Wain, '*Little Dorrit*', in J. Gross and G. Pearson (eds.), *Dickens and the Twentieth Century* (1962; London: Routledge & Kegan Paul, 1966), p. 175.

8 G. Thurley, *The Dickens Myth: Its Genesis and Structure* (London: Routledge & Kegan Paul, 1976), pp. 234–6.

9 G. D. H. Cole and R. Postgate, *The Common People* (1938; London: Methuen, 1966), p. 93.

10 See above, chapter 1, pp. 15–16.

11 Northrop Frye, *Anatomy of Criticism* (1957; Princeton, New Jersey: Princeton University Press, 1971), p. 34.

12 Ibid., p. 48.
13 Roland Barthes, *Sur Racine* (1963; Paris: Le Seuil, 1965), p. 49 (my translation).
14 Butt and Tillotson, *Dickens at Work*, p. 196. On Bloomerism, see also Dickens's article 'Sucking Pigs', *Household Words*, 8 November 1851, pp. 145–7.
15 Note to the Penguin edition of *Little Dorrit* (Harmondsworth: Penguin, 1967), John Holloway (ed.), p. 905.
16 See Clarendon edition, Appendix C, p. 835.
17 See Racine, *Phèdre*, II, v, for the obliqueness of Phèdre's declaration to Hippolyte. The situation, besides, is very close to that of *Phèdre* and other tragedies by Racine with its 'A loves B who loves C' pattern: John loves Amy, who loves Arthur, who loves Pet, who loves Gowan.
18 'The art of perceiving – HOW NOT TO DO IT' (I, x, 100) is clearly the Dickensian version of Carlyle's formula in *Past and Present*.

7 DICKENS'S DISINHERITED BOY AND HIS GREAT EXPECTATIONS

1 Dickens actually changed his mind about the father's first name. George J. Worth notes in *Great Expectations: An Annotated Bibliography* (New York: Garland, 1986), p. 17, no. 39, that in the *Harper's Weekly* text, which Dickens had not corrected 'thoroughly or at all', 'Pip's late father is still named Tobias rather than Philip'. Tobias is the name of one of the 'five little brothers' to whose memory the five little stone lozenges in the churchyard are sacred (and not the eldest, one would think, since his name comes fourth on the list). The novelist presumably decided on second thoughts to emphasize the sonhood of the surviving son and make his hero symbolically closer to the father than any of the dead children.
2 C. S. Lewis, *An Experiment in Criticism* (Cambridge University Press, 1961), p. 68.
3 G. Robert Stange, 'Expectations Well Lost: Dickens's Fable for His Time', *College English* 16 (1954), reprinted in George H. Ford and Lauriat Lane Jr (eds.), *The Dickens Critics* (1961; Ithaca, N.Y.: Cornell Paperbacks, 1966), p. 295.
4 Marthe Robert, *Origins of the Novel*, translated by Sacha Rabinovitch (Bloomington: Indiana University Press, 1980), p. 19, note 1.
5 Sigmund Freud, 'Family Romances', translated by James Strachey, in *The Standard Edition of the Complete Psychological Works of Sigmund Freud*, 24 vols. (London: The Hogarth Press, 1975), Vol. 9, p. 238.
6 Ibid., p. 237.
7 Victor Hugo, *Les Misérables*, translated by Lascelles Wraxall (1862; New York: Limited Editions Club, 1938), Vol. I, Bk II, 13, p. 105. The book came out in 1862 and was translated the same year.
8 See above, chapter 1, pp. 10–11 and below, chapter 8, pp. 138–40.
9 Sylvère Monod (trans.), *Les Grandes espérances* (Paris: Garnier, 1959), Introduction, p. xxi.
10 Like Pumblechook, 'self-constituted my patron' (xii, 90), Miss Havisham, who will come to be thought of as a 'patroness' (xxix, 219), is clearly perceived as a father- or *pater*- figure.

11 It should be noted that the murder of the uncle in Lillo's play is presented as a form of parricide: 'Murder the worst of crimes, and parricide the worst of murders, and this the worst of parricides!' exclaims Barnwell after doing the deed (George Lillo, *The London Merchant*, 1731, Act III, scene vii).

12 For an analysis of the theatrical rendering of the parricide theme and of the intertext, see Anny Sadrin, *Great Expectations* (London: Unwin Hyman, 1988), chapter 14, 'The Other Stage', pp. 198–214.

13 Sophocles, *Oedipus the King*, line 1001, my translation.

14 Robert, *Origins of the Novel*, p. 112.

15 G. K. Chesterton, *Appreciations and Criticisms of the Works of Charles Dickens* (London: Dent, 1911), p. 200.

16 Geoffrey Thurley, *The Dickens Myth: Its Genesis and Structure* (London: Routledge & Kegan Paul, 1976), p. 83.

17 Gabriel Pearson, '*The Old Curiosity Shop*', in J. Gross and G. Pearson (eds.), *Dickens and the Twentieth Century* (1962; London: Routledge & Kegan Paul, 1966), p. 83.

18 Ibid.

19 Thurley, *The Dickens Myth*, p. 289.

20 See above, chapter 3, pp. 35–6.

21 See Vladimir Propp, *Morphology of the Folktale* (1928), translated by Lawrence Scott (University of Texas Press, 1958). On Propp's theory, see Terence Hawkes, *Structuralism and Semiotics* (1977; London: Methuen, 1985), pp. 67–9.

22 See Tzvetan Todorov, *Introduction à la littérature fantastique* (Paris: Le Seuil, 1970), pp. 87–91.

23 See Wayne Booth, *The Rhetoric of Fiction* (University of Chicago Press, 1961), chapter 1, 'Telling and Showing'.

24 Cf. Northrop Frye, *Anatomy of Criticism* (1957; Princeton, New Jersey: Princeton University Press, 1971), pp. 34 and 37.

25 James Ridley's *The Tales of the Genii* (1776) is an interesting specimen of literary deception from the period of *Ossian* and the forgeries of Chatterton. The full title was *The Tales of the Genii or the Delightful Lessons of Horam, the Son of Asmar*, faithfully translated from the Persian Manuscript and compared with the French and Spanish EDITION. Published at Paris and Madrid. By Sir Charles MORELL, formerly ambassador from the British Settlements in Indi to the great Mogul, London. MDCCLXIV.

26 Frye, *Anatomy of Criticism*, p. 33.

27 Ibid., p. 34.

28 Chesterton, *Appreciations and Criticisms*, p. 199.

29 I am using the terminology of A. J. Greimas, *Sémantique structurale* (Paris: Larousse, 1966). For a summary of his theory, see Hawkes, *Structuralism and Semiotics*, pp. 87–95.

30 Wayne C. Booth, *A Rhetoric of Irony* (University of Chicago Press, 1974), p. 1.

31 Frye, *Anatomy of Criticism*, p. 40

32 Humphry House, *The Dickens World* (1941; London: Oxford University Press, 1965), p. 156.

33 Chesterton, *Appreciations and Criticisms*, p. 132 (about *David Copperfield*).

8 INHERITANCE OR DEATH

1 Montaigne, *Essays*, 'De la vanité', III, 9, my translation.

2 The Marshalsea prison was closed in 1842.

3 'I had the general idea of the Society business before the Sadleir affair, but I shaped Mr Merdle himself out of that precious rascality', letter to Forster, 4/?/56, Walter Dexter (ed.), *The Letters of Charles Dickens*, 3 vols. (Bloomsbury: The Nonesuch Press, 1938), Vol. II, p. 776.

4 *The Shorter Oxford Dictionary*, definitions 3 and 4.

5 See above, chapter 3, p. 39.

6 There is no mention of the name Akershem in P. H. Reaney's *Dictionary of British Surnames*, revised edition by R. M. Wilson (London: Routledge & Kegan Paul, 1976), but Reaney gives 'Acres, ackers, acors, akers, akess, akker: dweller by a plot of arable land (OE aecer). William *del Acr'* 1214; Adam *de Acres* 1346 ... Ackerman, Acraman, Acreman, Akerman; Robert *le Akerman* 1233, OE acerman: farmer, a husband or ploughman'. The remainder of the name, 'hem', might be a corruption of 'ham' meaning 'home' or 'hamlet'. Thus the entire name would indicate landed gentry (I am indebted to Barbara Hardy for this suggestion). But the suffix 'shem', might also be a corruption of 'sham', already to be found in the name of Miss Havisham, a lady whose property does not amount to much.

7 G. K. Chesterton, *Appreciations and Criticisms of the Works of Charles Dickens* (London: Dent & Sons, 1911), p. xi.

8 Ibid., p. xii.

9 I am thinking in particular of Trollope's portrait of Mr Alf: 'He was supposed to have been born a German Jew; and certain ladies said that they could distinguish in his tongue the slightest possible foreign accent. Nevertheless it was conceded to him that he knew England as only an Englishman can know it.' Melmotte is also 'said to have' married 'a Bohemian Jewess' but to declare 'of himself that he had been born in England, and that he was an Englishman' (1875; London: Oxford University Press, 1962), p. 8 and p. 30.

10 Honoré de Balzac, *Sarrasine*, translated by Richard Miller in Roland Barthes, *S/Z* (London: Jonathan Cape, 1975), p. 224.

11 William Miller, 'Dust Heaps', *The Dickensian* XXXI (1935), 147–8.

12 R. H. Horne, 'Dust; or Ugliness Redeemed', *Household Words* I (13 July 1850), 379–84.

13 Henry Mayhew, *London Labour and the London Poor*, 4 vols. (1851–62; London: Frank Cass, 1967), Vol. II, p. 171.

14 Ibid.

15 Humphry House, *The Dickens World* (1941; London: Oxford University Press, 1965), p. 167.

16 Harvey Peter Sucksmith, *The Narrative Art of Charles Dickens* (Oxford: The Clarendon Press, 1970), p. 31.

17 *The Shorter Oxford Dictionary*, definition 5, gives 1605 as the date of first occurrence.

18 Charles Perrault, *Peau d'âne*, 1694 (one of the tales of *Mother Goose*, 'The Donkey-Skin Girl').

19 'His very name suspiciously resembles the French word *merde*, with its be-

smeared and odorous associations', writes Edgar Johnson, *Charles Dickens: His Tragedy and Triumph* (Toronto: Little, Brown & Co, 1952), Vol. 2, p. 888.

20 Sigmund Freud, Letter to Fliess, 22 December 1897, *The Standard Edition of the Complete Psychological Works of Sigmund Freud*, 24 vols. (London: The Hogarth Press, 1975), Vol. I, p. 273.

21 Karl Abraham depicts the God of Genesis as a potter who shapes man from matter very like 'faeces' and who impersonates 'the almighty intestine function', *Études cliniques*, ch. x, 'La valorisation des excrétions dans le rêve et la névrose' (1920), in *Œuvres complètes* (Paris: Payot, 1966), p. 99.

22 Why 'forced sale'? The story does not say. Perhaps this too was imposed by the father?

23 Jean Starobinski, *L'Œil vivant* (1961; Paris: Gallimard, 1970), p. 192, my translation.

24 A. L. Hayward, *The Dickens Encyclopaedia* (1924; London: Routledge & Kegan Paul, 1969), p. 51.

25 Victor Hugo, *Les Misérables*, translated by Lascelles Wraxall (1862; New York: Limited Editions Club, 1938), Vol. V, Bk VII, p. 224.

26 I am using here the terminology of R. D. Laing, *The Divided Self* (Harmondsworth: Penguin, 1975), pp. 71–5 and *passim*.

27 I fail to agree with Masao Miyoshi who takes the early episode of John's immersion seriously, considering it as 'a kind of baptism for Harmon, who is then born again to a new life' ('Resolution of Identity in *Our Mutual Friend*', *The Victorian Newsletter*, Fall 1964, p. 7). The whole experience is in fact a false baptism, as deceitful in its own way as Riderhood's immersion which performs no cleansing ritual and fails to drown 'the old devil out' of the Rogue (III, iii, 445). Eugene's experience is certainly more orthodox, a sign that we cannot expect to find a very coherent Christian message in this story of 'drowning by numbers'.

28 'Golden bower', the expression actually used to describe Jenny Wren's hair (III, ii, 439), symbolizes the true values that the little dolls' dressmaker impersonates and that will eventually triumph thanks to the 'Golden Dustman'.

29 On the question of adoption, I owe the following information to Robert R. Drury, Faculty of Law, University of Exeter: 'Adoption, properly so called, was not possible under English law until the passing of the Adoption Act in 1926. Until this Act it was not legally possible to transfer the rights and liabilities of the natural parents to the adoptive parents. However de facto adoption was accepted quite generally throughout the latter half of the 19th century.' The attitude of the Boffins was typical therefore of contemporary practices even though their adoption of the young Johnny has no legal backing. Robert Drury also points out the possibility, open to any citizen, of giving the name of his choice to the adoptive child: 'As far as surnames are concerned, these could be changed as one liked. No formalities were necessary, but it was customary to change surname by a deed poll. The Christian name could be changed by Act of Parliament and also apparently by usage.' For more information, see the *Halsbury Laws of England*, 3rd edition, Vol. 29, p. 394.

30 In his work plans, Dickens himself notes how Boffin and his wife 'plotted'. See Harry Stone (ed.), *Dickens' Working Notes for His Novels* (Chicago University Press, 1987), p. 371.

31 Thus playing at 'guess what', the Boffins again remind us of Magwitch imparting the truth of the situation to Pip through a series of questions that sound very much like the terms of a riddle: 'Could I make a guess, I wonder . . .! As to the first figure now. Five? . . . As to the first letter of that lawyer's name now. Would it be J?' (*GE*, xxxix, 303). For a more detailed analysis of Magwitch's rhetoric, see Anny Sadrin, *Great Expectations* (London: Unwin Hyman, 1988), pp. 194–6.

32 *The Shorter Oxford English Dictionary*, italics mine.

33 *The Pickwick Papers*, xliv, 686; xlv, 704; lvi, 860.

34 *Little Dorrit*, I, viii, 84; I, xxxiii, 389; II, xiv, 577; II, xxiv, 678.

35 See, for instance, Dickens's letter to Thomas Mitton: 'I want to give the Governor some money', 21 November 1834, *The Letters of Charles Dickens* (Oxford: The Clarendon Press, 1965), Vol. I, p. 45, or his letter to Thomas Beard: 'I have made some arrangements concerning the settling-down for life of the governor which will a little surprise you', 13 March 1839 (Vol. I, p. 526).

36 Gaston Bachelard, *La Terre et les rêveries du repos* (1948; Paris: José Corti, 1958), p. 41.

37 Gaston Bachelard, *La Terre et les rêveries de la volonté* (1948; Paris: José Corti, 1976), p. 131.

CONCLUSION: OEDIPUS OR TELEMACHUS?

1 René Girard, *Violence and the Sacred*, translated from the French (*La Violence et le sacré*, 1972) by Patrick Gregory (Baltimore and London: The Johns Hopkins University Press, 1977), p. 188.

2 Ibid., p. 190.

3 Ibid.

4 Ibid., p. 172.

5 Ibid., p. 175.

6 Sophocles, *The Women of Trachis*, ll. 1204–7, my translation.

7 Girard, *Violence and the Sacred*, p. 191.

8 Ibid., p. 178.

Index